MINK COATS
and BARBED WIRE

MINK COATS
and BARBED WIRE

Ruth Turkow Kaminska

Introduction by Harrison E. Salisbury

COLLINS and HARVILL PRESS

London, 1979

ISBN 0 00 262310   2

Made and printed in Great Britain by
William Collins Sons & Co. Ltd., Glasgow
for Collins, St James's Place and
Harvill Press, 30a Pavilion Road, London SW1

To the memory of Adi Rosner

virtuoso trumpet player and gifted composer,
a superb musician, a magnificent showman,
and the father of my daughter.

ACKNOWLEDGMENTS

I express my deep gratitude to my cousin Charlotte Kamin Rouda and her family, without whose faith, encouragement, and help this book could not have been written, and to my friend Henry Moscow who edited the manuscript.

contents

A section of photographs follows page 112.

Introduction

No one can read Ruth Turkow Kaminska's touching story of her years in Stalin's prisons and prison camps without again asking: Why? Why did Stalin do it? Why did he confine thousands, hundreds of thousands, millions of innocent men, women, and children to custody, driving them year after year to death through hard labor, starvation, disease, and sadistic cruelty?

Why, in particular, did he torment this woman, a singer and actress, a woman of no politics, as harmless a human as might have been found in the whole dismal Soviet Union?

Why did he send into his camps and jails Ruth's husband, Adi Rosner, a gifted jazz musician, as fine a trumpet player as ever blasted a tone from the stage in Moscow?

Well, there is, of course, an answer. In Russia there is an answer for everything, no matter how unpleasant and irrational that answer may be. To begin with, Ruth and Adi were Jewish, and that almost automatically put them under suspicion in the darkening years of Stalin's first postwar purges. Secondly, they were not Russian at all. They were Poles who had been swept up into Russia willy-nilly, when Hitler and Stalin agreed to divide Poland as part of the Nazi-Soviet pact of 1939, which unleashed World War II. Thirdly, they were artists, musical artists, and not ordinary artists at that. They were celebrated and famous, and they were celebrated and famous for Western music and Western styles, just at a moment when Stalin had swung the helm sharply toward Socialist Realism and basic Russian chauvinism. And then there was the fact that they were a carefree young couple who enjoyed living their own lives, heedless of party line and propaganda. Well, when you add that up it is not surprising that they were swept up by Stalin's secret police in 1946. It is a wonder they were allowed to roam the Soviet Union and trip the light fantastic as long as they did.

In the annals of Soviet prison camp life Ruth Turkow Kaminska's story is not notable. She did not die of typhus. She was not raped by brutal prison guards. She was not even beaten unconscious by her interrogators. Compared to millions of prisoners her experience was idyllic. Bear that in mind when you read her story. It is not idyllic by our standards. It is idyllic only by the hellish standards of Stalin's system of crushing every spark of life and consciousness from his people before throwing them—emaciated, gaunt, and disease-riddled—onto the scrap heap of humanity that Soviet Russia became under his leadership.

Thus, Ruth Turkow Kaminska's story is in essence a cautionary tale. At every point, harsh as her fate was, she was saved from ultimate horror by various factors. One was sheer chance, the luck of the draw. As Ilya Ehrenburg once said, she had a lucky ticket. Another factor, quite clearly, was her own strong will. She never gave up. And finally she was a member of one of the world's most famous theatrical families. Her mother was Ida Kaminska, star of Warsaw's Jewish Art Theater. Her father was Zigmund Turkow, an almost equally famous actor. Ida Kaminska was now married to Meir Melman, another famous actor. Nor was this the family's first generation in the theater. They were known from one end of Europe to the other and in America as well. Adi Rosner, born and educated in Germany, was just as well known as a band leader, trumpeter, and composer. And the fact that Ida Kaminska was in Warsaw, not in the Soviet Union (having made a timely exit), was a decided help, even though her influential friends could do little during the worst Stalin years.

Ruth's connections helped with money and influence. How little they helped is also amazing, but no more amazing than the fact that her whole arrest and imprisonment was illegal from start to finish. She was not a Soviet citizen, had violated no Soviet laws, and even under Soviet law should not have been committed for more than six months—not five years—for the trivial offense she was falsely charged with committing.

It is these circumstances that make Ruth Turkow Kaminska's story so important as another example of the pointless cruelty Stalinist Russia was capable of—a tendency, alas, still not fully eradicated from the Soviet criminal detention system. In other circumstances one would describe this as the "Soviet criminal justice system," but nothing would be more absurd than to associate the word "justice" with the operations of the Soviet judicial mechanism, its police, and its jails.

Ruth was saved by Stalin's death March 5, 1953. By that time she had served her term of exile, but the constant and increasing difficulties that the police put in the way of her living a normal life were the inevitable portents of rearrest and worse suffering. But the death of the old dictator produced a major amelioration of police practices, which, despite such abominations as police insane asylums for dissidents, continues to this day.

Had Ruth and Adi Rosner lived in normal times in a normal country their life undoubtedly would have been marked by trials and tribulations, largely flowing from their own stormy temperaments. But there is no reason to believe that stark tragedy would have overtaken them. By the chance of coming to age in Poland just as Adolf Hitler and Josef Stalin opened the terrible minuet that each thought would make him master of the world, their existence moved off the conventional rails of exuberent young love onto the path of doom and danger. Despite all perils Ruth Turkow Kaminska survived to tell her story. It bears our closest attention.

Taconic, Connecticut
May 1978

HARRISON E. SALISBURY

I
Don't
Want
To Be Brave
Anymore

chapter **1**

Warsaw
September 1939

On September 1, 1939, Germany invaded Poland. Betrayed by the Soviet Union in the agreement between Adolf Hitler and Josef Stalin known as the Molotov-Ribbentrop Pact and abandoned by its allies, Britain and France, Poland fought heroically. But Warsaw was bombed day after day, night after night. The Second World War had begun.

I huddled under the grand piano, trembling in Adi's arms. The whine, whoosh, and crump of the bombs had subsided and I wanted only to sleep. Then one last, straggling bomb struck just above us. I sprang up, hitting my head on the underside of the piano.

"Mama, Mama!" I screamed, as ceiling debris showered down and fine dust clouded the abandoned nightclub in which we had taken refuge. "Mama, Mel, are you all right?"

"Everything is all right, children," Mama said, calm as always, from behind the big drum across the room. "Go to sleep."

Mama was Ida Kaminska, beautiful at thirty-eight and world-famous as the star and director of Warsaw's Jewish Art Theater. Mel was Meir Melman, her co-star and husband. Adi was the man I loved. And I was an actress in Mama's company, and a political leftist with all the idealism of the nineteen-year-old.

"Children," Mama had said. No one objected now to my relationship with Adi.

I smiled at the idea of objecting to anything when only survival mattered. A few weeks before, different things had seemed important. Then, everyone in the family had felt impelled to voice opposition to Adi.

"He is nine years older than you!"

"He is divorced!"

"He plays jazz in nightclubs!"

Even Grandfather Turkow had traveled all the way from Warsaw to Lodz, where we were performing, to thunder, "He is a playboy!"

I did find it difficult to picture Adi as my husband and the father of my children. But at the touch of his hand, I felt something I had never felt before. I would have followed him anywhere.

We had first met in Warsaw several months earlier. I was appearing with Mama and he came backstage to compliment me. Other girls in the cast called him a Casanova, which surprised me because he was slight, short, and dark, and his carefully trimmed mustache struck me as affected. He was not my type.

We met again in Lodz, where I was playing my first major role in Mama's theater, and Adi was on tour with his band. Wherever I went, he showed up. A basket of flowers from him arrived at my hotel each morning, another backstage each night. At first, I was annoyed, then flattered, and I found myself thinking more and more about him.

Adi, born and educated in Germany, was known throughout Europe for his virtuosity as a trumpeter, band leader, and arranger-composer. However, his credits did not impress Mama. I was her only daughter and had always been the center of her attention. She hoped for someone she could consider more nearly worthy of me.

For the first time in my life, I faced a serious personal conflict. I loved my family too much to hurt them, yet I wanted to be with Adi even if the world collapsed. Now I was in his arms, and the world was collapsing.

As long as I could remember, I had heard my parents and other adults speak of "before the war" or "during the war." As part of the post-World War I generation, I imagined that war would be an exciting, dramatic experience. Since Adi had come into my life, I was convinced it might take something like a war to solve my personal problems. The war had come—but it was clearly not the way to solve anyone's problems.

Day after day, Warsaw was shelled and bombed. Night air raids began with fire bombs that lit up the entire city. Everything that could burn, burned. An acrid pall of smoke hung in the air. Our sixth-floor apartment was among the earliest to be destroyed and we roamed from friend to friend for several days, seeking companionship and shelter.

For the first few days the authorities managed to warn of each raid. Radios and loudspeakers in the streets sounded: "Attention! Attention! It comes!" Everyone scurried from homes and shops for shelter. Always, the falling bombs seemed aimed right at us. I was sure their ominous sounds and our fears would drive us crazy.

One day, after Mama, Mel, Adi, and I joined some people crouching behind an apartment house stairway, I could stand it no longer. "Come!" I ordered. "Let's go!" I was determined to reach a cousin's apartment building in the center of town. The building was constructed of reinforced concrete, and I thought that there we would escape the shrieks of the bombs by hiding in the basement. Dashing into the street, we hugged still-standing walls as we ran.

When bombs fell near, we huddled in shop entrances or building doorways, mindful of jagged glass. Sometimes explosions came so close that reflexively we threw ourselves to the ground. Adi was with Mel; Mother held my hand, like a child. Soon I realized other people had entrusted their fate to me, too. Half a dozen of them stopped when we stopped, ran when we ran. They had mistaken my desperation for leadership.

Normally it would have taken twenty minutes to walk to my cousin's house; that day it took more than an hour. When we reached the building we went through the deserted courtyard and down to the basement. In the dim light, we could only sense the presence of many people. We sank to the floor and fell asleep. We were soon awakened by a big man who obviously had taken charge.

"This shelter is only for the residents of this building!" he rasped.

We promised to leave at dark. Later that night, Adi led us through fire-lit streets to the Esplanade Nightclub where his band had occasionally played. It was in the cellar of a building still intact.

That was how Adi and I came to be under the piano and Mama and Mel behind the big drums when the bomb struck. Within hours, others joined us, taking places behind the bar and in the wings of the stage. Establishing territoriality made us feel more secure. As more buildings crumbled or burned, friends and members of Mama's theater and of Adi's band moved in. Even my father, Zigmund Turkow, himself a famous actor who remained friendly with Mama and Mel, joined us with his new wife. After a time people simply sprawled wherever they could lie down. In the dark, we could hear couples making love.

Within a few days, we established a routine, as though life had always been like this. We ventured out, never going far, and dashed back at warning of a raid. Then came the last announcement over the loudspeaker. The choked voice was our mayor's. "Here speaks Warsaw for the last time. Warsaw on fire. Warsaw in blood. Warsaw in tears."

Then, abysmal silence.

The bombings continued, but now we had no warnings. Planes flew overhead constantly, so we never knew a raid was in progress until we heard the bombs' whine. It was now that Adi begged Mama to accept his love for me. She could not refuse: we had to worry about water and food and survival, not the suitability of a fiancé. And so we became a family.

Between raids, Adi and Mel set out together to forage for supplies. From the rubble that had been apartment houses and shops they salvaged treasures—a pot, a trinket, costly perfume from a bombed drug store.

Across the street from our shelter, a bakery still functioned in a cellar, and whenever the bombing let up, people queued in front of the cellar window which served as a counter. Our men seldom brought back bread because time after time a new wave of bombing sent them racing to the shelter. But one of our shelter mates usually returned with bread. We admired his courage until we learned he was deaf and never knew a raid was on until he saw flying debris.

After a while, hardly a building remained undamaged. There was no electricity, no gas, and virtually no water. The city was effectively dead, so the Germans reduced their night raids.

We used the lulls to go out, stretch our limbs, look for food and candles, and try to learn how friends had fared. The first time I saw people carving up dead horses, I retched. Later, I hardly noticed.

One night, as I was going out with Adi and two other men, we had difficulty opening the door. Once out, we discovered we had been pushing against the burned body of a man, full of glass slivers which seemed fused to him. The stench was the stench that rose from all of Warsaw, that of singed flesh and smoldering wood. Near the body were the remains of a horse and a wagon that contained more charred bodies, including those of several children. They probably had been racing to our shelter when a low-flying Nazi pilot spotted them and dropped a fire bomb. The planes by then were flying so low that their pilots could pinpoint and destroy a single baby carriage if they wished. They wished.

A thick, black column of smoke rose from the direction of Philharmonic Hall, pride of prewar Warsaw. How many thrilling evenings we had spent there! With the smoke burning our eyes and nostrils, we were drawn to the sight, hopeful that one link to our former world had survived. But the building had been destroyed.

Directly across the street a segment of wall gleamed white, all that remained of a cinema. The whiteness was that of a poster for a Joan Crawford film. Miss Crawford herself looked down with laughing eyes and flowing hair, a mocking reminder of the world of just one month ago. I read the title of the film, *The World Is Beautiful*.

chapter **2**

To Russia with Love
October-December 1939

On September 28 Warsaw surrendered. The bombing stopped. We left the shelter to look for above-ground housing in some building that had survived. We were a bedraggled party. Mel and Adi had not shaved for days. We had washed ourselves little, our clothes not at all. Water—what there was of it—had more urgent uses.

I cannot describe the awful disorientation of walking in an area one knows well, but suddenly finds unfamiliar. Holes gaped where houses had been. From huge mounds of rubble in the streets a stiff, dead arm protruded here, a shattered bathtub, a doll there. Sometimes we sank deep. We knew where we had come from. We knew where—or at least in what direction—we were walking, but we never reached a recognizable place. Once we came across a sign that read, above a pile of debris: "Here used to be the street Graniczna."

We peered intently at everyone we passed, hoping to find someone we knew. When we finally reached a possible home, it had so little space left that only Mama and Mel remained. Adi and I found a room in a partly intact building. There were no doors—they had been burned. Most of the furniture was gone. But we were no worse off than other people.

For food we sold what we had. One day, a loaf of bread might cost a pair of woolen trousers, the next day a diamond ring. We searched constantly for a hydrant or pump that worked, and we carried anything that held water—I had a rubber hot water bag I had found, Adi had a pot. We could not drink from the Vistula because the river was full of corpses. Water and food remained desperately scant even after Adolf Hitler led columns of troops, tanks, and trucks into Warsaw on October 1.

From the beginning, the Germans singled out Jews, shaved off their beards, and set them to cleaning up the rubble without shovels. Age or illness won no exemptions. We had no idea what else might happen, though we knew from Adi and other German and Austrian refugees that Jews were in for a bad time. But we did not believe the Allies would let the Germans get away with what they were doing, and we expected that in three or four weeks the Germans would be forced back to their own borders.

But Adi was not the type to wait. Shortly after the Germans entered the city, Adi strode into Gestapo headquarters, introduced himself as a German whose mother was Italian—to explain his dark coloring—and imperiously insisted in flawless German that the Germans provide him with food since their bombings had stranded him in this impossible city. A soldier was assigned to accompany him to his lodgings with a motorcycle sidecar crammed with food.

Adi gave an address not far from our refuge, and when the German rode off, Adi carried the supplies "home." He burst in on me, his eyes shining with mischief. He had not told me of his plan because I would have tried to talk him out of it.

A few days more and I realized it was not only the Germans we might have to fear. A queue had formed at a water pump. In line was a bearded man in the garb of the Orthodox Jew. He had his water can in hand when four young Poles came along.

"Hey, Jew, now you will have to go to Palestine. The Germans will make you go, even if we couldn't."

The old man replied softly. "Good. Let us say that I could go to Palestine. But you? Where could you go?"

Shortly after that, a friend warned that Mama was on a list of important Jews to be arrested. (How he had learned that, we never knew.) Within hours, we fled toward the only border open to us, Russia's.

The party that straggled east included Adi and me, Mama and Mel, my uncle and his wife, a cousin of Adi's who sang with his band, and another bandsman. Some of the women wore layer on layer of clothes, to salvage all they could. Mama and I preferred freedom of movement and only donned raincoats over our fur coats, to make them less conspicuous; we carried what we could. Adi had a rucksack, which contained—besides money, documents, and elegant suits—his two most precious possessions. One was a gold trumpet, awarded to him as second prize in an international trumpeting competition that Louis Armstrong won. The other was a photograph Armstrong had given him. It was inscribed "To the white Louis Armstrong, from the black Adi Rosner."

We could not know as we trudged along that we were leaving a part of our lives behind us forever. Neither did we suspect that we were saying last good-byes to most of our relatives and friends. Indeed, many who remained pitied us for venturing into the mysterious Red world. But I could hardly wait to see the great experiment I had heard so much about. I was convinced that the Russians had organized the most advanced social and economic system ever achieved by man.

We had been told how to reach the Russian-occupied zone of eastern Poland (the Russians had moved in accord with the Molotov-Ribbentrop Pact) by people who had made the trip out and back. We had the address of a peasant in Malkinia, a border village, who would help us—for a price. That is, if we were not intercepted first by German patrols.

As we picked our way through the debris to the outskirts of Warsaw, we passed dozens of cars abandoned in air raids. Two looked serviceable but their gasoline tanks were empty. Somehow, one of our party foraged enough fuel to get us to Malkinia—and off we drove, in style.

The peasant whose address we had agreed, after some bargaining, to escort us through the woods across the border, but we would have to stay in his hut until twilight.

Well before then, German soldiers surrounded the hut. Had they just happened on us or did they have a standing arrangement with the peasant? They marched us to a nearby railroad station, ordered the women to sit on the platform pavement, backs to the building wall, and put the men to work cleaning train coaches. We overheard one soldier tell another in German that the coaches had been used to transport people with typhus.

While our men toiled, the Germans searched us and took money, jewelry, and fur coats, though strangely, they spared my coat. All the while they vilified us. One German, in a short black leather jacket, riding breeches, and boots, towered over us, his legs apart and his riding crop tapping his boots while he rocked on the balls of his feet.

"Actors, eh?" He had seen our identity papers. "All Jews are actors! Wait until your men are finished with the cleaning. Then I will order them to run and I'll have a little target practice."

Numb, we studied each German face for a sign of compassion.

After a time, Mama noticed an older man in railroad uniform watching us. Ambling close, he whispered that he was not German but Austrian and hated the cruelty he was witnessing. The next time he passed, he pointed to a gate.

"Tell the guard over there you have all been searched and released," he said softly. "Then, quick, get into the woods." He indicated the man with riding crop. "He's the worst. As soon as he leaves, I'll get word to your men that you are in the woods."

Perhaps he, too, wanted a little practice shooting at moving targets? But we decided to risk it and got past the guard at the gate.

How or when our peasant arrived, I cannot remember. But we found ourselves riding in his wagon, our men walking behind. Adi even had his rucksack. He had left it in the hut when the Germans appeared and the peasant had brought it along. And thus we reached "no man's land," between the German and Russian zones, where the peasant left us. Nobody followed us. As we walked, we saw in the distance—with a thrill—the caplike *buddenovka* headgear, adorned with a red star, that distinguishes Russian soldiers.

The border guard was a young peasant, not much more than a boy. But to us he symbolized not only safety but freedom. Hysterically, we crushed him with hugs—and those of us who could not hug him patted his shoulders and arms.

"You are in a free country," he said in Russian, which Mama translated. "No harm will come to you." We touched and patted him anew as though to convince ourselves that he was real. He pointed the way to a train that would take us inland from the border.

We trudged on and on, wearily. Suddenly, a band of young Polish peasants surrounded us, howling insults. One shouted, "The Germans are finally giving you Jews what you deserve."

We sagged. It must have been fifteen seconds before Adi realized our changed situation. "What the hell do they think they're doing!" he roared. "We aren't under the Germans now. This is Russia—freedom!" With a fury pent up since the Germans dropped their first bomb, Adi and his cousin turned on our tormentors, fists flying. The hooligans ran, wiping bleeding noses on their sleeves.

We had not felt so good in weeks. Fatigue gave way to euphoria, and we strode down the road singing and laughing.

At the rail station at last, we found a throng of people who also had escaped the Germans. The train, when it pulled in, was so crowded we had to climb through the windows. Even then, packed like herrings in a barrel, we remained euphoric. Everything struck us as funny—even the men who urinated out of the windows and teased the women who could not. We had no idea where we were going or what would happen to us. We knew only that we had left the Germans and their war behind. Russia, that fall of 1939, was at peace, and I believed what they said—that they had occupied a sizeable part of my country for our own good, to protect us from the Germans.

The train took us to Bialystok, which was a Polish city when I had visited there many times with Mama's theatrical company. I remembered it fondly. Now it was overcrowded with miserably dressed refugees. Many people had left everything behind. Some had started out in their shabbiest clothes, thinking that would be the best way to appear before Communist officials. Others, like us, had been robbed by the Nazis. Everywhere, there were chalked messages and notes pasted to walls. "Anyone with information about Ruchel Finkel from Krakow, please contact David Finkel at. . . ." Or "Berenstein, Moniek is living on the fifth floor in apartment 3 at. . . . Please contact."

Casually, the Russians substituted Soviet identity papers for our Polish documents. The Soviet government could not provide for people without papers, the officials told us, and since Poland no longer existed "there is nobody to look after your interests." The new papers restricted us to the Russian-occupied zone of what had been Poland, and we could not travel into Russia itself without a compelling reason and a special permit. I did not think much about it. The documents were so easily given that they seemed unimportant—except that Adi obtained a Soviet passport for me with his name on it, thus marrying me without formality.

Not everyone took the papers, though. Some refused them because they feared they might never be able to return to Poland when the Germans were defeated. Some had not made up their minds whether or not they wanted to remain in the Soviet Union even temporarily. One refused because, he said, "As a good businessman, I never buy any merchandise which is thrust upon me too eagerly."

But the Soviet soldiers were extremely friendly and in their ill-fitting uniforms with frayed overcoats, they appeared impressed even by the refugees' disreputable clothes. The Russians were no less confused than the refugees or the Bialystokers who had suddenly found themselves under Russian control. Some of the soldiers, who were buying everything in sight, wore *tallithim*—Jewish prayer shawls—as scarves. All wanted watches—for a watch one could obtain anything. All smelled strongly of a cheap version of Chypre perfume. When commanding officers took their families to dances or restaurants—as we soon saw—their womens strutted in nightgowns which they had bought from refugees and mistook for evening gowns. With their Clara Bow look, tightly waved hair, and lips painted in a dark red heart, they appeared as though time had stopped for them in the 1920s.

I was puzzled but when I mentioned my puzzlement to other newcomers, they shrugged. "What is there not to understand?" they asked. "It's obvious. The Emperor has no clothes."

Trading, not surprisingly, sprang up everywhere. Doctors, lawyers, engineers became merchants. Some even slipped back over the border to bring in merchandise in demand in Bialystok.

That was not for us, though we also had to find a livelihood, and naturally, began to think about organizing a theater. But theaters were government-run. We would have to wait until things were "in order."

Before long, however, the authorities began to register people according to their professions and invited us to appear to discuss work. I felt flattered at how well informed the officials were about us. It was not too difficult for them to have learned about Mama's achievements. (I remembered coming to Bialystok in 1937 to attend a special performance Mama gave during a tour celebrating her twentieth anniversary as a star. I had not seen her for some time and had missed her tremendously. I spent the whole day before the performance basking in her tenderness. I loved her warm, wonderful eyes, her sense of humor, her smell. I adored her. But that evening, as I watched her performance from the audience, I felt awed by her greatness.)

I marveled, though, at how much the officials knew about Adi. It was almost as if they had kept a file on him.

Within a few weeks Adi was offered the opportunity to create a jazz band under the auspices of the Byelorussian People's Commissar. We were fast running out of money, but Adi asked for time to decide. He felt we might do better in Lvov, which was larger than Bialystok and might provide superior accommodations. Mama and Mel had already gone there because Lvov was Mel's home town and his brother lived there; many of Adi's former musicians also were in Lvov.

It was a two-day rail trip, and we stood most of the way. I arrived wearing a pair of Adi's shoes because my own had fallen apart. Though the journey had left us broke, Adi headed for the exquisite George Hotel; Mama's flat was too crowded. The George was largely occupied by Soviet officers but the manager, who knew us both, found us a room "temporarily." Adi immediately called room service for food and wine and instructed the waiter to put the charges on our bill. I bathed and crept into a clean, warm bed, in which I remained for two weeks, feverish and in a state of collapse.

The day after we arrived, Adi went to the Bagatel Nightclub; he had had a contract to appear there three months earlier but the war had prevented his keeping the date. The Russian authorities had not yet put things "in order" in Lvov, so the owner felt free to hire him and paid him an advance. Adi's first purchase was a warm nightgown for me, to replace one of his white shirts in which I had been sleeping. Then he bought me a watch. Each day he returned with something for me—clothing, a comb, high overshoes. But we worried about being dispossessed—Russian army officers were increasingly crowding the hotel.

For years I had had a recurring dream which I had heard other actors also describe. You appear onstage but find nothing familiar. The other actors all know their lines and where they are, but you wander about bewildered—until you wake in a cold sweat. So it was now. The night we had arrived in Lvov I had seen the same railroad station, the same buildings, the same streets I had known. Nothing had been destroyed. Yet everything seemed to have suffered some terrible blight. The Lvov of my memory had been such a bright, happy place. As I remembered them, men of Lvov, on being introduced to a woman, bent deep at the waist and raised her hand to their lips. Meeting a woman they knew, they declared, "I kiss your hand and I fall at your feet." Such touches made Lvov known as "Little Vienna." Now the city was dark and the people different. Nobody could call it "Little Vienna" anymore.

During the fortnight when I was ill, I had much time to think. I recalled a vacation I had spent in Lvov. Several young men had courted me in that innocent time, and I remembered in particular two special friends. One was Jacob Bickel, one of the finest political cartoonists in Poland. He played the violin flawlessly, held the city swimming championship, and had earned the degree of Doctor of Psychology; his book on the theories of Sigmund Freud had been praised by Freud himself.

The other young man was Leonard Hahn, who chose the life of a physician and poet instead of the indolence his family's wealth would have permitted. Bickel and Hahn had two frequent companions, whom I also knew, who were considered playboys but who spent endless hours and a great deal of money on a Home for Jewish Orphans and Homeless Children.

After I returned to Warsaw, they all wrote witty, wonderful letters to me. We met again in the summer of 1937 at the resort of Jaremze in the Carpathian Mountains, not far from Lvov. We rose very early every day, had lunches packed, and spent the day climbing in the bracing air and bathing in the clear mountain streams. When our time there was up, they had begged my chaperone and me to spend a week in Lvov. She and I had stayed at the George, where I was now with Adi.

I corresponded with them until the war started. Now I wondered if any of them remained in Lvov. I wanted to see them, but I knew they would be shocked by my sudden "marriage" to Adi. I was concerned, too, about Adi's all-too-apparent jealousy.

I had just begun to go out again, after my days in bed, when the hotel manager told us he knew of a flat for us. A German woman was leaving and we could have her place and everything in it for a consideration. We traded my two-week-old watch for apartment Wisniowieckich No. 6.

It was not much, but we had never had a place of our own and we enjoyed that apartment. It consisted of one room with a tiny kitchenette and a washroom with toilet and sink. We enlarged the place with words. The table at the right of our bed, near the window, became our "dining room." An armchair next to the opposite wall, with a small lamp on the table beside it, was the "living room" or the "study"—depending on how we were using it. The bed was our "bedroom." Adi found a large washbasin at a market and we stood in it to wash: it was our "bathtub."

Once, when we left the room to visit my family, Adi asked gravely, "Have you turned off all the lights?"

"I am afraid I left the chandelier on in the living room," I replied. It was our single bare bulb.

For warmth we had a stove, and at first we burned wooden hangers from the wardrobe—we had no clothes to hang on them anyway. Whenever we went out, we looked for old doors, wooden gates, anything to feed our stove. When the weather turned really cold, we bought *makuchy*, large, round, wafflelike discs made of the residue of grain from which the oil had been extracted. They provided not only heat, but smoke, soot, and ash.

We also had a miraculous sugar bowl that never depleted to less than a cupful of sugar. It was several weeks before we realized how it worked. Each time Adi passed me the sugar for my tea I had said, "Thanks, I've already had some." And he had been doing the same. Then, one morning, we burst into laughter together.

We were in love, and it was all part of the fun. There was an air of adventure to everything we did—including surviving. The Russians were putting things "in order" now in Lvov, so Adi's engagement at the Bagatel had proved short-lived. For the same reason, shopkeepers were pulling down their iron shutters. Thereafter, they would dole out the remnants of their stocks to themselves, their relatives, and a few old customers. The miraculous sugar bowl could not provide food or the other essentials of civilized life. But Adi—who did not dare to speak German, who knew no Russian, and whose Polish was woefully limited—wrought his own miracles every day, ferreting out treasures in the unlikeliest places, bartering, selling at a profit, and delightedly bringing the fruits of his adventures to me. His pleasure was greater than that of the ordinary man bringing gifts to his bride. In the few months he had known me before the war, he had always wanted to do things that would overwhelm me. I was the daughter of a kind of royal family of the theater. Grandma Esther Rachel Kaminska had been so famous and so beloved a Yiddish actress that when she died in 1926 even Warsaw's Gentile-owned stores closed in mourning. Newspaper photographs showed vast throngs blocking the streets during her funeral. Her husband, Grandfather Abram Isaac Kaminski, was an actor, director, playwright, and founder of the Kaminski Theater where Mama played. My father, Zigmund Turkow, was a distinguished actor and playwright (and a talented amateur painter). Father's brothers were actors. (Grandfather Turkow alone shunned the stage.) Mama's second husband, Mel, was an actor. Mama had been acting since childhood and had become a star at sixteen. I started in movies at the age of seventeen. I was the girl who had everything, and Adi had felt frustrated.

Now, I could hardly have survived without him.

Lvov was jammed with refugees—and in every block we encountered old friends from distant places. There were hugs, kisses, excited questions, and exchanges of information: "Did you hear, so-

and-so is here from Krakow, but he doesn't know what happened to his wife." Newcomers outnumbered old residents, some of the more prosperous of whom had departed for places where they might be less conspicuous to the Russians. It was this, I finally realized, that made Lvov seem Kafkaesque—the physical city and the people who now crowded it existed in different dimensions.

Adi and I could take it in stride. But Mama worried me. She never complained and she still told witty, pointed, and poignant stories. But she had been used to servants and luxury, and now she was washing and helping with the cleaning of the little apartment she and Mel were sharing with Mel's brother and his wife. Mama did not seem depressed, but her plight depressed me. I wanted to cheer her however I could.

One icy day I saw a queue, shorter than usual because of the weather. I got in the line and then asked what was being sold. Eggs! Fresh eggs! What a present for Mama! I bought fifteen and put them in my muff—bags had long since disappeared from shops. My hands hardly fitted into the muff now and were growing numb, but I treated those eggs as though I were a setting hen. It was growing dark as I hurried to Mama. Then I hit an icy patch in the dimness. Egg yolks and whites splattered my coat, my muff, my shoes, and my stockings and froze where they landed.

By the end of December, the Ukrainian Commissar of Culture in Lvov invited my mother to organize a Yiddish theater. And a musician whom Adi knew came from Bialystok with a tempting offer for us. The Byelorussian People's Commissar of Culture had a great deal of money to spend on a big jazz orchestra. All he needed was a leader of Adi's talent. If we wished, I could be the band's vocalist. If we accepted, he would arrange accommodations worthy of us. We accepted—and the whole family welcomed the New Year of 1940 in Lvov with an attempt at the gaiety of the old days. We did not succeed too well.

chapter 3

First Lesson in the
Soviet Reality, 1940

We were soon to see the Soviet Reality about which I had heard. The Byelorussian Jazz Orchestra under the artistic direction of Adi Rosner—with a good many German refugee musicians and some fine Polish singers and dancers—had just begun rehearsals in Bialystok when Adi and I were bidden to Minsk, capital of the Byelorussian Republic, to discuss plans with officials.

The practical thing would have been for Adi to go ahead and for me to follow when he found a place to live. When Adi said good-bye, I went to bed. I could not sleep. Hours passed, and I wondered how I could spend whole days and nights without him. Then I heard running footsteps up the stairs. I knew it was Adi. To hell with practicality. We would go together.

For the first time we would be traveling not in newly occupied territory but in places that had been part of Russia for hundreds of years. An interpreter, permits for the Soviet Union's interior, new clothes, luggage, even pocket money, suddenly were at our disposal. We rode to Minsk in a luxurious compartment of the *miezhdunarodnyi* (international) train. At Minsk a chauffeured limousine waited to take us to the Byelorussia Hotel.

The city's wide, clean streets impressed us, after overcrowded Lvov and Bialystok, and the houses of light-colored stone seemed well tended. I was unprepared, though, for the lavishness of our hotel suite, with its thick rugs and handsome furniture. I thought the hotel must be a survivor from czarist times. But it was a new building—and from Soviet Reality I had anticipated something that smacked a little less of conspicuous consumption. I decided finally that the hotel simply represented Soviet hospitality to newcomers.

Downstairs, the huge, opulent restaurant was empty of patrons except for three men at an oversize table. The restaurant was new and not yet open to the public, the interpreter confided. Fawning over them, he introduced the three men at the table—the Secretary for Cultural Affairs, who wore an embroidered white blouse and no jacket, and two deputies of the Department of Cultural Affairs, dressed in what passed in Russia for business suits. The food, champagne, and cognac came in great quantities and were excellent. The only flaw was the obvious but mystifying unease of our interpreter; only later did I realize that he had been overwhelmed by the sight of food and drink that he had not known existed.

In a brief after-dinner chat, it was agreed that Adi would conclude contractual arrangements the next morning. "Now," we were told by the interpreter, "as you are probably tired, you may retire to your room."

We were too excited to sleep and said we should like to go for a walk and see what we could of Minsk. Our interpreter objected; it was dark and late and we would not be able to see much. "Tomorrow, we would be pleased and happy to arrange a tour for you. Right now, I would advise you that, not knowing the language, you should not leave the hotel." It sounded like an order—and we obeyed.

Next morning, after a limousine had sped Adi off to the Department of Cultural Affairs, I decided to look around the city myself. The first thing that caught my eye outside the hotel was an enormous delicatessen store with a huge assortment of cheeses in the window. On impulse, I went in and pointed to varieties I wanted. Every time I pointed to one, the salesgirl muttered *nyetu* which in Polish means "not here." I pointed again, saying *tam*—"there." Again, I elicited only *nyetu*. I experienced the same sense of puzzlement that I felt the night before, in the all-but-empty restaurant, and it bothered me all day—at least until Adi returned breathless with excitement.

We would be touring the Soviet Union. Adi, with the same bumptiousness he had exhibited before the Gestapo in Warsaw, had asked for six thousand rubles a month for sixteen concerts, additional pay for anything in excess of sixteen, and twenty-five hundred rubles more for serving as artistic director. The Russians had not quibbled. I would get twenty-five hundred rubles a month as the band's vocalist— and my pay alone, I knew by now, would be at least five times as much as the average Russian earned. Sound equipment would be no problem; the Russians would provide whatever Adi needed from the Electrit Factory, which had been moved from Vilna—in occupied

18

Poland—to Minsk. They would send an engineer along to supervise installation. A manager would accompany us to make arrangements everywhere, and we could keep the interpreter as long as we needed him. Adi wanted the musicians to appear in white tuxedos. No problem. The tuxedos could be made by top Polish tailors in Bialystok. For our own clothes, we could shop ourselves—and the Russians gave Adi an advance against his salary to pay for them. "They want you to have an elegant wardrobe," Adi said. Then his face reddened and he choked. "And they told me: 'Please get yourself a suit that fits. You don't have to wear borrowed clothes any more.'" They were referring to the handsome suit he was wearing, one he had had made in Amsterdam just before the war. True, it did not look like a Russian suit. . . .

At the opera that night, we sat with our hosts of the evening before, in a box reserved for officialdom. The rest of the audience was obviously of the working class. Stage sets, costumes, and orchestra were magnificent. The voices were splendid. But the stars were old and fat as they often are in opera everywhere—and the harsh Byelorussian language lent itself poorly to the tragic romance of *Romeo and Juliet*. The Montagues and Capulets sounded to me like Polish peasants.

I shopped for my wardrobe in Lvov with Mama. Her name opened the back doors of elegant stores and boutiques tightly shuttered because they were being nationalized. I was packing my purchases in Mama's apartment when she asked, "Tell me, did you notice how people were dressed in Minsk?" I recounted the officials' comment on Adi's suit, and after Mother had stopped laughing, I added, a bit belligerently I fear, "But at least I have not seen any beggars, and I am sure I would have noticed if people walked around in rags. Anyway, the costumes at the opera were gorgeous." Of course the Emperor was not naked!

The entire top echelon of the Byelorussian government attended our opening in Minsk. Adi had created an impressive show, a revue with singers and dancers as well as jazz musicians—many of whom had toured Europe with Adi—and with attractive sets, costumes, and lighting. We knew we were good, but early in the show we sensed an overwhelming excitement in the audience; only after we read the reviews did we learn that what had impressed them was the "Western style" of our jazz, which heretofore they had heard, if at all, only surreptitiously, on foreign recordings and broadcasts.

At intermission, our manager rushed into our dressing room—the Secretary of the Byelorussian Communist party, Comrade Panteleimon Kondratevich Ponomorenko, was coming backstage. I opened the dressing room door; the corridor was jammed with people, many of them in military uniform. "The Secretary's bodyguard," our interpreter whispered.

Ponomorenko could not find words, he told us, to describe his enjoyment of Adi's virtuosity on the trumpet. Then he complimented me, perhaps excessively, and said, "You are billed as Ruth Kaminska. Are you by any chance related to Esther Rachel Kaminska, whom I saw in *The Lady of the Camellias* and *Theresa Raquin* many years ago when I was a student in Odessa?"

"My grandmother," I said, "but she played in Yiddish."

"Good acting needs no language," he said. "Talent is what counts, and your group has it."

Our tour was to begin in Leningrad, and on the way we were to stop over for a day in Moscow. At the Moscow railway station, a limousine waited to take us to our hotel.

After a nap—the train trip had been overnight—we dressed for a reception at the Actors' Club.

I put on a new black suit with fox neckpiece, a blue chiffon blouse, a blue-black French hat, black shoes, and blue-black suede gloves, and got Adi's admiring approval. Adi wore his Amsterdam suit. When we saw the limousine waiting, we asked our interpreter how far it was to the club. It was just a few blocks away, so we decided to walk. The interpreter seemed less than enchanted, but assented.

As soon as we appeared on the street, however, we knew something was wrong. People stopped to stare. They followed us. Then they laughed at us and some shouted. When we asked the interpreter what they had said, he ventured only that our clothes seemed strange to them.

We turned back to the hotel and I was so hurt I cried.

"It is not your fault that you don't know how to dress," the interpreter said patiently. "You will learn."

At the Actors' Club luncheon, our waiter, a man in his sixties who spoke to me in excellent French, wore an impeccable black suit with a gleaming white shirt, and his goatee was painstakingly trimmed.

Each dish he put before us—black caviar, sturgeon, salmon, beef à la Pojarski, ice tarts for dessert—was presented with such a flourish that I pictured him serving a banquet for the czar. It surprised me to find such ways persisting in the "new order" of Soviet Reality.

I had one other, smaller surprise. Although my French was at least as good as the waiter's, I could not make him understand that I wanted a slice of lemon for my tea. It was puzzling. Caviar but no lemons?

That evening, we left for Leningrad on the luxurious Arrow Express. I loved Leningrad from the moment I first saw it that wonderful spring day. The sun was shining, the air clear and warm, the streets wide and clean, the architecture interesting and varied.

Built as St. Petersburg by Peter the Great more than two hundred years before to serve as Russia's window to the West, the city almost from the beginning was—and had remained—the center of Russian culture.

An apartment in the Europiesky Hotel was ours. The huge bedroom was furnished with antiques. The living room contained a grand piano, enormous mirrors, tapestry, and luxurious rugs and drapes—and a heated balcony. No wonder Rasputin had chosen this apartment for his orgies. There was a bullet hole in one of the mirrors—a memento of one of the vicious old priest's riotous parties.

I recalled that when I first saw the Byelorussia Hotel in Minsk, I had thought it was probably used only for welcoming special newcomers. Now, at the Europiesky, I began to realize that this kind of accommodations represented our new living standard, and I tried to reconcile it with what I had read of Communist theory.

In the ensuing weeks, I managed often to slip away by myself, and I walked countless miles. Each new street I saw seemed vaguely familiar, and I was puzzled until I remembered how well they had been described in the books I had read years ago—Pushkin, Lermontov, Dostoyevsky, Tolstoy. I felt like Alice in *Through the Looking Glass*—I seemed to have stepped through a mirror into the scenery of *The Copper Horsemen, Queen of Spades,* and *Crime and Punishment.* I almost expected to meet the characters of those books walking the Nevsky Prospect or crossing the picturesque bridges over the canals that flowed into the River Neva. The people I did see seemed out of place.

"You know," I said to Adi one day as we strolled, "I have the feeling that here in Leningrad, it is always Sunday. I have the impression that all of the servants have the day off and are on the streets. Their *gospoda*—masters—are out of town or sitting at home drinking tea."

Another thing contributed to Leningrad's perpetual Sunday look. It was my feeling that all the stores were closed. They were not. But there were remarkably few of them and few people walked in or out of them. When I attempted to shop—as I did in my first few days in Leningrad—shopkeepers looked at me in a manner that implied any normal human being should know better. The window displays in no way reflected what was on the stores' shelves. I learned later the things in the windows were called *attrapas*, which means props. I finally understood the *nyetu* at the Minsk delicatessen: in Russian it means "it is not available."

Once after an excellent meal, I was standing with a famous Soviet composer sipping cognac from dainty crystal glasses. From the window of our enclosed terrace, I noticed a crowd across the street. It was very late at night and I asked, "What are they waiting for?"

"Probably," he said, "for tickets to the Marinsky Ballet, or maybe for your concerts, because you have no idea how our people love art."

In the morning, I crossed the street to see the box office. It was a bakery, and it was regularly sold out of bread before dawn.

When Adi and I had begun to understand enough Russian to do without our interpreter from time to time, some of our more successful friends began to ask us if we had clothes to sell. We bestowed my stockings and Adi's ties as gifts, until we realized we might not be able to replace them.

A famous director gave me a different cause for surprise. At a dinner, he whispered to me in Yiddish, "Do you know I am Jewish and so is the great entertainer and movie actor Utyosov, and the composer Bogoslovsky, and the conductor Fayer, and even the Secretary of the Central Committee—" Something in my eyes must have stopped him. He asked, "Hard to believe? You didn't expect it?"

"It's not that," I said. "But why so confidential?"

He blushed. "Oh, no. Not at all. It's just that we are no longer nationalists here. It is of no importance."

"But you speak Yiddish so well," I insisted. "And you took the trouble to inform me about yourself and those other people." Our interpreter approached, but I continued in Yiddish. "Somehow, it seems to me that it is very important to you."

"Well, I see you are getting along very well without me," the interpreter remarked.

"Oh," the director stammered, "I find I still remember a little of the German I once learned and I was practicing it with Ruth Zigmundovna."

We were in the midst of rehearsals at the time, in the auditorium of the Park of Culture and Leisure, and we were frequently approached by actors and musicians who wished to join our company. We spent much time auditioning them and also listening to writers and composers with material to offer. Adi and I wondered how they imagined we could use a dramatic poem about a *kholkoz* chairman—head of a collective farm—who became a saboteur, or lyrics which began: "If my yield of milk will increase, the tractor driver, Vaska, will notice me."

One afternoon following a rehearsal, we were accompanied home by a writer who had presented such material. He was enthusiastic about Adi's trumpet playing, the band's style, and my "sophisticated Western manner." I took advantage of the conversation. "So you can see for yourself how impossible it is for us to use the kind of lyrics you proposed," I said.

"Maybe not yet," he said quietly. "But soon enough, you will." He was silent a moment, then said softly, "We have a saying here that the higher you rise, the lower you fall." Then he added, "Believe me, we, too, have many talented people, but they prefer to be on the safe side."

To my delight, Mama called one day from Lvov to say she and Mel were planning to visit us. Even though our apartment could have housed them easily, I asked our manager to arrange similar accommodations for them. I wanted to impress them and repeatedly, during their visit, Mama and Mel expressed amazement that such luxury was available in Soviet Russia.

But Mama and Mel had a surprise for us, too—an unpleasant one. They told us thousands of Poles who had fled from the Germans had been rounded up without warning and transported to the Soviet Union's interior or to Siberia. Husbands had been separated from wives, children from their mothers. Why?

Mama said the radio and newspapers had been expressing deep concern over infiltrators and traitors. On the air you could hear playlets about traitors who had been denounced by patriots. But many of the Polish refugees I knew had been outspokenly friendly to the Russian "experiment" as they called it. And the Russians we met assured us that their political and economic system was the best on earth, serving all of the people in the best possible way.

Then who were the traitors? Internal Russian politics seemed most confusing.

As we attended theaters, operas, ballets, movies, and art exhibits, Adi and I began to recognize the great names and faces as those of people we had entertained in our hotel suite or chatted with at receptions. They were wonderful party companions as well as great artists. We often wondered, though, that they never invited us to their homes.

My first visit to a Soviet home came about several weeks after Mama's visit. A young man, a student at the naval academy in Leningrad, unexpectedly called on us. His father, he told me, had been a high military official during the revolutionary strife of 1919 and 1920, and a committed Bolshevik. My grandmother, Esther Rachel Kaminska and her Warsaw theatrical troupe, were playing in the small Ukrainian town where the father lived, when fighting broke out. Stranded, they continued to perform each night and the officer became a frequent visitor to the theater and a great admirer of the entire family.

It was a lawless time with roving bands robbing and murdering in the name of the Great Revolution. One night the officer overheard a group of soldiers planning to rob my grandmother. The officer, at great risk to himself, organized the family's escape.

Now an old man living in Leningrad, he had heard my name and assumed I was the granddaughter of Esther Rachel Kaminska. He had sent his son to see me. He would have come himself, the son explained, but he was paralyzed as the result of fifteen years in a concentration camp.

"Concentration camp!" I exclaimed. "What had he done?"

"It was such a period," the young man replied. "But he is cleared now. He was rehabilitated." I was speechless. "The authorities have decided," the young man continued, "he did not deserve to be punished and he is cleared of all charges. It no longer even shows on his documents."

"But the fifteen years," I asked, "they don't exist either?"

"Juridically, no. You see, if my father had not been cleared, I would never have been admitted to the naval academy."

All the while he talked, his eyes darted about the hotel room. Finally he said, "Forgive me. I must seem a little distracted. But in all my life, I have not seen such an apartment. I didn't imagine that anything like this existed in the Soviet Union."

I had to pay my respects to the man who had saved my family, and I went with Adi to see him. He was a Meritorious Bolshevik, and accordingly was receiving the highest rate of pension. The whole family, five persons, lived in one room of a five-room apartment. Each of the other rooms was occupied by a different family, all sharing the one kitchen and bath.

One night, after our own performance, we were invited to the Movie Club. The movies were usually American and only a chosen few got to see them at special screenings.

That night they showed a very old Laurel and Hardy comedy. While others in the room laughed, I felt chilled and miserable. The film reminded me of my childhood in Poland when I had first laughed at the hilarious nonsense: homesickness welled up in me and I worried about the people we had left behind in Poland. I was in no mood for the reception to follow the screening but we could not back out.

The club dining room, with an abundance of red velvet and gold trim, looked like a stage set for an operetta. Enormous mirrors and pictures in gilt frames adorned the walls. But what took my eyes was the appearance of the starlets present. Just by their attire and their mannerisms, one could deduce what American film and which film stars they had recently seen. There were several Marlene Dietrichs, at least two Claudette Colberts—from *Cleopatra*, a Garbo, and a Mae West.

The Mae West, hips swinging, suggested we have a few words in private. Then, in an affected, sultry voice, she asked if I could sell her some stockings. The sheer hose of Westerners were cherished by Russian women, but the state factories did not produce them. I knew by now how difficult it would be to replace my own dwindling supply, so I said I had none to spare. But I found it significant that while ideology unendingly stressed equality—equality of opportunity, equality in possessions and in living standards—people persisted in wanting to express their individuality.

We spent that entire summer and part of the autumn in Leningrad. Our next engagement was to be in Moscow and just before we left Leningrad, our manager told Adi, "Look, Leningrad is the fur center of the Soviet Union. If you would like, I think we can manage to get a very fine coat for Ruth Zigmundovna before we leave."

A few days later, when I arrived home, Adi said, "Close your eyes and come into the bedroom. I have something to show you."

There, on one bed, was a magnificent mink coat, and on the other an ermine.

Before I recovered, Adi reached into his pocket and took out a small package. Inside was a diamond ring. "This is in place of the one we traded for food in Warsaw. Let it be my anniversary present." As I sat there in the bedroom, wrapped in my new mink coat, my ringed hand stroking the ermine, Adi explained he had just had another lesson in Soviet economics.

Our manager had simply phoned the commerce authorities in charge of the fur fair and had obtained commercial sample coats designed for Russia's fur trade abroad. Such furs never found their way into Russian retail stores. They were available only to a caste that included high officials, writers, composers, ballerinas, and actors. The gifts delighted me, of course, as they would have delighted almost any woman anywhere. But more than providing a lesson in Soviet economics, it seemed to me they exemplified the anomalies and paradoxes of the avowedly classless society in which I now lived. It did not matter how much money one had—one could not buy those coats unless one fell into the correct category. Obviously, though we were all equal, some of us were more equal than others.

chapter *4*

The Good Life in Moscow
1940-1941

Our hotel in Moscow, the tremendous Moskva, was in the heart of the city. Red Square and the Kremlin were to its left; the Bolshoi Theater the Maly Dramatic Theater, and the Hall of Columns were to its right. The hotel had been built after the revolution to accommodate delegates to the Supreme Soviet and to labor and scientific conferences.

Inside, so many people were milling about in the huge reception room beyond the lobby and the elevators that I was reminded of a waiting room at a busy railway station. From the moment we entered the elevator and all through the corridor on the seventh floor, the now familiar odor of Chypre followed us from the barber shop downstairs.

We were ushered into a four-room apartment. Its large salon contained a piano, an enormous desk, comfortable armchairs and tables, all polished to a high gloss. The furniture's style was executive modern but the room was attractive. Windows in the salon and bedroom had heavy draperies over silky curtains. The voluminous down quilts on the twin beds were encased in silk. Thick Afghan carpets were spread over the floor. Our terrace overlooked Red Square, the Kremlin, and the gilded spires of St. Basil's Cathedral, and we could glimpse the River Moskva.

Our manager told us this was to be our home even when we were on tour.

As soon as we unpacked, I telephoned Mama and she mentioned that she had received a letter from an old friend in Moscow, Doba Markovna. "Why don't you go see her?" Mama said. "Doba was one of the liveliest girls in school and we always had a good time when she was around."

Next day, our manager, who acted as our liaison with the People's

Commissariat of Culture which technically employed us, said offhandedly, "You know, the 'people upstairs' suggest that since you are billed as the Byelorussian Orchestra it might be appropriate to hire some girls to perform Byelorussian folk dances." "Suggestions" from "upstairs" were not to be questioned. So while Adi interviewed the folk dancers, I went to visit Doba Markovna.

She lived in a fourth-floor walk-up apartment in a project house. When I knocked, an old, bent woman opened the door. Her white hair seemed to have been chopped off, and a huge bandage ran around her head and jaw. Her face was paper white and terribly wrinkled. Her old sweater was at least four sizes too large, and high rubber boots of the kind fishermen wear protruded from under her somber brown skirt.

I told her I wished to see Doba Markovna.

"You must be Ida's daughter," she exclaimed. "I am Doba Markovna." A pause. "You are shocked? I can imagine your mother and I look as different as heaven and earth."

It was true. Mama and I were frequently taken for sisters. This woman appeared to be my grandmother's age, and though Mama had described her as vivacious, only her eyes were glowing and lively.

She invited me into her dark, untidy flat and suggested that I keep my coat on because the apartment was cold. (I had already taken it off—my mink was incongruous.) Silently I handed her the candy I had brought, realizing I might better have brought bread. She had been widowed for many years, she related, and had to feed three growing sons on her pension and an occasional job. Her health was poor and, I later discovered, she was undernourished because whatever she obtained went to her boys to give them a "proper start." She was happy to receive the candy, she said, because her doctor had prescribed sweets, but I was sure she would give the candy to her sons.

Still, Doba Markovna possessed something rare in Moscow. She had an apartment of her own. The three rooms, bath, and kitchen had been assigned to her husband many years ago, when he was an important official in the Department of Industry, and after he died, she had been allowed to keep the flat. She sublet one room, she said, "But if you ever need a room for your mother when she comes to Moscow, I would be very happy to have her here." I thanked her for her offer and invited her to visit me at the hotel. I told myself I would have to do something for her.

A Russian language teacher had been assigned to us, as well as an instructor in Communist party doctrine. In a few months I was able to dispense with the language teacher, but the "political instructor" kept coming to our apartment for a long time.

I had been anxious to meet people involved in Yiddish culture but it was not until after many weeks that I managed one afternoon to visit the Mikhoels Theater on Malaya Bronnaya Street where the Jewish State Theater had its headquarters. When I arrived they were rehearsing, and I was heartented at hearing Yiddish again after so long. It was a pity, said the actors and crew who surrounded me, that I had missed their director and star Mikhoels, whom I had been eager to meet. I had come to ask questions but they overwhelmed me with questions instead about Mama and her theater. Was it true, they asked, that there had been many Yiddish theaters in Warsaw before the war? Sadly, they told me, "This is the only one in Moscow and we try very hard to go on."

They had an exciting drama school, they said, but young people who entered it soon became discouraged by the lack of opportunity to act in a Yiddish theater and drifted into the Russian, Ukrainian, and Byelorussian language theaters.

"You may not remember," their famous actor Zuskind told me, "but your mother knows about the great actors we had and how high our standards were." Perhaps the great days would return in Birobidzhan, which, I knew, was the autonomous Jewish Republic the Soviet Union had set up in Siberia.

At first I thought that we were the only permanent residents at the Moskva and that the writers, composers, actors, and chess champions who were our neighbors there had apartments of their own elsewhere. But I was mistaken. Some had been on a waiting list for cooperative apartments for fifteen years or more, but most were not unhappy about the delay because the hotel provided them with more than the seven square meters per person available in permanent residences.

Of all those whom we met, the only unsociable one was the author and journalist Ilya Ehrenburg. How different he seemed from the mental picture I had formed of him after reading his books, which I admired so much. He struck me as someone who feared or should himself be feared.

The others were wonderful companions. We gave parties and were invited to parties, sometimes in our rooms, sometimes in restaurants. Wherever, the vodka flowed like the River Don. Vodka in

Russia was an entertainment, a need, and an escape, but I met many people whose careers as actors or writers had been ended by their heavy drinking. A popular Russian expression had it that "They drink to drown the worm that is gnawing at them."

Moscow, despite its cosmopolitan appearance, kept rural hours. All evening performances began at 7:30 to permit working people to attend. Buffet restaurants in the theaters often served delicacies not available in food stores, but at 10 p.m. all restaurants closed and the streets were deserted except for theatergoers hurrying to the Metro—Moscow's beautiful subway—before it too shut down at midnight. Only we performers were not ready to go to sleep.

The Moskva Hotel had two restaurants, one on the third floor and a smaller one on the roof, which enjoyed a fantastic view. Although both restaurants were closed officially, the third floor place remained open illegally for us because, as our friends used to say, "With money there is no problem." That restaurant became our private after-theater meeting place and dining room. It had about one hundred fifty tables, but after hours all were unused except for one large table set for us—with a white cloth and many, many covered dishes—ready when we came in.

The chef knew what we liked and knew how to prepare it for us, and the waiters did not mind staying because they were amply rewarded. The diners included people from the opera, the symphony orchestra, and the theater, and painters and writers found their way in, too.

The main purpose of the evening was to drink and to get drunk, but like lovemaking, it required its preludes. While the gourmets were still busy ordering the feast, the others would discuss their performances that night and dissect their reception by the audience. They all talked at once.

"Tania thinks that because she sleeps with the director, she can walk in front of me when I am giving my lines."

"They must have sent a group from a *kolkhoz* to us tonight. Every joke fell flat!"

All the while, they would be spreading thick slabs of butter on their bread to coat their stomachs against premature inebriation. Then they tied their napkins around their necks and began the feast. Faces became redder and redder, voices grew louder and louder. Every bottle was tossed under the table as it was emptied. No one kept track of his own consumption, but rather of the total number of finished bottles, which measured the success of the party. Once we were surprised by a writer sitting next to us who suddenly put his arms about Adi and me and whispered, "You, you two! You come from the free world, free art. You were living! Now you are sinking in the same mud we are." He freed his right hand from around Adi's shoulders and poured himself more *vodochka*.

Some ended the evening with their heads on the table, weeping in self-pity. Some would sit with their eyes staring glassily into space. Others would stand and deliver dramatic speeches about how meaningless was life, whose only joy lay in getting drunk.

At such times, the waiters would begin to do their preassigned duty. At a sign from one of the more sober members of the party, they would quietly approach those for whom the evening was over. The unconscious ones were carried out. Others staggered out in twos and threes, leaning on each other. Few managed to wend their uncertain way home alone.

Back in our apartment, I often felt badly about having remained sober. I hated to be so keenly aware of the moment when all the gaiety and fun turned to bitterness and stupefaction.

Late in December, freshly cut evergreen trees appeared for sale in the squares near the hotel and near the Bolshoi Theater. Ribbons, candles, and tinsel went on display in shop windows. Looking from the street into the windows of homes, I could see trees, complete with colored balls, lights, and stars on top.

"How is it," I asked our manager, "that Christmas is still being celebrated in Moscow?"

"Oh, that isn't for Christmas," he said. "It is for the New Year's holiday."

"But the trees, with the stars on the top."

"Those are Soviet stars. We're getting ready for the New Year celebration."

"What about Santa Claus, the old man with the beard, dressed—"

"That's Grandfather Frost," he interrupted. "You will see many special festivities. This and the anniversary of the revolution are the most happy holidays for children, with gifts and excitement."

In addition to our regular performances we were invited from time to time to make special appearances in such cities as Kharkov,

Kalinin, and Voronezh, that could be reached by fairly short trips. In December, back in Moscow, we were invited to do radio appearances and recordings, in addition to our regular performances. The recordings, especially, required tremendous effort on my part because I could not count on personality, lights, and costumes to conceal my flawed Russian diction.

By the end of the month I felt the strain, and one morning I found myself shivering and in unbearable pain. Adi phoned our manager, who came right over.

"She needs a doctor," Adi said. "To whom are we assigned?"

"What are you talking about, being assigned?" demanded the manager. "You mean you plan to sit here and wait until somebody decides to show up? Or perhaps you intend to take her to the Polyclinic and have her wait on a bench for hours with all the others? You should have learned better than that by now. We'll have a top man right over." He went into the other room to telephone. When he returned he said, "Ruth Zigmundovna, I am going to take a taxi and bring over Professor Lukomsky, a top ear, nose, and throat specialist." Shortly, he was back with the doctor.

I was off the stage three weeks, and after I was permitted to leave my bed, I was told that I might take short walks. For the first walk, I had the company of our manager and his wife, Sophie Alexandrovna. Because of the cold, we paused in a department store in Gorky Street. Sophie Alexandrovna was excited when she saw a display of Modelny shoes in light beige—the "latest thing." I thought they were ugly, but said nothing. I had learned to keep my mouth shut. But when I saw the price of those shoes, I forgot myself.

"Five hundred rubles! Can that be right?"

"Yes, of course. It's a Modelny shoe, one of our best," said the saleswoman.

"But five hundred rubles!" I repeated. "That's a month's salary for a working girl."

"Yes, but what working girl needs Modelny shoes?" asked our manager. "She doesn't need them; she doesn't buy them. You, on the other hand, are in the public eye. You need them; you can afford them," he explained reasonably, as to a child. Then, with a smile, "I am afraid you are still quite ignorant in ideology."

I knew what ideology he meant: "From each according to his ability, to each according to his needs." But I was not prepared for such flexibility of interpretation.

As a practical matter, though, I was beginning to wonder what I would do about shoes when my old ones became too worn to be used on stage.

"I will make shoes for you," Adi said.

Adi's father had owned a shoe factory, but with Adi's ability to accomplish anything he undertook, he probably would have been able to make shoes even without the knowledge he had acquired by osmosis.

Yet even Adi could not just go to a store to buy leather. Soon, I noticed him paying special attention to a man who lived in the hotel. Whenever Adi spoke to him, he fingered the man's leather coat, and one day he marched in with the coat under his arm.

I got a lovely pair of shoes that fitted perfectly and even had a belt to match. The shoes' soles were of the flat sturdy leather that had held the blotter on our hotel room desk.

Among our professional friends, we admired in particular a well-known writer, Vladimir Oppenheim, a slight, handsome man. One night he invited us to his home to talk over some of Adi's ideas for future shows. Later we turned to everyday things, and Raya Andreyevna, his wife, showed me her latest dress, which she said she had purchased from a *komis*.

"Do you know," I told her, "although I have passed those places, I haven't yet had the time to go in and see how they actually operate. How do they work?"

"Well, let us say you receive parcels from relatives abroad and you want to sell some items. Or you have a good coat you want to sell. You take the things to the *komis*. They evaluate them. Then if you agree on the price, they display them with price tags greater than the amount you agreed to take. The difference is their commission, hence the name, *komis*. You get your money when they sell the items."

"Of course," she admitted, "the prices are higher than from our state production, even though some of the things are slightly used. But it is the very best place to go for foreign-made merchandise."

I said I should like to go there.

"If you wish, I will take you and introduce you to the manager, so you'll be able to buy things even before they are out on the counters. He keeps things aside for favored customers. He might even call you if he gets something in that he knows you will like. This way, he can charge more than the recorded price and put something aside for himself. But it's worth every ruble. Naturally, they cannot hold things aside too long because they worry about being caught by a sudden inspection."

I wondered where so much foreign merchandise came from, and Raya explained that some elderly people, mainly women, made their living by supplying the *komis*. Their relatives abroad sent them parcels of clothing, and some of the women specified they needed evening gowns and fashionable garb in general. They prospered by selling the stuff, but I wondered if their foreign relatives really believed that old auntie led so flourishing a social life that she needed so many evening gowns.

Our men rejoined us just then and the talk turned to our impending tour of South Russia. "Volodya, let us show our pictures," Raya suggested. "We can give them a preview of the places they will visit."

While she turned the pages of the photograph album, talking about the people and the scenery, my attention was caught by the picture of a man. The face—pale, unshaven, reflecting exhaustion—seemed familiar, but I could not place the man, dressed in rough work clothing with a dark quilted jacket of the kind many Russian laborers wear.

Raya started to turn the page, but I put my hand on it. "Wait, who is this?" I wanted to know. "I think I know this face."

"You do," came the quiet reply. "It's my husband, a few years ago when he was released from concentration camp."

"He, too?"

"Oh," she said lightly, "it was such a time. It was due to a mistake and he has been rehabilitated."

A few days later, Raya Andreyevna took me to her favorite *komis* in Stolechnikov Pereulok. I was amazed at the things people bought. They were so frenetic as they pointed to merchandise over the heads of people in front of them that some nearly came to blows.

"Give me that! That's mine! I saw it first!"

I knew the Soviet system caused strange spending habits. If someone whispered that an item was in short supply, people would rush out to buy it and hoard it. They bought radios like those they already had, all kinds of photographic equipment, watches, and as far as I could see, some things of no value at all. I was seeing them in action, and for the first time I was seeing them behave without inhibition. Russians could not—or had better not—go on strike or march in unauthorized demonstrations. So shopping, I realized, served as an outlet for their emotions, satisfying the urges and cravings they shared with other human beings.

The milling crowd shoved and elbowed me from all sides, separating me from Raya. I made my way to the door to wait outside. Some time later, Raya emerged with her hair messy, hat crooked, coat open, and face inflamed. Proudly she displayed her purchase, an outrageously red, Japanese silk kimono with tremendous gold dragons on it.

"Don't you think this will be perfect for Volodya?"

I tried to picture her serious, quiet husband in that geisha costume, and murmured that I hoped he would appreciate it.

chapter **5**

Command Performance
Spring, 1941

Our tour of South Russia was about to begin. Our manager called us before 5 a.m., and, sleepy and grumbling, we rode in the bitter cold of dawn to Moscow's Vnukovo Airport. The plane awaiting us, for my first flight ever, was an unheated box with a long wooden bench on either side of the fuselage, presumably a troop carrier. We were headed for Tbilisi in Georgia, the native land of Josef Stalin—and we were all airsick the entire way.

As we touched down at Tbilisi airport I saw flowers in bloom, and when we got off the plane the heat was so intense that I took off my stockings.

It was a different world from the Russia we knew, but Tbilisi was no primitive backwater. The Tbilisi Hotel was first class and our rooms were charming. After our concerts, which began almost as soon as we had unpacked, townspeople thronged backstage to invite us to weddings and feasts, and we accepted often. So we encountered some of the customs peculiar to Georgia. One governed toasts. When someone proposed a toast to you, he held his wine-filled cowhorn—or glass—lower than yours, to show his deference. But, returning the courtesy, you placed your horn or glass below his. He then lowered his, but you were not to be outdone.

At the weddings we attended, many toasts were offered to absent brothers, uncles, cousins. "Why so many away?" I asked a table companion at one party.

His reply was slow in coming. "You would have to understand our people better. Some of them were not enthusiastic about the Soviet form of government and the collectivization of their farms and the confiscation of their wealth in gold and silver. By making strong objections they were considered to be opposed to the Soviet system, and fighting it. That is counter-revolutionary and a serious crime."

"But it seems that nearly every family has missing ones."

"The government feels it must protect the revolution," he said. "You realize, of course, that the Soviet Reality was created to benefit all of us and so sometimes things must be done which we cannot all understand."

That night I tossed and turned and punched my pillow. I changed into a fresh nightgown but still I could not sleep. My table companion's words brought to mind the Meritorious Bolshevik who had spent fifteen years in prison and then had been "rehabilitated." I remembered my friend Oppenheim. And I recalled the writer who had quoted the saying, "The higher you rise, the lower you fall." I felt compelled right now, this very night, to sort out my impressions of this country. But what could I think? I was drowning in contradictions.

This country, this government, had taken us in, given us asylum, and heaped wealth and fame on us. But had I the right, as a result of my favored treatment, to close my eyes and refuse to see, refuse to question?

My increasing doubts did not prevent my enjoying the beauty and diversity of the country. In Kutais, the only other Georgian town in which we performed, we were drinking and devouring shashlik at the annual wine bazaar when we saw a man coming down the mountain. He wore a felt hat and a jacket of uncured sheep hide, and he carried a shepherd's staff. When he came near us, he peered into our faces and asked, "Yid?"

Adi and I nodded. He pointed to himself and said, "Yid." That was all. When I mentioned the encounter to Jewish friends, they said, "Ah, that must have been a Mountain Jew. They came up from Assyria many centuries ago, and they speak a language called Tat. They live high in the mountains and they're very religious—in their own way." The only Yiddish word that they knew was "Yid."

In Yerevan, the capital of Armenia, where our next series of concerts was scheduled, we found a very European people—among them talented actors, painters, and jazz musicians—rather than the rug merchants I expected. Professionals and ordinary folks alike wildly applauded our jazz, so different from anything they had heard.

We played Baku, the capital of Azerbaidzhan, where oil derricks rose from the Caspian Sea. Flat-roofed, Byzantine-looking houses of white stone climbed the mountainside and mosques pointed their minarets heavenward. The new government buildings, however, looked as though they all had been designed by the same architect. They seemed to epitomize the government's attempt to homogenize the diverse peoples, and they were dissonant notes in a beautiful harmony. A companion from the area murmured wistfully, "They might have tried to adjust, somehow, to the surroundings."

Since we had started our tour in Minsk, we had not taken a vacation. Now after three months in the south, we could rest for two weeks before appearing in Kiev.

Adi and I were just beginning to unwind in the crystal air of the Caucasus mountain resort, Yessentuki, when our manager told us to pack and be ready to leave in two hours. "Don't ask questions. It's an order."

A special plane took us and our company back over the Caucasus to the Black Sea resort of Sochi, where we landed in a tropical downpour. We were soaked just scurrying from the limousine into the Primorskaya Hotel. The hotel had not known we were coming until the last moment, and we had to sit in the lobby, wet, waiting for our rooms to be made up.

After a time, our manager rushed in with some officials and, without removing his dripping raincoat, spoke to the hotel manager, telephoned, rushed outside, came back wetter than ever, conversed with the officials, and telephoned again. Nobody could ask him anything. We had never seen him so distraught.

Once, as he hurried past us, he snapped, "As soon as they give you the keys to your room, unpack, rest, and wait."

We unpacked, but we could not rest. Others in the company kept knocking at our door to ask if we had any news. To pass the time we began playing cards. Within minutes, nearly all of our staff of thirty-five had crowded into our room. The bids grew larger from play to play. Some lost their money quickly and stood behind those still in the game, offering advice. The pot was enormous—it had reached thousands of rubles. Tempers frayed. The ballet dancer accused the first violinist, who was acting as banker of the game, of closing the bets too soon. The first violinist appealed to everybody in an injured tone to say it wasn't so. Then the door opened and the manager, pale and exhausted, came in. Wet, almost whispering, he told us, "Comrades, a big event brought us here." We had guessed that.

"Tomorrow," he faltered, "tomorrow, we will have a concert

which—comrades—which—" One girl helped him take off his coat. The first violinist sprang up to put a chair under him. Adi handed him a glass of cognac. After some minutes, he pulled himself together enough to speak more calmly.

"Tomorrow, you must be excellent. Give every bit of your talent. Mobilize all of your possibilities. And now—now, please go to your rooms and try to have a good night's rest." He was still sitting in the puddle formed by the water dripping from his clothes when the last of the company left. His jaw quivered and he began to cry.

"Adi Ignatzevich. Ruth Zigmundovna! Tomorrow will be the biggest day in my life—in all of our lives! I cannot say anything more."

We hardly slept that night. By morning, everything was dry and the sun was shining. Our technical staff had been at the theater for hours. We would be escorted there at 5:30. "Be sure to bring your identification documents with you," we were told.

That evening at the stage door, NKVD (secret police)* officers and civilians checked each of us. One officer looked at the pictures on our documents and compared them with our faces. Another inspected pockets and handbags, still another checked our names on a list. When we were allowed to enter the theater, the atmosphere was so tense that we avoided speaking to each other even in our dressing rooms.

Curtain time. The lights went on. The curtain rose. Before us was an empty theater. Only the closed curtains of the boxes at the sides of the stage indicated that this was not some ghastly joke.

Any performer—but especially a musical revue performer—needs a live audience. We spent two hours delivering jokes without getting a laugh, two hours singing songs and playing music followed by silence. When the reverberations of our imposing brass and tympani sections finally subsided and the curtain rang down, there were no curtain calls. We left the theater in dispirited silence.

None of us slept that night. Some timidly knocked on colleagues'

*The Soviet Union's secret police will be identified throughout this book by varying sets of initials. The initials used will reflect the official title of the police agency at the time it is mentioned. In my early years in Russia, from 1939 to 1943, the secret police were called NKVD, for Peoples' Commissariat of Internal Affairs. In 1943 the agency was divided in two, one part retaining the NKVD designation and the other becoming NKGB, which stood for Peoples' Commissariat of State Security. In 1946 the Soviet Union decided that ministry was a more seemly term than commissariat, so the NKVD became MVD, for Ministry of Internal Affairs, and the NKGB became MGB, for Ministry of State Security. In 1953 the two agencies were combined into one Ministry of Internal Affairs, with the initials MVD. In March 1954 the MVD was renamed KGB, for Commissariat of State Security.

doors and tried to make jokes to break the somber mood, but their humor fell with a thud.

Our manager, who had not bothered to reserve a room for himself, sat in our room, still wearing his raincoat and hat. His fingers drumming on the desk, he got more on our nerves every moment. From time to time, he rose and paced the floor with his hands behind his back, occasionally taking off his hat to scratch his head.

"If only I could get drunk," he said, hollow-voiced. Two minutes later he repeated, "If only I could get drunk."

At 6 a.m. the funereal atmosphere was shattered by the telephone's ring. We jumped. Our manager reached for it with a shaking hand. His first "hello" stuck so deep in his throat that he coughed and started again.

Then he removed his hat, wiped his forehead and the back of his neck with his handkerchief, and stood stiffly as he spoke.

"Yes, Comrade," he whispered.

"Yes, Comrade."

"Thank you, Comrade."

"Thank you!"

"Thank you! Many thanks!!"

After he hung up, he remained silent, staring at the phone. Then he said softly, "I have been told the Boss liked the performance."

Then, seeming to grow taller, he said loudly, "Now, we are really in business!"

Nobody to this day has told us that we had performed for Josef Vissarionovich Stalin—the Boss.

chapter **6**

Summer, 1941

We abandoned our vacation. Our manager boarded our plane for Kiev—the plane that had taken us to Sochi—with two bottles under his arm, and immediately applied himself to fulfilling his wish of the day before.

I anticipated arrival in Kiev with special excitement. Kiev was near enough to Lvov for me to visit Mama. And though I did not know Kiev, it had a special meaning for me: I had been born there—while my parents were touring with my grandmother's theater.

When I telephoned from Kiev's Hotel Continental to tell Mama I would be seeing her soon, I did not hear the enthusiasm I expected. Pressed, she admitted she had not been feeling well. I suggested she see Professor Bloch, a friend of the family who headed the gynecological clinic in Lvov. I would go with her. I did not tell her that I, too, wanted to see him professionally; I suspected I was pregnant.

My reunion in Lvov with Mama, Mel, his family, and many friends was both rejuvenating and saddening. We babbled endlessly of our experiences and exchanged information about people we knew. But I was frightened when I learned that all contact with family and friends in German-occupied Poland had been broken. Not a word leaked across the new Russian-German border.

The second day after my arrival, Mama and I went to see Professor Bloch. He examined me first and confirmed that I was about three months pregnant. I discussed Mama with him.

"Please," I begged, "if there is something suspicious about Mother's health, don't tell her. Tell me. Her mother died of cancer and anything out of order frightens her."

I waited for what seemed ages for her to come out of the examining room. When she did, Dr. Bloch was smiling; Mama was blushing. "The case is not serious," the doctor said. "The same illness and the very same timing."

Mama expostulated, "I was expecting to become a grandmother, not a mother!"

During the next week, everyone we knew from Poland who was in or near Lvov came to visit. Among them was the poet Peretz Markish, a handsome, charming, and witty man. Once, the talk turned to what life had been like in the thirties, during the waves of terror. Markish related that when he had learned one day from colleagues that some officials had been inquiring about him at his union's offices, he had taken flight without even getting in touch with his family.

The secret police found him in three days. "We've been looking all over for you," they said. "You certainly have been traveling around." With that, they hustled him off to the Kremlin to receive the highest decoration the government awarded.

Everyone laughed heartily at his story.

Too soon, after eight days, we said good-bye. Mama's theater company was to leave within days for Rovno, near the old Polish border, and Adi was calling three times a day, insisting I return at once to Kiev.

On the way back, I kept thinking of my childhood. I remembered how Mama had always insisted that love could overcome any adversity, and all during my youth I had an unshaken faith in the truth of that. Busy as she had been, she had always stopped to listen to my childish problems and had taken the time to solve them. I remembered how my home itself—the four walls—spelled safety, security, and peace.

Then I recalled again the Nazi invasion of Warsaw, the first time I had faced real hatred and known naked terror. When I saw the first building disintegrate on that day in September 1939, I had realized how insecure stone and mortar could be. Home to me now was wherever Mama was.

Adi was waiting for me at the station. I had worried about telling him of the baby because he had not wanted a child. But to my delight he had been expecting the news and seemed pleased. "About you," he told me, "I guessed. But I never imagined Mel and I might be pacing the hospital corridor together."

Our reputation had preceded us to Kiev. Newspaper stories and whispers conveyed that even the Boss had enjoyed our concert, so people lined up for tickets. We expected Nikita Sergeyevich Khrushchev, then Secretary of the Communist party of the Ukraine, would attend our concerts. But I met Khrushchev first at a party. His children, too, were there, well dressed and looking like *stilyagi*—youths with a weakness for Western-style clothes. They differed remarkably from their father, who resembled a jovial *kolkhoz* chairman and exemplified the new kind of man the Soviets had created—from peasant to political boss. I had been more impressed months before by Comrade Ponomorenko, who as Secretary of the Byelorussian Communist party held a parallel office but seemed much more statesmanlike, much more intelligent.

A few days after my return to Kiev, in the midst of a rehearsal, I began to bleed. Adi said he would not be able to go on with the evening's performance. So our manager went into action; he got in touch with the local authorities of the Ukrainian Republic. I was taken to the VIP hospital and assigned a luxurious two-bed room for myself. A distinguished specialist was summoned to consult with the hospital doctors, and they decided to call Professor Bloch.

Two hours later, the tall, dignified, aristocratic Dr. Bloch entered my room, face pale as wax. The local government people had ordered NKVD in Kiev to locate Dr. Bloch and bring him by special plane. They did not say why they wanted him, so NKVD used its standard operating procedure. NKVD Kiev phoned the NKVD men in Lvov who went to the doctor's home and ordered him to come along "at once!" His wife was sure she would never see him again.

At my bedside, Dr. Bloch could only stand and shake his head speechlessly. Finally he took out his handkerchief, wiped his forehead, and wryly told me what he had just been through. The Russians involved in his "abduction" laughed boisterously and slapped each other's backs and their own thighs over what they considered a glorious joke.

My bleeding proved to be nothing to worry about, and Dr. Bloch was escorted home the way he had come, but now with a huge fee in his pocket.

Once Adi learned that neither I nor the child was in danger, he went to the theater for the performance. After dinner I had the nurse turn on the radio: the concert would be broadcast. For the first time, I was to experience an opening night from the audience side.

I could hear from the sounds in the auditorium that the place was filled. Then everything became quiet. I could picture the lights dimming and the curtain about to rise. A burst of applause greeted the orchestra, already seated when the curtains parted. I knew how impressive they looked, spread out on the dais, in their white tuxedos. Then I heard thunderous applause. I knew that was for Adi as he took his place on the podium.

I could visualize him turning to greet the public and I pictured the way he held up his trumpet to begin. It was a special gesture, almost a signature, that signaled the start of a performance. Many musicians had tried to copy the mannerism, but I never saw one succeed. The first number was Adi's special arrangement of Toselli's "Serenade," and I lay back on the pillow, enjoying the flawless playing. I had always known how great a trumpeter Adi was, but there in the hospital, listening to him over the radio, I felt he had outdone himself.

In three days I was out of the hospital. Adi and I had just returned to our hotel room. I casually turned the radio dial and suddenly heard angry German voices talking of "Soviet pigs," "Stalinist swine," and "Stalin the Butcher." What were we hearing? Germany and Russia were at peace. We twirled the dial; Russian broadcasts were the usual. We turned back to the station on which we had picked up the Germans. They were still at it. From time to time we twisted the dial, playing the radio softly, our ears close to the set. We tried to pick up stations outside the Soviet Union, a forbidden practice.

At dawn we stumbled again on German voices talking to each other. Slowly we realized we had chanced on a report by German military pilots. They had to be nearby. We heard their chilling words: "We have completed our task at the Kiev airport. All planes on the ground have been destroyed, and we have blown up the ammunition storage area with no retaliation from the Russians."

A little later the voices returned. Now they reported they were flying over Ukrainian wheat fields. *"Armut und Elend,"* they said. *"Armut und Elend"*—misery and abandonment. To the German pilots, the breadbasket of Russia, as yet untouched by war, looked impoverished and abandoned.

It was not until late morning that the Russian radio presented Molotov. Germany had broken the Molotov-Ribbentrop Pact and attacked Russia without warning.

I panicked. Mama was in Rovno, near the border. The radio told us nothing about that area. Later in the day, Mama telephoned that she was safe so far but that the entire place was afire. I dashed down to the office of the Commissariat of Culture and begged the officer in charge to help arrange for the evacuation of Mama and her company. He looked at me in astonishment.

"Do you really believe," he demanded, "that the Germans can enter Russian territory with the Red Army standing there? You know, my dear, for such propaganda, you could get yourself in big trouble." After a time he smiled and became patronizing. "Ah, don't worry. I know you Westerners and I understand your fear because you have seen what happened in Poland. But the Soviet Union is not Poland."

By evening it was clear that the Germans had broken through the Russian lines, for that night our manager informed us we were to return to Moscow. I was frantic with worry about Mama. I was sure she would try to join us in Kiev and I persuaded our manager to allow us to remain behind as long as possible, although the rest of our troupe would leave for Moscow.

Throughout that week, all day long, wagons clattered and trucks roared, loaded high with people and belongings, going east from Kiev. By the week's end, we too had to leave, on orders of the Commissariat of Culture. The railway station was crowded. If anyone was frightened he did his best not to show it, for fear could be taken as disbelief in Russian invincibility.

Besides civilians, there were many soldiers going west toward the border. One group recognized us and crowded around, reassuring us. I felt like crying. They were headed for the front and they were comforting us!

"Don't worry," the soldiers said. "We will teach them a good lesson." Some were Jews who said they hoped to avenge their brothers. The plight of Jews in Germany and Poland had made them identify themselves as Jews for possibly the first time. Most of the others were Russian or Ukrainian. They were all young and excited, ready to defend their country and "Father" Stalin. My heart ached for each one of them. All I could say was, "Those poor boys. Those poor boys."

Shortly after we reached Moscow it became clear that the Red Army contingents rushed west had been destroyed. In the weeks that followed in that hot June I remained for the most part in our Moscow apartment near the telephone, worried about Mama and her troupe in

Rovno. I worried also about our troupe members' families in Lvov. The only time I came alive was when the telephone rang. But it was never Mama on the line.

Finally a telegram came. Mama, Mel, and some members of their company had reached Kharkov—deep in the Ukraine—and all were well.

Several days later we received our orders. We, too, were to be evacuated inland. We had one hour's notice. "Pack one small suitcase each," we were told. "Only take what is absolutely necessary."

We were going to Omsk, several days' ride to the east. It was the second largest city in Siberia, an important junction on the Trans-Siberian railroad and in the center of the Soviet Union. Even if important cities to the west fell to the Germans, it was safe to assume that Omsk would stand. The government was transferring important industries and scientific institutes there.

Our train had only rows of wooden benches facing each other, two by two in the unpartitioned cars, and was so crowded with people and luggage that one had to emulate a gymnast just to reach the one toilet. Although we had been told to bring "only necessary items," some evacuees had brought bedding and fixed their benches up like beds.

Despite the crowding and discomfort, camaraderie prevailed—we were all actors or performers. We spent hours discussing war strategy. At what point would the Germans stretch their supply lines too far and be finished off? Would they advance until the Russian "General Winter" defeated them as he had Napoleon's troops?

It was there, on that train, that I felt the movement of my child for the first time.

Our journey ended near Omsk, across the deep, swift River Irtysh in a suburb called Kirovsk. Soldiers led us to a not quite finished school, where other young soldiers from a nearby barracks set up iron folding beds without mattresses. The building had not yet been wired for electricity.

I unpacked by flashlight. It was while I was looking through our few belongings to find something to cover the metal bedsprings that we were invaded by bedbugs—thousands of them! We scooped up our things and fled. (Later, I learned that the school building had been constructed from used bricks and apparently the bedbugs survived in hiding until people arrived.)

We slept in an outbuilding the army used for storage, and next morning Adi and I took the early ferry that crosses the Irtysh to look for accommodations in Omsk.

We found ourselves in a city teeming with refugees. It was hot that morning, and all day it grew hotter. We spent the day walking from door to door, but the industries that had moved to Omsk had brought their workers with their families and housing was scarce.

As the afternoon waned, we became hungry and tired. The air grew muggier. Clouds were threatening a storm.

The ferry back to Kirovsk was just about midstream when the storm broke. The wind carried the boat well downriver before the pilot could pull ashore and let us off. Kirovsk was upstream and we trudged wearily along, soaked. In the mud I could hardly follow Adi, and at one point I started to sink into what must have been quicksand. Adi pulled me out, but my shoes disappeared.

When a bolt of lightning lit up the surroundings we saw a large stone and decided to rest. Sitting there, trying to rub the mud from my feet, I asked Adi what day it was. It was July 20, my birthday. I was twenty-one. I had come of age.

chapter 7

Motherhood
Summer and Autumn, 1941

Looking back, I recognize that the summer and autumn of 1941 were the time of my basic training for survival. Life, I discovered, could be hard even without falling bombs. Adi and I obtained a room in Omsk only because its owner recognized us. She was a public prosecutor with daughters named Stalina, Lenina, and Revolutsia, and she had attended our concerts while on business in Moscow. The room was so tiny that the big rubber tree with which we shared it brushed our faces with its leaves when we were in bed and kept us from using the desk. Omsk's heat was searing. Food, despite rationing, was difficult to obtain; for such necessities as soap, one bargained unashamedly in the teeming market with other refugees. Everywhere one encountered throngs of people concerned about their loved ones in the combat zone.

Approaching motherhood made it impossible for me to work, but Adi had been transferred from the jurisdiction of the Ministry of Culture to that of the Ministry of War to prepare for concerts at army posts and factories. While he rehearsed I was alone. I had to depend more on myself.

I continued to await word from Mama, knowing she could trace me through the Ministry of Culture. Finally a telegram arrived saying she had gone to Frunze, the main town of the Republic of Kirghizstan, farther out in Middle Asia. Adi immediately decided I should join her in Frunze, where the winter would be warm. Omsk winters were notoriously severe and I had no warm clothing. Adi of course could not go. I wired Mama to expect me.

Russian rail travelers did not just board a train to take a trip—they settled in. The Soviet Union was so vast that the train might be one's home for a fortnight.

Some passengers boarded in loose, comfortable outfits. Others queued up at the privy to change clothes as soon as the train began to move. And then there were those who changed into pajamas for the duration, wearing their medals to show themselves off with distinction.

Even when dining cars were available, most Soviet travelers preferred to eat their own food at their seats. So days before a trip, bread and cakes were baked, eggs boiled, and pork roasted; the smell of pork fat and boiled butter, which needed no refrigeration, permeated the train.

If in peacetime a long journey required careful preparation, during the war it took heroic artistry. Civilian passenger trains had the lowest priority for trackage and might wait at a siding for two days if troop trains and military supply freights were coming through. Since one never knew beforehand how long a trip would last, it was impossible to estimate how much food to take. So at every stop, local people appeared with edibles for sale or barter. The price one paid depended on one's experience and acumen and on supply and demand; availability of food varied from area to area, as did the length of the trains and the number of hungry passengers.

Adi decided I would need a companion to handle such matters and chose Lopek to travel with me as escort, bodyguard, and forager. I seemed to have run across Lopek all of my life in various places. Lopek had adopted his name from a character played by a famous Polish comedian, and his enormous nose reinforced the likeness. In fact, he called himself Lopek de Paris, because in his first escapade he had ridden from his home in Vilna to Paris under a train. This feat, he believed, had established him as a free citizen of the world and not even the army had ever tried to fit him into its scheme of things. Lopek was a machine fueled by vodka. It got him going in the morning, kept him moving all day, and seemed to be responsible for his unfailing good humor. Whenever he appeared after a lengthy absence, he made himself indispensable. In the theater, he was every bit as good as any professional backstage helper; unusually imaginative and inventive, he could always "find" essential props. The last time we had seen Lopek was in Kiev. Now he had turned up in Omsk.

It was mid-September when Lopek and I set out in two compartments in a car reserved for VIPs. Adi had provided us generously with food and vodka, the latter partly to keep Lopek going and partly for barter. Knowing Lopek, I took a supply of books. He was not a brilliant conversationalist.

The stations at settlements we passed were crowded with refugees; they had no homes and the station provided shelter during storms. Everywhere we stopped, the waiting crowd surged forward, peering at passengers who alighted in the hope of finding a familiar face. They begged for news of the war—the Germans were still advancing. Many clambered aboard to trade, and a few, Lopek told me, remained with their stocks. In spite of the difficulties of travel and the patrolling by the militia, people amassed fortunes carrying items from one place to another. In one city needles were plentiful; in another, a twenty-four hour journey away, the trader could get ten times as much for them as he had paid. Tea was an especially important commodity in the southern republics. For an investment of one thousand rubles and twenty-four hours on a train, a tea trader could realize a twenty-five thousand ruble return. For tea, customers would give up gold or even vodka. Speculating and profiteering were crimes, and in wartime, the penalties were particularly severe. But the desire for profit outweighed fear.

Finally the next stop was Frunze. Long before we pulled into the station, I stood at the head of the car.

When I saw Mama and Mel, only my condition prevented me from jumping off before the train stopped. We clung to one another, tears streaming down our faces. Then we looked at one another's abdomens and laughed. The walk to the Hotel Kirghizstan where Mama and Mel were staying was a delight. Everything was green, stately poplars lined the wide road, and in the clear air we could see the mountains of Tien Shan to the east. I had come nearly to China!

Lopek took the rest of the vodka and shuffled off. "See you," he promised.

Mama and Mel had been searching for an apartment. I joined in the quest and we found a hut in which the owner, a prison guard, sublet to us a large room, a primitive kitchen with a rough board floor, and a corridor.

Within weeks, we had money trouble. Mama and I could not work, and Mel, as a foreigner, could not obtain any. Adi had given me all the cash he could spare and had promised to send more regularly. But every day the post office told me none had arrived. Finally, one day, a postal clerk confirmed that Adi had deposited a huge sum for me in Omsk. But Frunze did not have that much on hand and could not honor the draft. I pleaded for a little on account, but rules were rules. Adi had to redeem his original draft and send us a smaller one which arrived after two more weeks.

Neither Mel nor Mama was capable of bartering in the market, and when Mama tried once to sell a fox neckpiece, she was struck dumb. Thereafter friends did their buying and bartering.

Preparing our apartment for our babies, I whitewashed the walls, sewed curtains for the windows, and used a good part of Adi's first draft to buy two box mattresses which I mounted on pieces of wood to keep them off the floor.

Mama was the first to go to the hospital. She was only seven months pregnant but my brother was born that day, October 16. Since the tide of war seemed to be turning at last we named the boy Viktor, for victory.

Since the hospital food was bad, I fixed something for her each day and Mel walked there with it. At home, I prepared a bed and made a quilt for my brother. (I arranged for a car to pick up Mama and the baby when they were ready to leave the hospital; I spoke to the driver for a city official and promised to pay him the moment more money arrived from Adi.)

How tiny the baby was when they brought him home! Because he was premature, feeding and caring for him were a full-time affair, on which, in a frenzy of motherhood, I focused all my attention.

On his twentieth day, my own pains began—also prematurely. After I signed in at the hospital, the doctor in charge told Mel he might as well go home as it would be quite a while before anything happened.

After they "prepped" me, they put me on a sofa in the corridor until they could get a bed ready. For what seemed hours nobody paid any attention to me. The sofa was broken and every spring dug into me viciously. I desperately needed a blanket. But every time I tried to draw the attention of passing doctors and nurses they asked whether this was to be my first child. When I answered, they said I had plenty of time and scurried off.

Then, at the far end of the corridor, a door opened and I saw an unoccupied bed. Unnoticed, I made my way to the room and crawled under the blanket. I gathered from the conversation that most of the women in the room had had their babies.

Several times, the pain made me yell for a nurse. The women scolded me to be quiet.

Suddenly, I felt such intense pressure that I grabbed the bedpost. In a moment, I heard my child cry. The women began to shout for a nurse. I joined my child in crying. A nurse ran in, took one look, and ran to find the doctor while the women in the room clucked.

"I thought you already had your baby and just wanted some special attention," said one.

"The poor thing was having a baby and we didn't even allow her to make a sound," said another, shaking her head.

All this time, I was holding my slimy daughter by her feet, just as I had caught her when she was born. Someone came in and wrote numbers in indelible pencil on my wrist and on my daughter's. I was still sitting there holding her by her feet. Finally the doctor arrived and asked me where the afterbirth was. I had no idea what he was talking about.

They took the baby and moved me to the operating room where they started to push out the afterbirth. I must have awakened every patient in the place with my screaming. When I asked for something to relieve the pain, the doctor snapped that the few drugs they had were for soldiers.

Just then, I heard a tiny mewl. It was my baby, whom they had apparently forgotten on the table nearby. When I saw her I grew frightened. They told me she was so small and weak she would have to be fed through the nose. I was determined to breastfeed her, but for three days, no matter how I insisted, they did not bring her to me. I was afraid she had died.

At last they brought her to me, wrapped in cotton and gauze. She was very, very small, like my brother, and very red and screaming. They may have been feeding her through the nose, but she grabbed my breast at once. My ecstasy in motherhood was boundless. I was sure no woman had ever loved her child as I loved mine, with the possible exception, of course, of my mother.

My time in the ward provided another insight into Soviet life. My wardmates recognized me as a Westerner and asked many questions. "Is it true that in the United States there are houses more than twenty floors high?" I said it was true.

"Are they higher than that?"

"Some could be over thirty stories high."

"This means that it's as if we put one of our houses on top of the other, one over the other, thirty times?"

"Yes."

"You see," one woman said triumphantly. "It's true what we are taught, that in the capitalist countries they don't care for their citizens." What was the connection?

"Well," she explained, "you can imagine what it means to go down from thirty floors with the garbage or to bring up the water. And how do they whitewash these houses on the outside?"

It would have been useless to explain. I laughed, turned over, and took a nap.

Now we had two tiny babies to care for in the hut. Our biggest problem was diapers, for which we used any material we could tear up. We had to boil them constantly because they were interchanged from one baby to the other. Mel got the water from a small, fast-running stream, carrying it in two pails suspended from his neck by a wood yoke. Even so, there were times when I felt I could not go on. All my life, my every need had been satisfied, first by my parents, then by the Soviet government. Now the difference between my life as a performer and life in the real world of the Soviet Union was all too evident. Most other refugees had merely altered their geography, I had altered my whole way of life.

Adi had planned to come to Frunze for the birth of our child, but once he received my telegram that she had arrived, the authorities saw no reason for him to rush to join me. We agreed to name the child Erika, using the first syllables of grandmother's name—Esther Rachel Kaminska.

Adi and his band finally reached Frunze when the children were about three months old. The first thing Adi did was to get in touch with the town council, whose officials, realizing he had government backing, offered to help me in any way they could. Life became easier.

About then, a contingent of Polish fighting forces led by General Anders was organized, and many of Adi's band members, refugees like us, left with their families to join the general in Buzuluk. Adi wanted to go but with two premature babies, we could not afford to exchange even the meager facilities of Frunze for camp life.

Adi recruited Russian musicians as replacements, and finally the band left Frunze. I planned to join Adi as soon as our daughter was stronger, but shortly after he departed she became ill.

At first, I noticed a spot under her nose and treated it locally. When it did not heal, I called a doctor who gave her a shot and told me she had to be hospitalized because of the danger of infection to the other baby, as well as for her own sake. His diagnosis was diphtheria.

I bundled her up and wheeled her in an old baby carriage down the badly rutted road to the hospital. The staff would not allow me to remain with her even when I pointed out that I was still nursing her and that she had never had a bottle.

"Rules are rules. No parents are allowed inside." They pointed to many other parents in the halls, some crying and screaming because they could not see their children. I was determined to get inside.

A doctor beckoned me and said I would be allowed to hold my baby while they gave her a shot. They did not ask whether she had had any treatment. Distracted by their adamantine admittance policy, I did not think of volunteering information. Almost immediately after her shot, Erika began to swell, apparently from an overdose. Frightened, I insisted I would not leave the child there, and the head pediatrician, Dr. Riebkova, coolly told me it was quite all right with her if I took the child home to die. The doctor and a nurse practically pushed me out the door. Once on the door's other side, I remembered the town council's promise to Adi, and I phoned the chief councilman. He obtained a pass to the hospital for me and armed with it, I returned and banged on the door until they let me in.

Erika lay in a large room with about fifty other children, all on dirty, wet beds, all screaming. I picked up my daughter and carried her around all night, while trying to comfort the other children. Many obviously were dying. There was no sign of medical personnel. But hours later, when I frantically went looking for someone to do something for one of the children, I found them all in the staff room, talking, reading, and eating.

After that, it took me no time to learn that the staff was selling medicine on the black market. I saw trucks deliver food and fruit which were distributed immediately to the staff. No wonder they kept out parents.

Every moment that I was not occupied with caring for Erika, I did what I could for the other children. Their clothing and bedding were filthy. Most of the children looked like aged monsters with a layer of skin covering their bones, I saw some fall trying to reach for water. I engaged in battle with the staff, demanding food and care for the children.

But on the third morning the staff appeared in clean white coats and hurriedly put the place in order. They even turned over the mattresses and covered them with clean white sheets—the very first I had seen in that place. Dingy rooms were cleaned and fresh fruit was placed on tables between the beds. When the head doctor brought me a clean white coat and insisted I put it on to look like a staff member, I knew something was up.

"Because of you," she muttered, "all the high officials in Frunze are coming. I knew when I allowed you to stay I would have trouble."

When the officials arrived, they inquired immediately about Erika. Dr. Riebkova whispered, "Why didn't you tell me before?"

"Tell you what?"

"That you are somebody."

"I thought in the Soviet Union everybody was treated equally. I didn't think it was necessary to ask for anything better for myself."

"Please, don't talk about what you have seen here. I will be as grateful to you as I can be." She was offering a bribe.

"Please, don't make things any worse," I responded icily. "Just know that you are lucky that I am not a denunciator."

While the officials were inspecting the facilities, Dr. Riebkova had given orders to disinfect a small, unused operating room on the floor below. In it they put beds for Erika and me, a small carpet on the floor, draperies on the windows, a large platter of fruit on the table, and a vase of flowers on the windowsill.

My only revenge was when I warned Dr. Riebkova, "As long as you treat the children properly, I won't say anything. But remember, I intend to visit these children even after I take my daughter home."

When Erika was well enough we both returned home. Our little house always was filled with visitors. People were attracted to Mama because of her sense of humor and her wisdom.

One friend who seemed always present when we needed help was Hymie. As long as I could remember, he had been part of our entourage. When he was eleven years old, he would skip school to work backstage at my grandmother's theater. He wanted to act but he was not actor material. However, he so desired to be part of the theater world that he became my grandmother's stagehand and property man and then Mama's; he sensed what they needed from a flick of a wrist or the raising of an eyebrow.

Hymie had been with Mama on the tour to Rovno, and he had left his family in Lvov, which the Germans raced through. Like so many people he knew, he kept himself going with the desperate hope that somehow his wife and their nine-year-old twins had escaped the Nazis and would walk in the door any day. Meantime, he gave my brother and daughter all of the love he could not lavish on his own youngsters. Often he would go for a walk and pretend he was again the proud father of twins, carrying one child on each arm. We were delighted because his jaunts sometimes permitted us the luxury of a nap.

Later Hymie confided to us that our infants had been the biggest smugglers in Frunze. Like other refugees, he bought, sold, and traded, and his black market deals were made under cover of our babies' blankets. "Who would look under a baby's sweater for a watch?" he asked.

Erika had become well enough to travel, and Adi was insisting that we join him. I would go, but with mixed emotions. He had made me for a time the happiest woman in the world. He was a passionate lover and a tender, adoring, and thoughtful husband. But I had learned that Adi could not say no to an attractive woman, and attractive women could not say no to Adi. His unfaithfulness had broken the spell under which he held me. He tried to assure me that he loved only me and that his affairs meant nothing to him, but I was not persuaded.

I understood his insistence that I join him. Knowing how easy it was to stray, he feared that I too would err, and he wanted me within sight. Often, I considered leaving him, but under the circumstances that would not be easy. For now I dressed Erika for the trip and set out to meet Adi in Tashkent, the city nearest to Frunze in which he would play.

chapter 8

Feast and Famine
1942-1943

Adi awaited me at the Tashkent station. The band had a new manager.
He had appeared one morning and announced, "From now on, I will be
your manager." We never learned what had happened to our old
manager. Rumor said he had told a political joke to someone with no
sense of humor.

Within days, the band resumed its travels to such places as
Samarkand, Bukhara, Alma-Ata. The influx of refugees had brought
middle Asia close to famine. Flies buzzed in vast swarms, sanitary
facilities were overwhelmed, the heat was excruciating. And typhus
was wiping out whole families within days.

Just before the band was to leave this tragic region for Siberia and
the Far East, our manager suggested: "Ruth Zigmundovna, probably
you will soon be able to join the band again and you'll surely need
someone to help you with the child. Maybe you can find a woman who
would be willing to travel with you." I found the idea of having a maid
in the Soviet Union rather strange, but I did not object.

My choice was Yelena, a cleaning woman in our Alma-Ata hotel.
Middle-aged and dried out, she had no family and she slept in the
hotel's basement storage room. She assented ecstatically when I
offered her a job.

Because trains were overcrowded and hotels often inadequate
where we were to go, our manager had two private cars attached to a
train. One was a regular passenger car to which were assigned more
than thirty people of our troupe. The other, somewhat smaller, was
more than big enough for Adi, me, our baby, her nurse, and two
singers. The manager dictated the arrangements. I had learned to take

special treatment almost for granted, yet it sometimes puzzled me that the others never questioned such inequities.

At Novosibirsk our cars were detached from the train and sidetracked for the duration of our engagement. Novosibirsk in central Siberia was, like Omsk, swollen by evacuated technicians and engineers. But it had had time to digest the influx of refugees and had become a cultural center. One of Leningrad's best theatrical troupes and the Byelorussian Yiddish Theater from Minsk were there, and the Jewish actors were much more cheerful than those I had visited in Moscow. For one thing, Jews were enjoying more official favor, possibly because Russia now was fighting the fascists who victimized the Jews.

Because we were giving concerts for the army, we were permitted to buy things at exclusive places that most people probably did not know existed. With special ration coupons meant only for wives of high officials, I acquired a mink coat to replace the one I had left in Lvov. I outfitted Yelena. There were all kinds and classes of ration cards and we received them all. Most people had to wait in line for meager food allotments, but enough food was delivered to me to supply a restaurant. Butter and herring came to us in barrels, and once, so many slabs of bacon and so much pork that it took two men to carry them. I attempted to share the supplies with the other members of the band, but the manager scolded me: "You are not the one to decide who is to receive more food and who is not. We decide. In the Soviet Union there is no need for charity."

After Novosibirsk we headed for Vladivostok, and frequently after our concerts our hosts would reward us—more food!

At Vladivostok, we mostly entertained the fleet, but we gave some public concerts as well. Because everyone was looking forward to the opening of the second front by the Allies, there was even more interest than before in our Western-style music. The government's attitude toward Western art forms was in a period of thaw, as the official sponsorship of our tour evidenced. But the relaxation was hardly complete, one of our musicians discovered. He was a great jazz buff and he had met an American newspaperman who shared his enthusiasm. The journalist invited the musician to his hotel to listen to some recent American records. Our musician was arrested.

We found ourselves in a difficult position one day when an American government representative staying at our hotel invited us to his room for a drink after our performance. We said we usually were so tired after our concerts that we did not go out, but he said he would call us after the show.

Our manager told us to refuse.

"But how would it look," we argued, "if we say no to him? Anybody here in the hotel knows we never go right to bed the moment we return. It will look as if we don't have permission to speak to him—as indeed we don't have."

The manager was almost convinced but he did not want to take the responsibility of allowing us to go. Finally I proposed that he go along, too, to ensure that we did not say anything that should not be said. "Don't you see?" he replied, perspiring, "I don't speak any English." Of course! We needed to be censored. But he agreed reluctantly to accompany us for a short visit. And so we all went up and stood around, stiff and awkward. Before long we said lamely that it had been a long day and we left.

The good life proved too much for Yelena. I suspected she was consuming Erika's vitamins and oranges, and when she was not eating she was sleeping and neglecting Erika. After one particularly serious instance of neglect, I sent her packing—but we had to get a special permit for her to leave the area.

Finally, our tour took us to Birobidzhan, the controversial Autonomous Jewish Republic that we had been hearing about for years. In Poland I remembered it had been called "the hope of the Jews in Russia." When our train slowed down all of us pressed close to the windows to glimpse the town.

There it was! A small white building bore an inscription from left to right in Russian and from right to left in Yiddish. That turned out to be virtually the only Yiddish accent in the place.

Arriving at our hotel, we had to step into mud to get through the door. This was not some new settlement—it had been established years before. The whole place, which could not be called a city, looked untended, almost empty. Hardly anyone spoke Yiddish, except a few administrative workers and actors at the theater where we were to perform. They advised us to take the light bulbs out of our dressing rooms and back with us to our hotel, because we probably would not find any there after the performance. For dinner we were invited to a club. The main dish was pork.

Now our tour hugged the Manchurian and Mongolian borders where we performed only at army bases and for border patrol units. We stopped at Blagoveshchensk, Komsomolsk-na-Amure, Chita, Ulan-Ude. In such places we were received by generals who resided on huge estates. Soldiers worked everywhere but they got close to the generals only to shine their shoes.

The officers were happy to have us; it gave them an excuse for a party. They were justifiably proud of their table, the food for which was grown on the grounds or in hothouses. I could imagine I was visiting a nobleman's country estate during the reign of the czars and only the toasts, *Za Stalina, Za Rodinu*—"For Stalin," "For our homeland," reminded me that this was the Soviet Union, not feudal Russia.

The generals usually were circumspect in conversation and avoided politics. But one night an officer whose tongue had been loosened by female company at dinner—as well as by a great deal of vodka—began to expound Russia's view of the world.

"Nobody has to be afraid of us," he said. "We don't want to conquer anybody. We don't have to. We have other ways. We have people everywhere. We have a long reach. America, England, France—they'll destroy themselves and our people will show them how. Then the whole world will be Communist."

If the Russians did not want to conquer anybody, why, I asked, had they attacked Finland?

"Oh," the officer said, "that was a preventive war. Finland was too close to Leningrad."

I refrained from saying that the Finnish mouse hardly seemed a threat to the Russian lion, though the mouse had fought like a lion.

At last Adi and the orchestra departed for Moscow to entertain the soldiers who had so heroically stood off the Germans; Erika and I headed for Frunze to see Mama and Mel. It was summer, 1943.

My train was nearly a day late. At my first glimpse of Mama, she was standing on the little bridge over the stream that went by the house. She was holding my brother and I ran to her carrying Erika. I thought we would crush the children in the fierceness of our hugs.

It was a joy watching the two children become acquainted. I was struck by my brother's beauty. He had large, black, serious eyes and a perfectly shaped head and face. I could not say my daughter was beautiful, but she was wonderfully vivacious. She had begun to talk early, and once she began it seemed she never stopped. She immediately set about making her new companion feel at home, heedless that she was the newcomer and visitor.

As soon as the children were fed and the excitement had subsided, Mama handed me two letters that had arrived in the same post. One was from Adi in Moscow; he asked me not to stay in Frunze too long because he missed me. The letter was full of endearments that were undoubtedly sincere, but it would not have surprised me to learn that he had written with a girl on each knee.

He wanted me to join the band as quickly as possible because they were starting to rehearse a new program. He reminded me to try to find a new nurse. If I would send him her name, he would obtain a permit for her to live in Moscow, which was still a restricted city. Mama was amazed that it could be done so easily; she knew people in Frunze who had been born in Moscow and had lived there until they were evacuated, but had been denied permits to return.

I finally remembered the second letter which lay in my lap. The return address was Alma-Ata, Yelena's home town. But the letter was from a Ludmilla Kozlova, whose name meant nothing to me.

Ludmilla introduced herself as a girl of seventeen. She worked in the same hotel as Yelena, who evidently had nothing but wonderful stories to tell about the time she had spent with us. Ludmilla was applying for Yelena's job. She could care for a child, as she had brought up many younger brothers and sisters. Her life at home was unbearable, for her stepfather, drunk nearly all the time, beat her unmercifully. The letter was in grammatical Russian, and that impressed me because before we had sent Yelena home, we had noticed Erika was starting to speak the crude dialect that Yelena used.

When those two letters arrived simultaneously, I decided that some force was sending Ludmilla to me. When the papers for Ludmilla arrived from Adi, it was time to part from Mama. I would stop at Alma-Ata on my way to Moscow to meet Ludmilla. She was at the station when we arrived and ran to us, recognizing us from Yelena's description. I liked her immediately. She seemed to be a simple country girl, but vivid and intelligent-looking.

She took me to her house to meet her parents, who had to give their permission for her to go. I had seen misery caused by the war's displacement of people, but the poverty of Ludmilla's family and neighbors was another kind of poverty—"normal" for them and permanent.

The family, with children everywhere, was crowded in a one-room hut. There was no electricity, no water inside. Children slept on the floor, the father and mother on the stove.

Ludmilla's mother had no objection to my taking her. "For plenty of vodka," she declared, "you can do what you like with her."

It was early autumn, and when we left Alma-Ata Ludmilla was wearing her father's old army overcoat and galoshes; she had never possessed her own shoes. But even before we boarded the train, she proved she was not so simple as she appeared.

"Do you know," she said, "on our way, I am sure we will have many opportunities to trade. We should be aware of things to buy and sell." She bought salt at a place called Aralsk, on the edge of a huge salt lake, and at another station she traded the salt for geese and turkeys, which she assured me would not spoil on the cold train.

Finally we arrived in Moscow, where Adi was once again in apartment 704 at the Hotel Moskva. It was good to be back.

chapter 9

Awakening
Moscow, 1943

When we arrived at the Hotel Moskva, Ludmilla was afraid to go through the revolving door. As we were about to step into the elevator, she asked if this would be her room. I explained that this was an elevator which would lift us to the seventh floor.

"Are there stairs?" she asked, her eyes wide with fear. I had to shame her to get her into the elevator. She closed her eyes tightly, her face paled and she clutched my arm. When the elevator stopped, she was amazed that she had not felt a thing. In the apartment she ran around touching the draperies, the polished tables, the rugs and bedspreads.

After she had calmed down I told her she could take a bath. She was glad to, but hesitated to use the scented soap. She found it hard to believe that it was not a treasure for special occasions. She caressed it, fascinated by its fragrance.

Several days later, she bashfully presented a letter to her parents. I told her, "This is your private letter, and I should not read it." She insisted and when I read it, I understood. After the usual Russian greetings, the letter began, "I am dressed and I live as a princess in a fairy tale. Every day, as often as I want, I drink cocoa. I can have a bath every day with scented soap and I have never seen such white bread as we eat here. As much as Yelena told us, she did not really describe such a life as we have here, and Ruth Zigmundovna is an angel." Showing the letter to me was her way of expressing gratitude. Her gratitude went so far that once, when I awoke very early, I found her preparing to scrub the floor. I explained she had nothing to do but watch and feed Erika and take her out.

"But I feel terrible not doing anything," she protested. "For what are you paying me and giving me all these things?" Taking care of a baby was her pleasure, not to be considered work, and she had come prepared for hard, physical labor.

But Ludmilla learned fast. Before long, she was telephoning stores, introducing herself as Adi Rosner's secretary, and giving them orders to deliver.

We were rehearsing a new show when news came of the victory at Stalingrad. We decided to prepare a special number to commemorate the occasion. Adi was reorganizing the band, for still more members had left to join the Polish forces. But as soon as the word went out that Adi Rosner was looking for musicians, we had a parade of talent; even men who had played with famous orchestras for twenty years wanted to join our group. There remained only one important position to fill, the job of stagehand. We both came up with "Hymie!" He arrived from Frunze in due course.

It was just then that Adi published his first hit song. We were sitting in our living room with a composer of many popular songs. He said to Adi, "You know, the public loves your kind of music, but only to listen to. Nobody here would ever be able to sing your stuff. I'll bet you will never manage to write popular music. You must be born in Russia to write a tune that will catch on here."

Adi took bets. "Oh?" he said. "I can write Russian hits any time I wish."

With that, he drew the musical staff on the back of a package of Kazbek cigarettes. He spent about a minute chewing his pencil and then filled the lines with notes. Then he covered the pack with his hand.

"You want to bet it will be a hit?" Three minutes had not elapsed.

"Sure. How much?"

"You name it."

"Your new camera for my watch?"

They shook hands and, according to the Russian custom, I had to punch their hands apart to seal the bet.

Adi gave the cigarette pack to the other man. He studied it for a few minutes. Then he said quietly, "I used to have a watch."

What Adi wrote caught on. Other compositions followed and soon it became almost commonplace for us to turn on the radio and hear one of his songs. Royalties mounted day by day. The taxes on

Adi's income, apart from the royalties, came to twelve to fifteen thousand rubles a year. I was getting five hundred rubles a concert for a minimum of sixteen concerts a month, and we used to joke that I paid Adi's taxes. But there was plenty left over.

The most exciting thing about being back in Moscow was meeting old friends, and I was very happy the day I heard the animated voice of Raya Andreyevna Oppenheim on the telephone.

She had been evacuated to the Bashkir Autonomous Republic. She had had a difficult time, especially since her Volodya had not been with her. He had volunteered for the army and had been assigned as a war correspondent. He had been wounded and she was waiting for his discharge.

When I first met Raya and Volodya, I had been struck by their relationship, which seemed unusual. He was quiet and she was voluble, and their intellectual levels, I suspected, were unequal. But friends had told me of what she had done and gone through when Volodya had been sent to concentration camp. Many loving wives in similar situations had obtained divorces. Divorce was a minor formality, and wives of imprisoned husbands were under constant pressure to apply for it.

If the wives were party members, the authorities advised them that it was not necessary to remain loyal to an "outlaw and traitor." Superiors at work suggested they would be better off freed of marriage. Family and friends nagged: "You know, if they say ten years, it could be longer. What if he gets in trouble while he is away, and they add on time? What if he returns a physical wreck?" But nobody ever persuaded Raya.

Until Volodya's arrest, they had been well off because Vladimir Oppenheim was a famous writer whose work earned high royalties. With his arrest, Raya sold everything for cash. She used the money to travel ten days each way to be with him for half an hour. She sent him enormous parcels, aware that they always had to be shared with others. She wrote daily. Though she had been pregnant when Volodya was arrested, shock, worry, and endless running from official to official, trying to have him released, had caused a miscarriage and they had never had any children. All of her tenderness and maternal feelings had been lavished on Volodya after his prison term ended.

Fifteen minutes had not passed since Raya phoned me when she was knocking on the door. She was living at the nearby Savoy Hotel instead of at her apartment, because, as she told me over tea, she left everything she possessed in Bashkiria. "It was so hard seeing all the misery around me that I just couldn't take any of my belongings back to Moscow with me. Whatever I had was so badly needed by my neighbors."

So now she had to refurnish the apartment. "Will you help me shop?" she asked.

After one tiring shopping trip, she asked Adi to let me stay with her overnight. Adi would be rehearsing far into the night and Erika was in good hands.

We had crept into bed. Raya was lying on her back and had a book on her stomach. She seemed more serious than I have ever seen her.

"Ruth Zigmundovna, I would like to—you won't think I am foolish to ask—but can you tell me something about your previous life? I mean, life before the war. Somehow, the longer I know you, the less I believe what I have been taught."

"What do you mean?"

"I mean," she said hesitantly, "I have been told that in capitalist countries only a very few people ever had the opportunity to get higher education, especially someone who is Jewish. And yet—you are Jewish, and surely you are educated.

"I have also been told that all over the world, Jewish people live in ghettos, just as the black people do in the United States. I even wonder about that.

"You see," she continued, "we were friendly with a black engineer named Williams. He came here as a member of the American Communist party, but after being here for two years, he wanted to go back. If things were so bad for black people in America, why would he want to return?"

"Did he go?"

"No. He couldn't get permission. Later he committed suicide."

She sighed. "I have wondered so many times about that man. And there is something else I wonder about. All of the people who have come here—even the refugees, when they first ran away from the war—were so much better dressed than we were. And I heard that in other countries there are such wonderful stores to shop in, and you can buy things whenever you want. Tell me, what is the truth?"

While she was speaking, she turned toward me and her book slid to the floor. She bent down to retrieve it, but remained in that position so long I thought she might have had a stroke and I jumped out of bed to help her. Suddenly she spoke.

"Of course, you know, Ruth Zigmundovna, that I was only joking. I wanted to see your reaction. I know very well that there is not a place on earth where my Volodya would be able to be a writer and have it as good as he has it here. And about that black man I told you about, everyone knows he was a terrible alcoholic and that is why he committed suicide."

I started to ask what had happened to her, but she covered my mouth with her palm. Her eyes were large and frightened. With her free hand she pointed to a dark spot on the wall under the night table between our beds. I recognized a microphone. The Savoy was an Intourist hotel.

Raya Andreyevna gestured me to talk.

"Of course," I said lightly, "I knew you were teasing me. Who would take such nonsensical talk seriously?" I laughed.

She said, "You know, we still have to be careful because there are always infiltrators, traitors. They envy what we have done here. They are jealous of our happy life and they envy us such a leader as our Father Stalin." We put out the light and went to sleep.

Theater life went on. I began to think seriously about a new stage wardrobe. The better department stores had nothing suitable and since theatrical people were entitled to obtain whatever they needed for the stage, I tried the theatrical workshops. They could turn out authentic masterpieces for shows about Peter the Great or Ivan the Terrible, but when it came to stylish evening gowns, I discovered, their clothing was impossible.

And so I prowled through some of the *komis* looking for fabric, and I found an artist willing to brighten the plainer materials; I would make my own outfits out of whatever was available. It was a challenge to make do with what you had at hand. We all played the game. There was a chronic shortage of flour, so women baked tasty cakes from farina or the crumbs of rolls.

Sometimes you had to pay a bribe, called a gift. Usually it was enough to give a clerk stockings for his wife, or a vial of perfume, accompanied by a few endearments. For more important things, the gift had to be larger. This system created a category of people who made their living as "deliverers" although officially they had other titles—barber, driver, cashier. The government frowned on such pursuits and the penalties were severe, but many government people were integral to the setup. The deliverers could not deliver without cooperation from producers and middlemen, and you never knew whether you were dealing with a deliverer or a denunciator.

Their only defensive weapon was blackmail. "If you mention my name and don't protect me, I will swear that you were a customer of mine and I will take you with me if I am caught." A lot of suicides resulted.

I could not see how anyone who obtained money this way could possibly enjoy it. They could not dress better because they would attract attention. They could not eat better, I thought, because they were jealously watched by neighbors who shared their kitchens. But a young woman whom Max, one of our musicians, admired, explained it to me. You cooked a meager meal in the kitchen and the real meal in the bedroom over a kerosene stove. After the meal, you went for a walk and dropped your garbage, well wrapped, in a trash pail on another street.

This young woman said that even she, when she went to work, often carried a small suitcase containing better clothing purchased from a *komis*. If she had a date after work she would change into something nice, and then, before returning home, she would put back on the outfit she had worn in the morning.

"But," she sighed, "I am afraid I will never get married. My parents would never trust anyone to come into our house. They are afraid of being caught."

Hymie, who knew the family, agreed that she never would be allowed to marry. "They cannot afford to let anybody in on their secrets," he said. "They're swollen with money. They keep a stand in the market. It's owned by the government, of course, but they operate it. They sell fabrics, trimmings, elastic—sewing necessities."

"And from this they get rich?"

Hymie knew all the angles. "They give everybody short measure and hold back something from every bolt of cloth. They even stretch elastic. They use the extra stuff to make garments at home—a blouse or a dress. It's off the books and the profit is all theirs. And they do what the managers of the *komis* do; they put aside their best merchandise for customers willing to pay higher prices. Naturally, they always keep a present put aside for the inspector's wife. Their only other expense is to pay somebody to sell them unusually attractive stuff—if they can find it."

"Aren't they afraid of getting caught?"

"Sure," he answered. "That's why they live like they do, without friends."

As I became aware of these things, I found myself sliding into depression. I missed home—Warsaw—so terribly that it became almost a physical thing. Not that I missed the city itself—I knew nothing was left of it. It was the life we had led there. I remembered how we used to sit at home, my parents and their friends, freely discussing events and ideas. How I missed those discussions! Here, the talk was almost always about things, not about ideas.

Even the young people I had met—this girl whom Max admired, and her friends—were so different from the young people I had known in Poland, from the young person I was myself before the war.

Here these kids were intelligent and alert, and they also enjoyed a lively discussion. But the subject would be the hero of a book, or why such a character had done this or said that. They were familiar with every line spoken by every literary character.

Once one of them had just declared that under the Soviet Reality such poets as Pushkin and Lermontov would never have been permitted to reach such a state of frustration as to have their lives ended by duels.

"I wonder," I murmured, "if the Soviet Reality could produce such poets as Lermontov and Pushkin?" Everyone in the room grew tense. Quietly I asked, "Do you never discuss things that are happening around you? Life? Politics?"

One youngster finally replied in a flat voice. "What is there to discuss? We are Communists. That is beyond discussion." Soon after that, they said good-bye and left. I realized then that I never could feel truly at home in the Soviet Union.

chapter 10

The Waning War
1944-1945

Led by four goose-stepping generals, fifty-seven thousand Nazi soldiers marched down the streets of Moscow in ranks of twenty—officers first, then enlisted men. With their decorations and ribbons on their uniforms, they strode so arrogantly that they might have been a conquering army. But they shouldered no rifles. Splendidly mounted Russian cavalrymen with bared sabers rode alongside them. And Muscovites lined both sides of the streets, some stonily silent, some shouting epithets, some spitting at the Germans.

"Murderers! Pigs! Hitler kaput!"

It was July 1944. The Germans had been surrounded and captured by the Byelorussian army.

Hour after hour the Germans passed, even the walking wounded who brought up the rear. They looked as arrogant as their generals. On the heels of the last rank of Germans came the Moscow sanitation department with every piece of equipment it possessed. No litter was visible but water wagons doused the pavement and sweeper trucks whirred their huge brushes. The vast crowd got the point and roared in appreciation. The sanitation crews and the Muscovites—with the militia doing its best to keep order—followed the Nazis all the way to their prison camp in a Moscow suburb. To my mind it was the biggest and best show Moscow ever produced.

The war, though, was by no means over. The Germans were fighting hard for every square inch of territory. But every day on the radio, the *svodka*—the special army report—listed newly liberated places. Many evacuees were returning home.

Victory was certain, and with a new Soviet mood of warmth

toward Russia's allies, I was allowed for the first time to sing in French in Adi's newest show. I had two French songs—one about Paris, which was still occupied, and the other a love song called *Vous Qui Passe Sans Me Voir* ("You Who Passed Without Seeing Me"). Only the first verse of each song was sung in French; the rest was in Russian, translated by a poet who worked with us. The translations had nothing to do with the original, but it did not matter. The audience went "aaahh" when I appeared on stage. I had made my dress of white chiffon painted from light pink on the top to deeper and deeper lavender blending into dark purple at the bottom. The skirt was many layered, and when I first appeared I had the bottom of one layer wrapped around my head like a hood—the entire dress seemed to be dark purple. When I let the hood fall, the lighter colors became visible. As the dress changed, so did the lighting and when I sang about the liberators that Paris was expecting I seemed to be standing in sunshine. In the mood of the time, it could not miss.

We were giving the show not only in Moscow, but at the fighting fronts and in defense production centers far in the interior, performing from the beds of trucks. As the Byelorussian army moved forward in heavy combat, we were close behind. In Vitebsk, the population—or what was left of it—was just emerging from hiding in the woods to return to homes where only the brick chimneys remained. In Vilna we talked with people who had survived among the partisans and who told of incidents so disturbing that we felt ravaged just listening to them. One man who had been hiding in a cellar with several families related a story that still haunts me. The Germans had discovered the refuge, raped the women and then made one- and two-year-old children suck their penises. Most of the children had strangled before their mothers' eyes.

It was in Vilna, too, that I had an emotional experience of a different kind. I happened to be on hand when the buried treasures of YIVO, the Yiddish Institute of Research, were dug up. Just before the Germans had moved into Vilna, people had taken the trouble to hide documents, books, and artifacts of their cultural heritage, so that it would survive even though they would not. As I watched the excavation I was handed carefully wrapped documents and mementoes of my own family; the Institute had had a collection devoted to my grandmother and some of it had been among the things buried.

Minsk had been destroyed. Because we followed the army so closely, I learned firsthand what had happened to the people there. In the remains of the government house of Byelorussia, *Dom Pravitselstva*, we found German newspapers published in the area, in which executions of Jews were described and depicted in photographs. We spoke with people who had been partisans behind the German lines and had witnessed unspeakable happenings. In some villages parents had been forced to watch while the brains of their children were dashed out against walls. We listened. We knew they were telling the truth. But we could not really comprehend.

In each city the Russians took, they tried the captured members of the German command. In Minsk I even attended one such trial and after hearing the testimony of eyewitnesses, I almost enjoyed the subsequent executions in Minsk's main square.

After we had given a number of concerts in the surrounding area, most of our troupe received medals and decorations. I was very moved when the Secretary of the Byelorussian Republic and the head of the Byelorussian guerrilla movement—the same Comrade Ponomorenko we had met previously—shook our hands and thanked each one of us personally for helping to bring some joy into the lives of his soldiers. I felt indebted to them, not they to us.

From this trip we took home an impressive war trophy. We were allowed to buy a Ford automobile that the Germans had left behind. We proudly drove back to Moscow in it.

We returned from a number of such trips with treasures the Germans had stolen in France, Denmark, and Belgium and then had strewn along the path of their retreat. Each abandoned article was recorded, appraised, and inventoried by Soviet military officials who decided what should be done with it. Occasionally such valuables were appropriated by the men assigned to catalogue them. One general helped himself to oil paintings destined for museums. Their value was enormous, as was the length of the prison terms given the general and his famous folksinger-wife, Russlanova. But many of the items were placed on sale. Among our acquisitions was a demitasse set complete with sugar bowl, creamer, and tray, all handmade of solid gold. Another was an oriental carpet.

One evening, Adi announced that he wished to buy me furs to replace the ones I had left in Lvov.

"Why?" I asked. "You don't have to replace things. I don't hold you responsible for Hitler just because you were born in Germany."

"But I want you to have everything you have lost, and more."

"Let's wait until our next quarrel," I suggested.

The first thing he did buy for me was an eight and one-half carat blue-white diamond ring. The stone had been in an earring given by the czarina to the circus performer Durov. He had had the stone set in a ring, which his family now had sold cheap, for one hundred fifty thousand rubles.

I did not even know where I could keep such a ring; so I wore it with the stone inward except on the stage. Once after a gala performance an opera singer said, "You know, Ruth Zigmundovna, you can afford to wear real jewelry. Why do you wear all this junk?"

"What are you talking about? Every piece I wear is real."

She paled and screamed, "Fool! You could be murdered for that!"

Adi kept his promise about the furs, too. He made his selections on the advice of a sad, gentle, elderly, pudgy little German Jew named Blaustein who lived at the nearby Hotel Metropole and often played cards with us. Before the war Blaustein had commuted between Germany and Russia buying furs for an American firm. He had only two interests in life—his family and furs. The war had trapped him in Russia and he was desolate that he had procrastinated in getting his family out of Germany. He had not heard from them and we tried to cheer him up. Otherwise we probably would never have become friendly. It seemed unlikely he would play an important role in our lives, but he would.

Mama was as depressed as Mr. Blaustein. She and Mel and little Viktor had finally been able to join us in the capital in the spring of 1944. Mama was working with Ilya Ehrenburg, who was preparing a chronicle of Nazi crimes against the Jews. He had correspondents on almost every front, who, as soon as a territory was secured, sought out survivors and partisans and sent them to Ehrenburg to tell their stories.

Most of these people spoke only Yiddish or Polish and Ehrenburg had asked Mama for help. It was hard for her to talk to me about the stories she heard.

I was present at one interview with two young women who had been frozen during "scientific experiments" by Nazi doctors in a concentration camp. Instead of hands, the women now had hooks fashioned from their own hand bones.

Night after night we talked of relatives and friends in Poland, trying to measure their chances of survival. Could this one have managed to join the partisans? Could that one have been hidden by a Polish family? A cousin might have survived as an "Aryan" because of her blonde hair and blue eyes. Some had been so resourceful that they seemed indestructible. There had been a large group of Warsaw Jews—tough, athletic types—whom even the Polish police used to avoid. Surely some had survived.

But the more news we received, the less hopeful we became. From one partisan we learned that my grandfather Turkow had died of natural causes. We were grateful.

Surprisingly, the few survivors who straggled out did not fit into any groups we had expected would manage. Indeed, the people who had done the most heroic things were the ones for whom heroism had seemed least likely. And some whom we recalled as strong and respectable people had turned out to be cowards or traitors. I wondered into which group I might have fallen had I not escaped when I did.

Of course we hid our depression and our concerns from Erika and Viktor, and we were lucky that we had Ludmilla to care for them. With two of them to fuss over, she was busier than before, but if anything, happier.

But one winter day she came running in, out of breath, holding Erika and Viktor by the hands. When she breathed well enough to speak she gasped, "Oh, Ruth Zigmundovna, I am afraid that I may have got you into trouble. I took the children to the Lenin Mausoleum."

"So? What's wrong with that?"

"Nothing," she said, "if the children had not asked why Lenin was in there without Stalin next to him."

I laughed. But Ludmilla was frantic for fear that someone might have overheard and would make a case against the children's parents for wishing Stalin's death.

In their innocence, the children were living an idyll, which was interrupted by near-tragedy. It was to give a special profundity to the relationship between Erika and me.

Adi and I had decided Ludmilla was too intelligent to remain a nursemaid, and we sent her to a preparatory school so that she might enter Moscow University. In her absence, our apartment became the noisiest of playgrounds. All the neighbors' children preferred it to their own apartments because Erika had so many toys.

One afternoon, the children were shrieking throughout the rooms. I was unable to quiet them and Adi, who was trying to compose music, blamed me for his inability to concentrate. "You are as crazy a mother as your own mother is," he shouted. "Why can't they, just once, play in someone else's house?"

Next day, I sent the children upstairs to friends. We experienced the luxury of sudden quiet. Adi sat at his desk to work while I soaked in the tub.

The telephone rang. Adi, as usual, did not bother to pick it up. I shouted, "Why don't you answer the telephone?"

I heard his impatient "Hello!" then a cry, "What?" He dashed out of the apartment. I sprang from the tub, flung on a robe, and ran after him. In the corridor, I heard Erika's screams. A second later, Adi came running down carrying Erika and followed by children, their terrified parents, and neighbors who had run into the hall. Erika's face was contorted. Adi held up her arm, which looked like raw meat.

The children had been playing hide and seek and had not noticed an electric hot plate on the floor with a pot of boiling soup on it. Erika had been pushed and had fallen, her arm and elbow landing in the pot. The other children thought she shrieked in excitement over the game and shouted with even more glee.

Then the mother in the next room realized something was wrong. She tried to remove Erika's sweater, but flesh came off with the garment. A physician arrived almost immediately and after anointing and bandaging her arm he wanted to hospitalize her. Remembering Frunze, I insisted I would care for her myself, with his help.

For weeks the doctor visited her daily. I stopped working to nurse her. She was in constant pain, unable to eat or sleep. Any air turbulence or loud noise increased her pain. If anybody walked in the next room her eyes widened with fear, and she would tolerate nobody near her but me.

Sleepless night followed sleepless night. I told her stories, sang songs, applied lotion, sponged her feverish head. If she closed her eyes for a moment, I fell asleep, too. And yet her slightest motion, even the opening of her eyes, woke me instantly.

Once I saw her serious eyes staring at me. I panicked. "Is something wrong? Do you feel sick?"

"You know, mama, I was just thinking that I don't want to grow up."

"What?"

"Mama, I was just thinking that when I am grown up you will be an old lady and you won't be as beautiful as you are now, so I'd better stay as I am."

Because Erika had been born prematurely, I had always felt more than a normal maternal concern for her. The accident and a case of whooping cough that followed had heightened that concern; I must always be there to watch over her.

In the spring of 1945 Adi and I went on tour to the south of the country again and we took along Erika and Ludmilla, for whom school was over. It was in Baku in May, just as we left a concert, that we encountered bedlam on the streets. Strangers were hugging one another, shouting, "The war is over! The war is over!"

We were feverish with excitement, but now faced new decisions. Should we return to Poland? Could we?

11

You Can't Go Home Again
1945-46

Shortly after the war's end, we learned that the Soviet Union and the new regime in liberated Poland had agreed on the repatriation of Poles who had spent the war years in Russia. Registration offices were being set up for those who wanted to go and we told our manager of our wish to register to return. "What's your hurry?" he replied. "You will have time to register after the tour is completed. What makes you want to go back there?"

We said Mama had decided to return and we wanted to keep the family together. He reminded us our contract specified the tour's length. Until the contract was fulfilled, no office would process our application.

When I telephoned Mama on New Year's Eve, she told me she and Mel had applied for repatriation. I approached our manager again. "Everything in due time," he responded.

That New Year's Eve was the first on which I felt a need to get drunk. I did; it was easy because I had not eaten. Minsk was in rubble. The elegant Byelorussian Hotel no longer existed. We lived in barracks and food was scarce.

Shortly after New Year's Day we again approached our manager. We assured him we would be forever grateful to the Soviet Union, that we knew we owed our lives to it. Nevertheless, we had always assumed that we would return to Poland. We had relatives and friends throughout the world, and if the border were closed we would have little chance of ever seeing any of them.

The manager listened coldly. He emphasized our fame, our wealth, our position. It was as though he could understand the ordinary refugee wishing to return, but Adi and Ruth Rosner?

As repatriation applications were processed and exit permits issued, musicians left us—some sooner, some later. By the summer of 1946 many were gone. Mama's application was still "in process." Closing of the borders was rumored to be imminent. Diatribes began to appear in the newspapers against prominent people for being "worshippers of Western culture" and "internationalists." It was enough for someone to be labeled "cosmopolitan" for his neighbor to stop greeting him.

However, our concerts continued to be crowded. So we were astonished when on August 18, *Izvestia* published an editorial entitled "Vulgarity on the Stage." Signed by Comrade Grosheva, the article left us white and shaking. Was it now "such a time" for us?

"Adi Rosner hasn't learned a thing about art during his seven years in our country," the article read, "although he has had plenty of opportunity to do so. He and his jazz remain as they were, untouched by the Soviet Reality. He and his band are worshippers of Western culture. Everything they do on the stage might be acceptable somewhere in Western Europe or in United States nightclubs, but not on the Soviet stage . . . . It is time for us to think about the people who have been the recipients of our awards and merits. We mislead our youth when we decorate people like these, who, to our regret, have such an enormous influence upon our young people." And then the article went on to discredit Adi's musicianship.

Whenever anybody became the object of such criticism, he was expected to confess to wrongdoing and promise to do better. But it occurred to us that by damning us, maybe the authorities were informing us that we were free to leave and would no longer improperly influence their young people.

We told our manager this was to be our last tour. When our contract had been fulfilled, we felt we would be free to register— despite our manager's persistent objections. Then, suddenly, registration ended, except in Lvov for people who could prove they had lived there between 1939 and 1941. We had. Our passport still showed our address there, Wisniowieckich No. 6, Lvov.

Our tour over, we returned to Moscow to say good-bye to Mama and Mel; they were to leave for Poland on the November 27 train from Moscow. We went around to friends to say good-bye before going to Lvov, whence we would depart. Some begged us to change our minds. Most turned icy cold and refrained from saying good-bye. Some were "not at home" when we telephoned; they had heard the news.

We were glad that Ludmilla, who had been studying engineering at the university, would not have to share our difficulties. She had been sent as a trainee to a place near her home.

For the first time Adi had to make all of our travel arrangements. Even Erika was unusually quiet when we boarded the train for Lvov. Only the knowledge that Hymie would be greeting us in Lvov cheered us. Good, loyal Hymie, who could have left from Moscow with Mama and Mel, had elected to travel with us from Lvov to Warsaw to be of help. He had gone ahead.

We made our trip in as much silence as we were permitted. For a time we had to abide an excessively lively fellow passenger who introduced himself as Mischa; he said he recognized us from our concerts, he knew all of our hit songs, and he referred to many of our shows. He wanted to know whether we were on our way to give another concert. We did not want the veil to fall over his face as it did with anybody to whom we mentioned repatriation, so we said we were bound for a holiday resort near Lvov. He insisted on buying us cognac, but we ended the conversation as soon as we decently could. We were not in the mood for fans like Mischa, and he was not someone we expected we would hear from again. But we did.

Hymie was waiting at the station. Repatriation registration, he said, had turned out to be no problem for previous Lvov residents like himself. The last train carrying repatriates was to leave November 28. The Commissioner of Repatriation, Mr. D., himself a refugee from Warsaw, was planning to leave on that train.

On the train also would be Dzigan and Schumacher, a popular comedy team recently released from a concentration camp. I had never been able to find out how they had got themselves into disfavor.

We settled in a spare bedroom in a flat where Hymie had rented a room, and immediately Adi went off to register. He returned outraged. "Imagine," he sputtered, "D. had the nerve to ask me for twenty-five thousand rubles and to sign a paper hiring him as our impresario in Poland."

On principle, I was against the idea and told Adi he should insist on his rights. Why pay a bribe for something to which we were entitled? But Adi changed his attitude as he spoke. He shrugged. "Why should we argue about it? The money is no problem. We won't be able to do anything with it anyhow. They'll never permit us to take rubles out of the country." (I wondered how D. expected to take money out.)

Meanwhile Erika, who had been cranky all morning, began to cry.

She grew steadily worse over the next two days. Normally, I would have asked a prominent pediatrician to see her. That was no longer so simple. We had lost influence and we did not want to call attention to ourselves. Judging by our experience in Moscow, we felt that everyone took our plan to leave the Soviet Union as a personal affront.

Once again, Adi went to the Commissioner of Repatriation. He returned on the run, waving the registration cards that would permit us to board the November 28 train. But that evening it became clear that Erika's illness was more than a cold. Her temperature rose in spite of medication. The next morning our landlady sent for a pediatrician she knew, who at first could not even diagnose the illness. Later that day, when spots appeared all over her body, even we could see she had measles.

The train was leaving in six days. It would be the last train out. The doctor assured us that Erika had a mild case and two days before we were to leave, Erika was feeling better. But then we learned that our train would be unheated, drafty, crowded, and even lacking window glass. Dare we travel with the child?

Next evening, after Erika fell asleep, Adi and I packed. I had an excruciating headache. I was weary from lack of sleep and worry about Erika. I was overwhelmed, too, by a sense of emptiness. Until we had decided to return to Poland, everything had been provided for us. Now the magic wand seemed to be operating in reverse.

Tomorrow, we were setting out to remake our lives in the Poland we had left seven years before. It could never be the same after the war, the German occupation, the atrocities. Aside from Mama, Mel, and Viktor, who would there be? Was Poland the right place to start over?

Just thinking about the trip worried me. I had journeyed often between Lvov and Warsaw, but Lvov was a Polish city then. Now there would be a border to cross, and the distance seemed to expand, the way a familiar street in Warsaw had grown so long when the bombs were falling.

From the living room came the voices of Hymie and the landlady. In spite of my headache and my mournful mood, I had to smile when I heard her giggling at something Hymie had said.

In the bedroom Erika was sleeping peacefully, but picturing her pale, wan face, I suddenly said, "Adi, perhaps her sickness is a sign? Maybe we shouldn't leave? How can we take chances with her health?"

At that moment there was a loud knock on our door. Four burly men in leather coats and uniforms strode in, accompanied by the janitor.

"Adi Ignatzevitch Rosner?"

Adi nodded.

One man remained near the door with the janitor. The others motioned Adi, Hymie, the landlady, and me to the dining room. One of them looked through the apartment to make sure nobody was hiding. I asked him not to wake my daughter, and he just looked into her room from the doorway. Then they requested our documents and scrutinized our repatriation permits, made some notes, perfunctorily examined the suitcases open on the floor, and asked who owned each of them.

Then one of the men looked at Adi. "You will come with us."

I felt as though someone had punched me in the stomach. But immediately I recalled their interest in our suitcases. Perhaps they did not want us to take the valuables we had purchased. We had the gold coffee set with us, wrapped in clothing, and jewelry we had hidden quite ingeniously to prevent theft during the border inspection. They could have it. It would not be the first time we had left everything.

Why did they want Adi to go with them? To keep us from leaving? Or was there something else? I remembered Dr. Bloch, who had been picked up here in Lvov and taken to examine me in Kiev. Perhaps this was a mistake. Raya's Volodya had been the victim of a stupid mistake. The old Bolshevik officer in Leningrad had been the victim of a stupid mistake. "My God," I thought, "mistakes in this country could take ten years to rectify!"

Numb, I went through the motions of saying good-bye to Adi. We were quite formal. We did not want to show fear before the four men, who exuded implacability. I have since tried to remember them individually, but even then I could not distinguish among them. They may have been normal human beings, but from the moment they entered the flat they were faceless, impersonal extensions of Soviet law.

I picked up one of Erika's sweaters and pushed it into Adi's pocket as he put on his coat. For a lucky charm? A memento? I did not know.

After Adi and two of the men had left, the remaining two informed us we were under house arrest. I could go to my daughter, but none of us could leave the apartment.

I went to the bedroom, closed the door, turned out the light, and lay down beside Erika. She put one arm around me and with the fingers of her other hand twined my hair as though to keep me from leaving her. Through the crack under the door, I could see only the shadows made by the men's feet. From the sounds, I gathered they were going through our suitcases thoroughly. All night I lay awake as shock gave way to fear.

In the morning, I tried to question the two men, suggesting that if I knew what the trouble was, I could help clear it up. Adi's Russian was poor—perhaps I could go down and answer the questions. They knew nothing. There was nothing they could do. They had orders.

I spent most of my time in the bedroom with Erika; I wanted as little contact with those men as possible. Whenever I did pass them to go to the kitchen or the bathroom, they were sitting at the table eating. The landlady apparently kept them fed. What little food I prepared, I took to the bedroom. Whenever the phone rang, one of the men answered. I was never told who called or to whom the callers wished to speak.

My head reeled with worry. What was happening to Adi? What of my family in Warsaw? I pictured them waiting at the station to meet the train from Lvov. When the last passenger had climbed down, what would they think?

I was glad that Erika slept much of the time. I could not answer her questions—"Where is Papa? Why doesn't he come to see me? When will I see Mama Ida?"

Day and night were almost indistinguishable. I comforted myself at times that Adi would somehow talk his way out of trouble. Or perhaps he would be able to get in touch with some of our many friends among high officials in Moscow. But by now the borders must be closed.

Then there was Hymie. He could have left from Moscow with my family. Now he was trapped in the apartment with me.

Erika, feeling better each day, became more persistent in her questions. Where was Papa? Why didn't he come? Why didn't I play with her? I tried. I did not want her to sense my fear. But she knew. She even asked for food, but she struggled to eat it—she was only trying to please me.

After three days the men disappeared without a word. The moment I realized I was free to go, I dressed, left Erika with Hymie, and went to police headquarters.

At the entrance to the NKGB building, which had recently been renamed the MGB, there was a booth manned by a uniformed guard. When I asked about Adi, the guard wrote down Adi's full name and mine and inquired by telephone. After a brief conversation, he told me, "Yes, your husband is here and you are allowed to bring him coffee, cigarettes, and clean clothing. But no one will see you today."

Somehow I felt reassured. Adi had not been taken elsewhere. Even the appearance of the building cheered me. Constructed of white stone, it had no bars on the windows and gave no indication that people were imprisoned here. Surely Adi was just being questioned. But for days and days?

Next day I returned, dressed carefully because I did not want my appearance to betray worry. The guard took the coffee, cigarettes, and clothing that I brought and told me to wait. He gave the things to another guard who left the booth with them. After a while, Adi's worn underwear was handed to me. When I insisted on seeing someone in order to find out why Adi was being held, I was told, "No one will see you today. Come back tomorrow."

Every day for a week the guard at the booth said, "Come back tomorrow; nobody will see you today. You may leave the things here."

Each day I went with a clean shirt, underwear, coffee, and cigarettes. Then I would wait. When the soiled clothing was returned to me, I knew that at least Adi was still in that building.

Finally, on December 7, I was told that Major Ivanov would talk to me. The guard handed me a pass and escorted me into the building, up a flight of steps and down a long, wide corridor.

On one side of the corridor were closed oak-paneled doors. The doors bore no numbers or names, but from the space between them, I gathered that the rooms were large and occupied by fairly important persons. Opposite each door was a bench. I was told to sit on one of them, and the guard left me. At either end of the corridor and between some of the benches were large windows through which light streamed.

Occasionally somebody passed me and went into one of the rooms. A red carpet runner muffled footsteps. Some of the passersby wore civilian clothing, some MGB uniforms. A few stared as they passed and I wondered whether they recognized me or whether they just did not see too many people here dressed as I was—in my expensive Western clothes.

I looked at my watch. I had been waiting two hours. I hoped Hymie was at home and would feed Erika. He was such a comedian that she probably would eat while he entertained her. I was sure that by now she was asking, "Where is Mama?"

I was beginning to feel I was part of a nightmare. The occasional MGB man who passed seemed out of focus as though I were looking at his reflection in a distorting mirror. Once again, as I had so many times since that night, I relived the moment when the four leather-coated men walked into our flat.

The door I was facing opened and I snapped back to the present. "You have to wait," the emerging officer told me as he started down the corridor. "The major is still busy."

For ten days I had had no news of Adi. The last train to Poland had left. My child lay at home, still not entirely recovered, and here I was sitting endlessly, looking self-possessed when I wanted to scream and kick that door in.

For something to do, I took out my compact and looked at myself in the mirror. My image surprised me. I appeared unlined and unruffled, as though waiting for a friend who was to meet me for lunch.

One o'clock. Three hours. I had come of my own free will, but I could not get up and walk out of the building. My pass had to be stamped by Major Ivanov and returned to the guard at the booth. I began to feel as though a web were being spun around me. To snap the strands, I stood up decisively and knocked sharply on the door. The officer who had previously come out opened it immediately. "I am Lieutenant Vishnevsky. There is something you want?"

"Listen," I told him, "I don't know how much longer the major plans to keep me here but I left my child at home and cannot wait any longer. I'll come back tomorrow. Please stamp my pass."

The lieutenant said it would not take much longer and made no move to stamp my pass. So I asked him to direct me to the ladies' room. There, I did not know by what impulse, I rummaged through my handbag. In addition to identity papers for myself and my daughter and the exit papers for our trip out of the Soviet Union, there was a copy of a telegram I had sent earlier that week to Doba Markovna. I had presumed that when Mama reached Poland, and I did not follow on the train from Lvov, she might try to communicate with Doba. So I had asked Doba to try to inform my family that my husband was sick and in a hospital. In a code common in the Soviet Union, sick stands for arrested and hospital for prison.

I had a book with telephone numbers and addresses of friends all over the country and I tore up the pages and flushed them down the bowl, together with the copy of my telegram. I felt it was something I had to do, though I did not know why.

When I returned to my bench, the lieutenant's door was open and he invited me in. I entered a large office with a huge desk at one end and an armchair behind it. It was a cheerful room, with large windows covered by sheer curtains. On the wall behind the armchair hung two familiar pictures, one of Lenin greeting his people, the other of Stalin holding a child.

In the center of the room stood a chair. In a corner were a small desk with a typewriter on it and another chair. The lieutenant offered me the chair in the middle of the room. Thinking it misplaced, I moved it over to the desk opposite the armchair. He told me the major had just called and would be in soon.

In a moment, the door opened wide and a rotund man in a MGB uniform loaded with decorations bounced in, a broad, friendly smile on his face. The lieutenant sprang up from his place and seated himself at the small desk with the typewriter. The major took my hands in his.

"How very glad I am to see you! I attended so many of your concerts! I love your songs, especially . . ." And he hummed a bit of a tune. It was from one of my hits, "Good-bye, Farewell—And Don't Be Angry."

"Now, what did you want to see me about?"

I told him I had tried many times to talk to him because I wanted to clear up any misunderstanding about my husband. It could not be anything but a misunderstanding, and perhaps I could help with explanations because my Russian was better than Adi's.

"But the thing that worries me so much right now is that I left my child at home. Perhaps you have no idea how long I've been waiting."

The major smiled broadly and the corners of his eyes crinkled. "Don't worry. It has all been taken care of. The landlady in your apartment will care for the child until you return."

I relaxed. It seemed to me I had known this man for years. He was just like the officials we had been meeting at our concerts, who were always so cordial. It was good to be with somebody who knew us, who remembered.

I began to feel that the nightmare would soon end, and I became lighthearted and talkative. I asked if I might smoke a cigarette and he lit one of his own for me.

"You have been here so long you probably haven't eaten. Let me have something sent up for you," he suggested.

I was so excited at finally having a chance to speak to a friendly person that I did not feel hungry. I just wanted to finish the business at hand and go home. Even sending down for some tea would delay me and so I shook my head. "No, I'll have something to eat when I return home. Thank you."

"Well, as long as you're here, we have to go through some formalities. Have you any papers, any identification?"

Silly question. In the Soviet Union, nobody went anywhere without papers.

I started to look through my purse when he said, "Hand me your purse." He put it in his desk drawer without glancing inside. My elation vanished. Then I wondered—how did he know my child was at home, and that the landlady would care for her?

I became aware of the major pushing documents toward me. "Would you be kind enough to fill out these papers?"

Conscious that my hand was shaking, I told him lightly that my Russian was not so fluent that I could fill out documents, and I suggested that I dictate to him. The questions began.

"Have you ever been a party member?"

"No."

"You weren't interested in politics?"

"Not so much as in art."

"Ach, you artists. You always think that art has nothing to do with politics. Now, what is your name?"

"You know my name. Ruth Kaminska."

"But Kaminska is the name of your mother, isn't it?"

"I use it as a stage name."

"Ah, so. Yes, I know, actors usually do things like this. But what is your real maiden name?"

"Ruth Zigmundovna Turkow."

He began to write. "Ruth Kaminska—ah, yes—Turkow. And where is your father?"

"My father is in Palestine."

"Oh, in Palestine? Your husband's name is Rosner, isn't it?"

"Yes, of course. You know that. And that is why I am here. I have to know what has happened to him."

"So, Ruth Zigmundovna Kaminska—alias Turkow—alias Rosner. And your mother's name?"

"Ida Kaminska. Famous actress." He knew that, too.

"And where is she?"

"Repatriated to Poland."

"Is that so?"

My heart pounded in my ears. From his tone, I began to tremble for Mama. Had she been prevented from leaving, too?

"And now your grandparents. Your father's side and your mother's side. Parents of your father first."

"Itta Gittel and Naftale Turkow."

"Actors?"

"Oh, no. Definitely not!" In spite of myself I smiled at the idea of my strait-laced grandfather as an actor.

"Parents of your mother?"

"Esther Rachel and Avram Itzhak Kaminski."

He wrote it all down. "They were famous actors," I volunteered.

Finally, still smiling, he told me to look over the paper, see if everything was correct and sign it. I told him also with a smile, that I was sure it was. I was too nervous to read the paper carefully. It appeared to be a simple *curriculum vitae*, and by this time I wanted only to get out of this place and return to Erika.

I signed the paper and handed him my pass. Instead of putting his signature on that, he took the document he had just filled out and told me he would return shortly.

"Wait here," he said.

The lieutenant, still at the typewriter desk, hid his face behind his newspaper as a sign that he had no intention of engaging in conversation. Again I was alone with my thoughts.

The mere mention of my family's name in this place had seemed like blasphemy, and my throat had tightened every time I named a loved one. To the major, those names were merely something to be written in the proper spaces on a form. To me they summoned waves of memories, as though my whole wonderful, protected childhood was trying to erase the bewildering present.

The reappearance of the major interrupted my thoughts. He walked into the room quickly, with a rolled-up sheaf of papers under his arm. He handed these to the lieutenant, and I sprang up eagerly.

"As for today," he said cheerfully, "it is enough. Let's go."

"Where to?" I asked.

Lightly, he replied, "To prison."

chapter 12

The Ice Cage
1946

All tension left me. Down to my fingertips, I felt nothing, as though I had received a massive narcotic injection. I was hearing somebody tell me that someone else was being sent to prison.

The tone of my own voice surprised me. Sounding self-possessed, I asked, "My child . . . ?" And then I stopped. I would not ask for pity.

"We just have to clear up a few things," the major said, almost kindly. He nodded to the lieutenant, who led me down the corridor and into the street, now dark and deserted. I heard only the sound of his boots on the stones and the beat of my heart.

I knew Lvov well but had never been in this section. We arrived at a large gray stone building with an iron gate over which hung a huge sign: First Inner Prison. In front of the gate stood a guard booth.

The lieutenant seemed to be having difficulty in getting me inside; he and the guard exchanged sharp words, but he apparently persuaded the guard to admit me.

We went through a long, dark passageway, then across a central courtyard. The whole place was quiet. The only light came from dim bulbs over doors. The lieutenant opened a small wooden door and led me to a tiny office just inside. It was difficult to see because cigarette smoke clouded the room. The dominant odor was that of handmade cigarettes rolled out of newspaper and makhorka tobacco, which grows wild and is coarsely cut. It blended with the scents of perspiration and unwashed feet.

A rumpled official sat behind a desk. The lieutenant handed him his sheaf of papers and left. The man at the desk pointed to another door and motioned me through it.

I found myself in a room almost filled by a concert grand piano. A small bulb provided barely enough light for me to see three figures behind the piano, next to the wall. When one approached me, I realized I was confronting a prison matron.

The events of the last days were so unreal that even the piano in this unlikely place hardly surprised me. As my eyes adjusted to the dimness, I distinguished the forms of two young girls. One was a peasant with long, flowing blonde hair; apparently her braids had loosened. The other was out of Brecht's *Threepenny Opera*, in rags that seemed like a studied costume. Through the holes in her outfit—it was midwinter—I could see her flesh. Her tangled hair looked as though it had not been disturbed by a comb for weeks.

The matron ordered me to strip. I put my things on the piano—probably the only use to which this magnificent instrument was put—and the matron crumpled every garment one by one. She removed two diamond rings, my watch, my girdle, and my dress belt from the pile and then put her hands through my hair, roughly pulling out hairpins. I felt vaguely outraged, but was too numb to react, except that now I understood how the girl's braids had become undone.

All this time, the huge woman was going over me and my things impersonally, unemotionally, professionally. Finally, gruffly, she told me I could dress. The only glimmer of interest in her eyes was for my things; she handled them almost appraisingly.

"What shall I do with my stockings?" I asked when I saw she would not return my girdle with its garters. "Without the girdle, they'll fall down."

"Everybody manages."

When I was dressed, she knocked on the door. A guard was waiting, holding a gun with fixed bayonet. He told the three of us to walk in file and ordered: *Ruki nasad*—"Hands behind you!"

I tried to hold up my stockings but the guard reminded me with his gun butt to put my hands behind my back. We recrossed the snow-covered courtyard, laced with traces of footsteps, and stopped at the iron gate. The guard opened it and in the sliver of light coming through, I could see a stone stairway leading down. The gate closed behind us with a grinding finality that echoed through the courtyard. We felt our way slowly down the staircase.

Ahead was a short corridor, one wall of which was stone, the other of rough wooden planks nailed to upright beams. All along the wall were wooden doors, tightly closed. The guard unlocked one and motioned us into a boxlike wooden cell thinly carpeted with straw. It reminded me of the animal cages in circus wagons, except that the animals see their keepers and their neighbors. As the door was locked behind us, I realized I did not know what time it was; the matron had taken my watch. I guessed it was eight or nine in the evening. With my stockings around my ankles, my hair falling loosely in my face, I felt a lifetime had passed since I had entered the MGB building that morning.

The two girls huddled on the floor. I stood. The whole place looked so dirty and bug-infested that I could not bring myself to risk the floor, and the only thing in the cage—besides us—was a small light bulb high in the ceiling, encased in its own metal cage.

I could not accept my situation as the two girls seemed to. I did not feel one of them. After all, I had come here that morning of my own free will! I had hardly been questioned. The major had not even completed my *curriculum vitae*. Detached, I waited numbly, convinced he would soon have me returned to his office to complete the form.

And so I stood, and stood, and stood, for what became the entire night. I kept thinking about Erika in that flat without me. It seemed to me I could hear her crying. Who could explain to her why her mother was not with her? First her papa had not returned, then I. Did anyone bathe her? Did she have a glass of milk before going to sleep? By staying awake, I felt as though I were watching over her.

I never knew when the new day began because there were no windows, but I felt as though I had been standing forever. The sound of the door being unlocked alerted us. Then a guard entered our cage. The girls jumped up, and I found myself standing more tensely. I suppose each of us expected to be summoned. It was merely breakfast time. We were each given a little warm water in a tin cup, and in the palms of our hands the guard put a bit of brown sugar and about ten ounces of black bread. The bread felt heavy and looked like clay. Although I had eaten nothing the day before, I handed the bread to one of the girls; they divided it.

It seemed as though all of my senses had concentrated in one—my hearing. My ears strained for sounds. The first sound always was the grinding of the gate. Then came footsteps on the staircase, footsteps outside our cage, the sound of the door being unlocked. A guard entered with a paper. I stepped forward. The girl in rags, Masha, elbowed me back. Both girls had been transferred from another prison and knew how to behave. The guard looked down at the paper. "Letter

D!" he called. The blonde stepped forward.

"Duda," she replied quietly.

"First name?"

"Oksana."

"Father's name?"

"Stepan."

"Right. Come along."

I never saw her again.

Now we were two. I finally gave in and sat on the floor, legs outstretched. Two pairs of ears listening hour after hour. Neither of us spoke. Late at night a guard summoned Masha "on the letter P." She returned before breakfast, more than a little drunk. Her behavior contrasted surrealistically with her rags. She spoke excitedly.

She had been interrogated by two generals because she was very important. They had assured her she would soon be free. She had been treated to a fine meal and to wine and to confirm her story she fished out of her rags a bit of meat wrapped in paper.

"I know you haven't eaten for two days," she said, "and I know you won't be able to eat what they bring you, so I saved something for you." I bit into the meat ravenously. As I ate, she began her story.

When the Nazis entered Kiev, her home town, she was fifteen years old and attending school. Almost immediately, she was sent to Germany with other young girls.

"I was transported to a small village and put to work for a German with a wife and family. I slept in the barn and he began to visit me at night. I was rewarded with food, silk stockings, and other goodies. Later, he had me transferred to cleaner work. I realized quickly that to make your life easier, you have to be smart. The German told me that they needed smart girls like me. I would never be hungry and would have an easy life if I cooperated."

"Did you?"

"Why not? I never had such a wonderful time. They put me into a special school where I learned to become a radio operator and to jump with a parachute. I slept with many of them, but I was always well rewarded. Some girls did it for nothing, but not me!

"When the Russians retook Kiev, the Germans dropped me by parachute in a wood out of town. I had instructions to hide my parachute and radio, find my way back to my home town, and wait until I was contacted with a password.

"I tore my clothes and got myself very dirty, to make it look like I had been walking for days. When I came to a house at the edge of the wood, I told them I had made my way back on foot from Germany. They fed me, gave me fresh clothing, took me to the train, and bought me a ticket to Kiev.

"My parents were so happy that they stayed drunk for a week. In order to return to my *Komsomol* (youth group) I invented terrible stories about my German captivity, as the Germans had told me to.

"I waited for instruction. But the Russians kept pushing the Germans back and then the Germans lost the war. Some of the girls who had been taken from Kiev with me returned home and ratted on me, and so—here I am. But I'm still smart. You are sitting here hungry, and I've had a feast with generals."

Probably because I had seen a Russian movie about foreign spies, I felt I had to be on guard. Had she been planted to test my loyalty? When she finished, I asked her: "How could any Russian girl sell her country to an enemy for silk stockings? I am not a Russian, But I feel it is your duty to tell them the whole truth. Perhaps if you admit you were a traitor, you could get a pardon. Don't think you can fool the Soviet officials. They know everything."

For the next few nights, Masha continued to be taken out, always "On the letter P—" During the day she was drowsy, but found energy enough to tell me how good things had been with the Germans and how bad and poor Russia was. I insisted she could never convince me— I had fled from Hitler because I was Jewish, and from me she would get no sympathy for Nazi murderers.

"And for your information," I told her, "I was able to wear silk stockings right here in the Soviet Union. If you lived according to the law, you could be happy here, too."

After that last exchange, Masha was not returned to my cell. I remained alone. Except for the guards who brought my miserable food, nobody stopped at my cell. I had long since made my accommodation with the straw floor; it became both chair and bed.

My longing for Erika was a constant, physical pain. Before my eyes was imprinted the way she had looked the morning I left her, a smile on her tiny wan face framed by silky curling hair, waving bye-bye with her little hand. I imagined I could still smell her fresh baby-hair smell.

I thought of the time Adi had angered me by teasingly trying to make me chose between Erika and himself. In the middle of the night he had asked, "Tell me, if there was a flood and you had a tiny boat and could save only one person, would you save me or the child?"

"I don't even want to imagine my child standing on the edge of the water with her hands stretching out for help. That's cruel and sadistic!" Now, I lived with the image of my daughter stretching out her hands for me.

Eventually, the door did open. A guard entered, a paper in hand. Though I was the only prisoner, he went through the ritual.

"On the letter R!" Masha had explained to me that the procedure was a precaution to prevent people possibly involved in a group arrest from learning who else had been taken. If my name were Kuznetzova and my first name Maria, and they asked for Kuznetzova, Dasha, they would be letting me know my sister also had been arrested. In such matters you could rely on them. They knew their jobs.

The ritual completed, the guard told me to come along, hands behind my back.

For the first time since I arrived, I faced daylight. The brightness of the sun on the snow-covered courtyard blinded me momentarily. It was a cold morning, so cold it left me breathless. I paused to inhale the clean, clear air. A kick in the small of my back started me moving. But I was so sure I was walking to freedom that I could almost feel the pressure of my child as I hugged her. In the middle of the courtyard, I saw that we were not going to freedom, not back to the major's office, but toward an iron door.

This time, the stairway leading from the door went up. Several times, the guard ordered me to stand facing the wall. I heard people passing on their way down but I could not see them. Finally we reached the third floor and I was introduced to Cell 320. It was no bigger than the wooden cage in the cellar; four steps in one direction, three in the other. The door slammed behind me.

It was unbelievably cold inside and I shivered despite the mink coat I still wore. High on the wall opposite the door was a windowlike opening with metal bars set in the stone. There was no glass, but outside the window was a kind of inverted wooden hood, open at the top, so that I could see a sliver of sky through the opening if I stood directly beneath it.

To the right of the door was a toilet bowl, the water in it frozen solid, with feces encased in ice. Next to it was a sink with a spigot, also frozen. The floor was covered by thick, uneven ice, deepest near a water pipe which had been leaking.

No chair, no bed. I paced, trying to keep warm. The ice under my feet penetrated my shoes; it seemed to bore into my bones. To keep my nose and ears from freezing, I raised my coat collar and breathed into the fur. But when the fur became damp, I felt the cold more intensely. After the time I had spent in the cellar I seemed to have no resistance, and the cold overpowered me quickly. I rapped on the door. Perhaps nobody realized that the water pipe had broken and turned the room into an ice box.

I kept rapping on the door until the pain in my knuckles stopped me. There was a peephole in the door and somebody opened it from outside. First I saw an eye and then a mouth with a gold tooth in front. The mouth said, "For hysteria we have a treatment, so don't bother me with your capriciousness!" It finished with, "Who the hell do you think you are, annoying people like this?"

I told him breathlessly I must see Major Ivanov. My sick child was home without me . . . I was freezing!

The peephole was already closed.

After a while, I found myself standing with my back to the door because there, nearest to the outside corridor, the ice on the floor was thinner. How long my legs held me upright that way, I have no idea. Suddenly the door opened so rapidly that I fell at the boots of Gold Tooth. On a routine check he had looked through the peephole and not seen anything. I had covered the hole by leaning against the door, and he had panicked.

He shoved me back into the cell and there and then taught me one of the first lessons of prison life—I must always be where I could be seen from the door. He kept muttering he could not understand how anybody could be so stupid.

By then, I was without will. I lay down on the ice in front of the window. I fell into a deep sleep that bordered on coma, from which I emerged slightly from time to time. I remember somebody trying to wake me. I recall being handed food. I did not know whether it was breakfast, dinner, or supper. I could not eat it anyhow. The only thing I remember wanting all the time I lay there was cold water to drink.

Several times I was handed lukewarm water that they called tea, but I let the cup sit on the floor until it became cold and then drank it greedily. Through my mental haze I seemed always to be conscious of the odor of fish—specifically spoiled anchovies. Despite the cold, a fire burned within me. Once, out of water, I crawled to where the ice was on the wall, out of the water pipe. I sucked at it but my lips stuck to the ice. Numbness set in—I had less and less sensation. And then I began to feel wonderful. I was a child again. I heard Mama's caressing voice comforting me, and I fell asleep in peace.

Somebody kicked me. I tried to open my eyes, but I had trouble lifting my eyelids. Everything was gray and in the gray light I saw first the boots. They seemed to rise way above me, ending in the mouth with the gold tooth. The mouth, spreading vapor, demanded to know whether I was still alive.

I tried to speak and a scream came out. Gold Tooth announced then that he was taking me to a doctor. He ordered me to stand. One foot had frozen to the floor. When he pulled me up, my shoe split and my foot began to bleed. As I stood, I realized why he was concerned. On the floor was frozen blood. I must have hemorrhaged. I felt no pain; I was barely aware of anything happening to me. Gold Tooth pulled me into a long corridor that seemed to me like a tropical garden because it was painted green, full of sunlight and warmth.

In the doctor's office the guard put me in a chair, the first I had sat on since Major Ivanov's office. The doctor was a woman; the sight of her white coat and the proximity of another female human being made me sure that here, at least, I would receive sympathy and kindness. I found myself thawing, first on the outside and then inwardly until I burst into weeping.

Brusquely, the doctor commanded me to stop crying instantly. "The time to cry," she told me, "was before you broke the law. Moscow doesn't believe in tears."

She took my temperature and listened to my lungs through my clothing. "Pulmonary," she diagnosed. When she saw blood on my clothes, she said "Hemorrhage" and gave me a few drops of a tranquilizer in water. She turned to Gold Tooth. "You can return her."

I remember her well. She was about my age, with a permanent wave and an empty, cold face. As I left, she resumed reading a book.

When Gold Tooth unlocked the door to my cell, he remarked, "Brrr, devilish cold." Once again the door locked behind me. After my exposure to the warmth I was no longer numb, and the cold penetrated to the backbone. I sweated and shivered and my teeth refused to stop chattering.

That night, at ad'boi (retreat), Gold Tooth came into my cell. "Up to five o'clock in the morning, just before the changing of the guard, I will put you in a warm place," he said. "Don't tell anybody. Until I go off duty, you can sleep there."

He led me into the guards' toilet. It was filthy, stinking, but heavenly warm. I took off my mink coat, folded it into a mattress with the fur inside and put it on the floor.

It seemed I had just fallen asleep when Gold Tooth woke me and took me back to my ice cage.

Apparently that incident coincided with the turning point of whatever my illness was, because from then on when food was offered to me I took it hungrily. At breakfast I was given ten ounces of bread and some *komsa*—small, stinking, salted fish. This, then, explained that odor. I also got warm water and a little sugar. For dinner there was soup of potato peelings and dirt that had clung to them, or groats in which I could see the worms. I hoped the cooking had killed them. Supper was water and sugar. The bread given out in the morning was for the entire day. Despite my hunger I found it difficult to eat.

From then on, I waited every day for the time Gold Tooth had the night watch. Without a word he would lead me into the kingdom of warmth. Blessed Gold Tooth!

Despite the fact that after each such night I felt the cold more intensely, and in spite of the lack of medical care, I knew from my rising hunger I was recovering from my illness. I had no idea how long I had been sick. Again I began to listen, awaiting the time they would stop in front of my door. My stockings were torn and filthy and I was concerned that I did not have soap, a towel, a comb, or a toothbrush.

I became more conscious of my surroundings, too. I heard things, not just the customary sounds, but others as well. Awful sounds of torment—screams and loud groans—came from a distance, and sometimes I thought I heard the cries of frightened children. I was never sure whether the sounds were real or imagined.

I used the warm nights not only for sleeping but for sanitation. As soon as Gold Tooth left me in the toilet, I took off my clothes and washed myself in the warm water. Then I put my coat back on, washed my clothes and dried them on the radiator. Then I would stretch out on the floor and sleep until Gold Tooth came.

One day the footsteps were for me.

"On the letter R—"

I was taken downstairs and through the courtyard to the gate where a captain waited. He told me to walk with my hands behind my back. He followed. There on the street, I recognized the way back to the MGB. Maybe now I would be freed.

It was dawn. A few people were passing by and I thought it was wonderful just to see them walking along of their own free will. But they kept their distance. The sight of me, walking with my hands behind my back, the guard following, quarantined me. People averted their eyes, as though they might catch my disease by looking.

I was ushered into the clean, brightly lit building where, despite the early hour, work seemed to be going on as though it had never stopped for the night. My escort took me back to the same corridor and the same door I had entered so long ago. He rapped and I recognized Major Ivanov's voice. "Come in."

The major was at his desk reading a paper. The captain saluted and announced he had brought the prisoner. Major Ivanov continued to read. In the stillness all I could hear was the paper's rustle.

I noticed the calendar on his desk. Three weeks had passed. The major folded his paper, laid it down, and only then raised his eyes to me.

He appeared to lose his self-possession for a moment. He began to talk quickly. "Uh, how are you?" It seemed to pop out of his mouth automatically.

I replied quietly, "Thank you. How are you?"

He shouted to the captain, "Wait outside the door!"

I did not know what had unsettled him. I was aware my clothes had turned to rags and I had lost so much weight that everything was hanging on me. I knew that my stockings were drooping down around my ankles and my hair was not combed. I did not yet know that my hair had turned partly gray.

I was twenty-six years old.

chapter 13

The Warm Cell
1946

The major probably pressed a button on his desk, because a lieutenant walked in with typing paper under his arm. As soon as the lieutenant was ready at the typewriter, my interrogation resumed.

It started with the same questions as the last time. Where was I born, what was my occupation, what kind of schools had I attended, where had I studied, where had I lived?

Did I have relatives in Russia?

"Just my husband and my child."

"Do you have anybody in other countries?"

"Oh, yes."

"Have you been in contact with them?"

"Constantly."

I dictated the names of my relatives. My father lived in Palestine. I had uncles in Palestine, South America, and the United States. Relatives in London. Then I started on the long list of cousins in Europe and in the United States. They included a journalist, judges, businessmen and, of course, theatrical people and musicians.

I invented a few to help convince the major that I could not just disappear without a trace in the Soviet Union.

The lieutenant was having trouble. The form provided a lot of space for relatives in the Soviet Union, little for those elsewhere. Soviet citizens who had relatives abroad rarely admitted it; having kin outside the country implied communication across borders and could prevent admittance to universities and promotion at work or in the army.

My situation was the reverse and I wanted to make the difference clear. By pointing out how close and dear each relationship was, I felt I was bettering my chances for release. After listing about thirty relatives I said, "I have finished with the closest ones." The lieutenant wiped the sweat from his forehead.

The major's next question was, "How is it that you know several languages?"

I replied, "Lenin said that knowledge is light, and I think that if somebody wants to be cultured (a favorite word in the Soviet Union) he has to try to learn whatever he can. I am sure that such a cultured man as the major must understand this."

"Of course, of course, I understand. I am a great admirer of Maupassant. But it seems to me you have used your knowledge to contact foreign agents."

What? The interrogation from then on centered on that point. Whom did I contact? How did I reach them? How did I use my radio apparatus?

I gasped. "What radio apparatus? The only radio I own is a small Philco." It was the kind made for American automobiles. He persisted in wanting to know how I operated it to send out information and receive messages from abroad.

"Major," I reasoned, "I bought that radio in a *komis*. Would they sell me a radio that could send messages outside the country? It's just an ordinary radio."

He glanced at his watch and announced a break. For perhaps half an hour I was installed in another smaller room, while the major apparently took a well-earned rest and refreshment. In the small room I was handed a glass of tea and a cigarette and savored both. The lieutenant remained with me but said nothing.

When the major returned and we resumed our positions in his office, I told him I could hardly stand the terrible physical conditions in the prison. He looked up at me sharply. "What do you mean, terrible physical conditions?"

He acted so innocent that I was convinced he had ordered me put in the icebox. He was trying to break me so that, in the hope of better treatment, I would sign whatever he wanted signed. I would sign nothing untrue, but felt it would be best to go along with the major's self-image as a benign, cultured person. I did not mention that I had heard people screaming; the more I knew the slimmer would be my chances of getting out. So I dropped the subject of my health and asked about Erika.

He assured me she was being cared for. Once more he questioned me about communicating with foreign agents and about how and when I used the radio for my contacts. The lieutenant, typing, recorded everything.

At the interrogation's end the lieutenant gave his typed pages to the major who passed them to me to look over and sign. I was in no hurry. I was happy to be sitting on a chair. Everything around me was warm and clean, and even the scent of the Chypre cologne now seemed heavenly. The interrogation had not frightened me; I was playing a game with the major, a kind of mental exercise which I had to win. What frightened me was the impending return to my cell.

But I could not postpone my departure forever, and since the typed transcript simply contained further facts concerning my background and a record of everything we had said, I signed it.

I was walked back to prison. It was dark out; I had been there the entire day. I realized that the glass of tea they had given me was to be my whole day's food ration since I had missed all meal times. I found myself wondering if dinner had consisted of potato peel soup, which I preferred, or the wormy groats.

After the day in the warmth of the major's office I was unprepared for the brutal cold of my own quarters, and I found it difficult to breathe. I postponed getting down on the icy floor as long as I could, but finally lay down from exhaustion. I curled up inside my coat and shivered uncontrollably. I was not aware of having slept, but I must have, because I was awakened by the arrival of "breakfast"—the warm tea.

I sat on the ice and relived the previous day over and over. What had the major wanted? What had happened to Adi? Where was my baby? What was going on inside her little head? What was she being told about the parents who had abandoned her?

By afternoon, worn out from torturing myself with unanswerable questions, numb from the cold, I lay down and closed my eyes. Now the guard enforced another rule. "Don't sleep. Don't sleep. It is daytime." I sat up a while, but soon again curled up on my side, huddled in my coat. The peephole betrayed me once more and the guard stormed in, furious. "It will go hard with you if you violate the prison rules. Don't sleep during the day."

I wondered what could be harder for me than my present lot, until I recalled the screaming I thought I had heard.

Shortly after I finished my tea, the door opened.

"On the letter R—"

"Rosner."

Our charade played out, once again I found myself walking deserted streets with my hands behind my back. I knotted my torn stockings at the knees to keep them up, but it did not help much.

Again the major's office. Again the routine questions to start with, and again questions about the radio.

"Whom did you contact?"

"I had no contacts."

"Why do you keep insisting? It will go harder for you!"

"You know the whole story. You know I won't change my answers because there is nothing to change. You know I am telling you the truth."

"You are wasting our time. We know that a man named Blaustein was one of your illicit contacts with the West."

"Blaustein? The poor little German fur trader who couldn't get news about his family. A contact? An agent? Major, you can't be serious. The only thing that pathetic man ever knew about were furs and his family."

"We know you were contacting him, among others. You might as well confess and tell us the names of others. We also know that you contacted an American in Vladivostok. We know everything, so you may as well confess."

"Major, we both know this is not only untrue but impossible."

"Why do you make things so difficult?" (He was acting as if his professional pride were on the line.) "If I don't obtain your confession, somebody else may take over and he won't be as patient as I. Don't you understand you have to confess to something? Perhaps we can drop the charge of high treason, but you cannot say you are innocent. We don't arrest innocent people."

"High treason?"

"It could be something less if you cooperate."

"I have done nothing wrong and I will tell you only the truth. I will never admit to anything I have not done."

The major was growing increasingly irritated. At this point he returned to the radio, demanding again how I had used it to communicate with the West. Finally the session ended and the lieutenant again supplied the typed transcript, which I read carefully. It was reasonably accurate and I signed it.

The lieutenant returned me to my icebox and there, sitting on the frozen floor, I at last understood fully the irony of the joke which had been making the rounds concerning Stalin and his lost pipe. The story went that Stalin mentioned to his adjutant that he could not find his pipe. The aide got to work. For three days the aide tried to find every person who could have entered the room when the pipe had last been used. He had each trace his movements that day and there was quite a furor. Then Stalin phoned him. "Never mind about my pipe. I have it. I misplaced it."

"That's impossible!" said the adjutant. "Three persons have confessed."

I think that was when I really began to comprehend what had always struck me as the peculiar reluctance of the Soviet people to speak of their own affairs and their apparent lack of interest in anyone else's thoughts and problems. I had always considered this to evidence selfishness or egocentricity. Now I recognized it as a precaution. They did not want the responsibility of knowing too much about you. And they did not want you to have information about them which might be misinterpreted. So many people confessed to so many things—my God! Is that what this was all about? Were they trying to use us to press a case against that poor Mr. Blaustein?

With little sleep, the tension of the interrogation, and the enervating cold, I dozed sitting up, managing to appear awake. *Ad'boi* had been announced before I stretched out to sleep. Again, I was jarred awake.

"On the letter R—"

Night after night, the routine continued. Each time the major asked all the questions he had before, but each time he added some element.

"Were you aware that your husband paid money to the commissioner in charge of repatriation?"

"No, I was not aware. I am sure he didn't pay anything."

"We know he did."

"He was asked for money and I told him not to pay anything. I am sure he didn't. We were entitled to our repatriation papers. There was no reason to pay."

"We have proof that he not only paid but that you were present while he did so."

An opportunity to see Adi? I knew that when prisoners or witnesses told conflicting stories, they were brought face to face. So with flashing eyes I said icily, "Let me confront Adi and have him say such a thing in front of me! You would soon realize I know nothing about any such payment!"

The questions turned back to the radio, to "contacts," and to poor Mr. Blaustein.

One night, after again trying to make me confess to being an agent, operating the radio, and using Blaustein as a contact, the major gave the interrogation a new turn.

"You are a stubborn person," he rasped. "You are doing yourself no good by these denials. However, there is one charge to which you must confess." He picked up a sheet of paper and read, "'Participation in an attempt to illegally cross the border.' This, of course, you cannot deny."

That made no sense, I replied. Adi had been picked up at home. I had walked into the MGB voluntarily. How could they charge me with an attempt to illegally cross the border when we had acted in accordance with an international agreement?

I kept talking and talking. There was no crime. It was a plan to take a train legally with other Polish repatriates—we had met the necessary requirements and had the papers. I became more and more excited. Why should I confess to a crime when I was guilty of none?

The more I spoke the more amused the major seemed. Laughing, he interrupted. "In spite of so many years in the Soviet Union, you show a typical Western political irresponsibility," he said. "The strength of the Soviet Law is based on our being sensitive to 'intentions.' Suppose somebody decides to steal government secrets. He has the documents in his suitcase. After a while, perhaps he becomes frightened or he reconsiders and tries to put them back. But if he is caught during the time he still has the papers in his suitcase, is he not a criminal? Isn't he a political traitor?"

I was astonished at the parallel. "Stealing secret documents is an illegal act. Ours was not. How can you make such an analogy? I think our imprisonment is only because you don't want us to leave the country." The pitch of my voice rose. "I don't understand it. We haven't anything bad to say about the Soviet Union. We shall always be grateful to this country for giving us refuge. Why are you doing this to us?"

"It is precisely because you people who have had such a good life here want to leave, that you make bad propaganda for us. Take away the prisoner," he rasped. "Enough for today."

chapter **14**

A Christmas Recalled
1946

During the period of nightly interrogations, there was one night when I was not returned directly to my own icy cell. Instead I was taken to a much larger cell containing four women. Exhausted, I had no wish to socialize. I lay down on the floor as far from the women as possible, to get as much sleep as I could.

The women spoke in Ukrainian. They probably assumed I was asleep and they had no reason to believe I understood Ukrainian. I could see I had interrupted a feast. On a shawl on the floor they had spread out a parcel of food. Its odor made me hungry, a feeling I believed had died. The more they ate, the fiercer grew my need to eat.

No longer able to sleep, I realized that my isolation had kept me from learning about life in this nether world. It had never occurred to me that prisoners could receive packages from outside. From the women's talk, I gathered that the food came from a *piridacha,* which is prison and hospital lingo for a gift parcel. This one, I gathered, was for the holidays. My God, had I been here that long?

The women were peasants from the Polish Ukraine, the area Russia had annexed, and came from villages around Stanislav and Lvov. They were Banderovites, followers of Bandera, the reactionary leader of a Ukrainian independence movement.

They talked about their homesickness, heightened by the holidays, and I realized this was January 6—Epiphany, the Greek Orthodox Christmas. Reminiscing, one mentioned that it had been on Christmas Eve in 1942 that the Germans had begun to liquidate the Jews in her village. I became alert, realizing from her words that here was not only a witness, but apparently a participant in the massacres.

As usual, I was using my mink coat as a cocoon. But to hear more clearly, I changed my position, moving the collar from my ears. The women noticed I was awake and began to question me. What was I charged with? How long had I been in prison? Where was I from? I said only that I was Polish, from Lvov. If they discovered I was Jewish, they would worry about how much I might have heard.

And so I told them that at the outbreak of the war I had been sent deep into Russia, as so many Poles had been. Now I had been arrested trying to cross into Poland illegally. My interest in everything that had happened around Lvov while I was in the East seemed perfectly natural to them and they spoke freely.

Their villages had had mixed Jewish-Ukrainian populations. Before the war, Ukrainians and Jews called each other by first names, attended each other's festivities, and paid their respects when someone died. They shared the life Sholem Aleichem depicted. But when the Germans descended, the barely submerged anti-Semitism of the Ukrainians became legitimized and they were able to take from their good friend Shloimke his cow and from Motka his *perine* (down quilt). They took them without scruples, as later they would take their neighbors' lives.

As my cellmates talked, they recreated the grisly picture. The Jews' huts were burned. The Germans were not interested in the Jews' meager possessions, but the Jews' neighbors were. They knew where Label kept his flour (having borrowed from him often enough) and where Malke put her Sabbath candlesticks (having visited her often enough). Several of the victims were mentioned with a kind of sympathy. How pretty young Rifka had looked before she was raped and murdered, and how wise and kind Moishe, the butter maker, had been.

When the last Jews from their village were being led to their deaths, Moishe, wearing his *tallith* and surrounded by his sons, had shouted in Ukrainian, "Remember well! There will come a time when our innocent blood will fall upon your guilty heads!"

The women were convinced that Moishe's curse was striking now. It was not that the Russians had imprisoned them—it was, they acknowledged, that it was now "in their blood" to denounce one another. As soon as one found himself in prison, he informed on his neighbor because he could not bear to think of another free and working his fields while he was locked up and his farm neglected.

The women did not look like political fighters. They were illiterate and probably believed in Bandera's *Samostina Ukrainia* movement in the same way they believed in witches and black magic.

When the guard began to bang on the iron cells, shouting *ad'boi! ad'boi!* the women shoved the shawl with all that remained of their feast toward me. I told them I did not feel like eating. I wanted nothing from them—I hoped I would be taken away, even if it meant going back to my icebox.

Sure enough, before morning, the guard put me in the cold cell again. I was relieved. It even gave me hope—I convinced myself the authorities did not want me to become acquainted with other prisoners because my release was imminent.

More nights of questions. More days of trying to keep warm and trying to sleep while appearing awake. And then came a night when my hope of release died. Repeating all the questions, the accusations, the major said, "You are entitled to know the accusations against you. First . . ."

First was code 54, high treason, and then the code numbers covering espionage, conspiracy, and other crimes. There were eleven charges. I no longer remember them all. The least of them was attempting to cross the border illegally.

About a week after the episode with the Ukrainian women, I was falling asleep after being returned to my cell when the door opened.

"On the letter R—"

I had returned not ten minutes before. I must have convinced them of my innocence. I was even surer of that when, instead of being taken to the major's office, I was led to the office by the gate. Same room, same rumpled official. Without a word, he handed me a paper. My hand trembled. It must be my release. "Sign it," he said. By this time, however, the habit of reading everything before signing it was ingrained. Under the heading *Arrest Order* and the date *January 4, 1947* was a statement that I had been arrested under charges. . . . There followed a whole column of codes and numbers.

January 4? I had been arrested December 7. My God! All the time I had been kept in this dreadful place, there had been no official arrest; they had had no legal right to hold me. I recalled the lieutenant arguing with the guard at the outside gate. He had had to persuade them to take me in, because there was no warrant. The entire time I had suffered there did not even exist—juridicially—and the file was beginning only now.

I was enraged. The officials tried to calm me by saying it was a mere formality. I kept insisting that any formality that did not agree with the facts was an untruth, and I would not sign any false documents. I kept shouting, "I was arrested December 7!"

"What's the difference?" he asked. "You are in jail anyhow."

"I want to make it clear to you," I insisted, "and you can make it clear to the major, that I have my principles. There is nothing that can make me sign anything which doesn't reflect the truth."

With my head high and my stockings down, I was led back to my icebox. But the next time I was taken to the admissions office, the document I was handed showed the arrest date correctly as December 7. I had achieved something at least.

On another occasion I was handed a list itemizing the things that had been found in the apartment. I was told to sign it to verify that everything was in order. It was not in order. There was no mention of my furs, my jewelry, the things we had purchased through the years. But this time I decided not to make a fuss. If the men who searched the flat had taken the things, there was no way I could press a claim against them. And perhaps our landlady had hidden some of our possessions. I signed.

The itemization of things the major had found in my handbag was correct. I confirmed that one hundred rubles was right, and the major asked me what I wished to spend the money on. "Soap and cigarettes," I told him.

He promised to have these articles brought to me. And then, solicitously, he inquired, "Would you prefer more of a cheaper brand or less of a better brand?" I told him I had had several cartons of American cigarettes in the apartment. If they were still there, I should like them. For the money, and to make them last, I preferred the cheapest brand.

This conversation cleared up one thing between us, without our discussing it directly. I understood I would be sitting in this jail for a while without trial.

But the major kept his promise. After days, I was given some liquid brown soap of the kind poor people used for boiling laundry. I also got the American cigarettes, which I smoked in small pieces to make them last longer, and a supply of cheap Russian cigarettes.

Once I had signed the arrest order with the December 7 date, I was taken to another cell on the second floor in a different wing. It was quite large but nobody else was in it. It was damp but warm, and if anybody could be said to be happy in such circumstances, I was happy.

The floor was of wood, and to the left of the door was a sink with cold and hot water. I undressed and washed my things, for the first time with soap, and put them on the radiator. Then I washed myself from hair to toe.

In the midst of this, I heard the door open. I wrapped my nakedness in my mink coat and saw a frightened guard, new to me, enter my cell. "Why did you stay for so long out of sight of the peephole?" he screamed.

I told him I had been washing myself. He shouted that he thought I had taken my life. There were baths directly under my cell, he said, and from time to time I would be taken to them. (That explained why my cell was damp.) Furthermore, when I slept I must remain on my back and my hands must stay in sight. Several times, while I was still in the cold cell, I had been asked if I wished to go to the baths. I shuddered at the words and refused. We had heard of the Nazi baths at Auschwitz and such places.

Now I found myself looking, almost dispassionately, to see if there were any way to commit suicide. There was no place to hang yourself. Then I understood why the light was always on in the cells and why my hands had to remain visible. The only way to kill yourself was to break the bulb—if you could get at it—and slash your wrists. But they had thought of that. Every bulb was in a metal cage. I wondered why they cared so much about my life when they seemed intent on destroying it.

There was nothing I could do, beyond trying to live within their rules. The only way to fight them would be to keep myself as healthy as possible. Grudgingly, and in spite of myself, I began to adapt to circumstances. In the cold cell it had been impossible; I was like a stray cat in the snow. But my new quarters were large enough to remind me of a normal but unfurnished room.

The walls had traces of paint, peeling because of the dampness. And there was that radiator! It was warm, so comfortingly warm! I had slept for so long curled up into a tight ball to get the most protection from my coat that sleeping stretched out was a luxury. Even lying on my back on a wood floor did not detract from the feeling I experienced as I closed my eyes that somehow something good had happened.

A night or two after I moved in I woke with the sense I was being watched. I was used to surveillance through the peephole but this was different. Then I saw on the floor right next to my head a pair of tiny eyes staring at me. It was a rat.

I sprang to my feet. The rat disappeared into a small hole a finger's length from where my head had been. My first impulse was to bang on the door. But the guard would laugh or take me back to the icebox where it was too cold for rats. By this time I was so lonely I probably would not have minded even the rat had it appeared in daytime. But having it near me when I slept revolted me. I rearranged my shoes, which I used for a pillow, so that the heel of one shoe filled the hole.

During the day, my only companions were roaches. The first sight of them made my skin crawl. But one needs company. After a while I started playing with them and could distinguish one from another. I raced them and put imaginary bets on them. I lined them up on a crack in the floor board and watched to see which one first reached a bit of sugar that had come with my morning tea. They apparently got used to me, too, for they would come quite near and wait. When I paced I took care not to step on them.

A longing for people came only occasionally, for when I had been with other prisoners, I had felt lonelier than when I was by myself. Alone, I could plunge into my remembered world or an imaginary world. In my thoughts I was with my child and experienced happiness, love, success, excitement. But it was a masochistic scratching of wounds. The pain of memory was sometimes unbearable. Everything always was, *was!* Always, things had happened in the past and would probably never happen again. But I knew I must not allow myself to succumb to depression or hate. I had to endure, to find Erika again, wherever and whenever.

Try as I might, though, the sessions with my memories usually ended in such frustration that I had to keep myself from banging my head against the wall. There was nobody to fight with, nobody to blame but the regime. Because of the State, I was no longer a mother, wife, or woman. I would end up crying wildly and with tearstained face I would fall exhausted into sleep.

Through all of one such night I heard my records played over and over. Only my records. The music returned me to the concert halls where Adi and I had played, the hotels, the excitement of opening nights. How well those people—my captors—knew the psychology of isolation, the longing, the self-pity. They had to be playing those records to break me and I stuffed my fingers into my ears. The day would come when I would face a court and have counsel. Then, even if I were not freed, I would have someone to help me plan for Erika. I had to find the strength to live.

I would not be leaving this place quickly. I had heard of prisoners who set themselves tasks and routines to pass the time. I had wondered why they bothered when they could end their miserable existences with their own hands. Now, I knew this was not so easy. And if I succeeded somehow in killing myself, my child would be sent to an orphanage. I was sure she was too young to remember her own name very long.

With no books, no radio, nothing but my mind, I vowed to take care of myself physically and mentally. I would exercise and rub my body with warm and cold water. I tried to bend and stretch to keep my muscles from becoming flabby. But my mental condition worried me. I began to hear Mama calling me, Erika crying, Adi screaming. I recognized these as hallucinations and feared that one day I would begin to believe they were real.

But try as I might, I could not make myself oblivious to one certain sound—the sound of a whistle which our family had used to summon me when I was a child playing in the distance. Now I would hear it mainly in the quiet of the night. It could not be real, yet it would wake me from deep sleep.

I imagined Mama going around and around the prison, whistling, to let me know she was there. One night I whistled in answer as close to the window as possible. I could not see outside; the window was high. But if anyone were trying to reach me, I had to respond. I began to dream about Mama's rescuing arms. I cried and I whistled until the guard came in and shook me. I fell to the floor and wondered how insanity began. Would I recognize it?

To prove that my brain was still functioning, I began to recall mathematical formulas, songs, Yiddish stories. I translated them into other languages I knew. But I could not blot out that whistle.

Then, from my piece of daily bread, I began to mold objects. Straw and whole grain were mixed in the bread, but by wetting it with saliva and mashing it I made it flexible enough to shape. The first thing I contrived was a cigarette holder. It kept the short butts from burning my lips, and I would not have to get so close to the guard to have him light my cigarettes, for we were not allowed matches.

Next, I made an ashtray and then a small plate. As I became more adept, I made a domino. Then playing cards. They were more difficult because even with my improved spitting and molding techniques, the deck was too thick to hold. But I could play solitaire. Making the cards was more of a challenge than playing with them.

Eventually, I created masks and heads. I molded Major Ivanov many times, stretching his image into funny faces. And each night, before I went to sleep, I would lay out tomorrow's program. So much time had passed since my last interrogation that I began to think they would never send for me again.

And then, "On the letter R—"

After walking down the flight of stairs to the main floor, I in front and the guard behind, I turned as usual toward the outside door. My guard punched me in the back and told me to continue downstairs.

We descended a winding metal staircase for what seemed to be at least three more flights below the main floor. My guard rapped sharply on a heavy iron door which opened slowly. The door was on tight springs, and as it opened, the creaking of the springs sounded like the family whistle. I was pleased that I was not going mad. But I had lost my one spark of hope that someone was searching for me. A swift blow from behind restored me to reality.

chapter **15**

Brief Encounter with Hymie
Spring, 1947

In a cubicle, a tall, thin official, wearing glasses so thick that his eyes seemed to peer from behind binoculars, took my fingerprints. To me that represented the ultimate degradation—it stamped me as a *ZeKa*, a convict! Moments later I was led back to my cell where I experienced excruciating loneliness. I had placed such hope in that whistle.

I was beginning to wonder if they had forgotten my existence when I was told, "Come with belongings." My heart danced. Against all logic, I was sure that this time I was going to be released; it could not be anything else. My hands shook so violently I could scarcely put together my belongings and my bread sculptures. I decided to leave the soap and the iron cup in which it had come; I would not need them anymore. But the guard ordered me to take everything. Probably to leave the place clean for the next inmate, I thought.

In torn shoes on stockingless feet, I shuffled down to the courtyard with the guard. It was a clear evening; the snow was melting. I headed toward the gate, but the guard set me straight with a rough, *Kuda!* "Where to?" I must have looked at him with the eyes of a beaten dog, because in a softer voice he said, "We are going to see the prosecutor."

We went into a small entrance off the courtyard and up half a flight of stairs. Standing on the stairwell landing was the prosecutor, a middle-aged peasantlike woman in uniform. She was neither rude nor friendly—indifferent, almost bored.

An open file with my name on it lay on a windowsill above the landing. I could not help thinking what an absurd place for official procedure. The prosecutor told me my interrogation had been completed and I was entitled to read the testimony of witnesses before I signed it. I tried to read by the dim light.

A statement by Mr. D., Commissioner of Repatriation, attested that I had been present when money passed between Adi and himself. There was a report by Mischa, the young man who had introduced himself on the train from Moscow to Lvov. He had found us suspiciously uncommunicative and evasive. Nothing incriminating, but the man had to offer something to earn his pay.

There was testimony from my landlady. She had spoken well of me as long as she was unsure of my destiny. As she was questioned again and again, she began to remind herself that I had aroused her suspicions: I admired the Western world and appeared critical of the Soviet Union. It struck me that at first she might have saved our things for us, and that later it dawned on her that our things could become hers; I had signed the document that omitted most of our valuables.

I asked the prosecutor in a small voice, "When will the trial be?"

"Probably soon."

I had been charged under Ukrainian penal code 16-80. The 80 stood for "crossing the border" and the 16 for "participation in attempt of." The other articles—including code 54, "crimes against the country," and treason—had disappeared.

The woman was still putting my file together when the guard took me back to the courtyard. The moon was shining so brightly now that I could see something strange about the paving stones. Under the thawing snow were Yiddish letters, names and dates. I was walking on gravestones. The dates of birth and death were close—1942 and 1943, the years the Nazis had been there. I could not step on those stones. I shook off my shoes quietly so the guard would not notice and made my way barefoot in the cold mud.

This time he led me to the old wing of the prison. "Now you will have company," he said. I had been in solitary for so long I had grown used to it. Alone, I had managed to cope with my situation. But with others?

The new cell had a wooden floor and was unusually clean. There was a sink with running water, but no toilet; in a corner, an iron pail with a cover served as a commode. For the first time, I learned the word for it: *parasha.*

The room, smaller than my warm cell, had five occupants. Without any greeting, they made room for me. Four were Ukrainians and one Polish, and it did not take long to sort them out. The oldest of

The theatrical Kaminska family, about 1910 (clockwise from top): Esther Rachel, Regina, Ida, Joseph.

The Turkow family, about 1922 (from left to right): Grandmother Turkow, Rachel Turkow, Grandfather Turkow, Isaak Turkow, Ruth Turkow Kaminska, Ida Kaminska, Sarah Turkow.

Ruth in the Yiddish-language movie, Al Che (I Have Sinned, *1936 with co-stars (from left right): Herbert Scherze J. Schumacher, Kurt Katsch, S. Dzigan.*

Adi Rosner, conducting his orchestra in Lodz, Poland, 1939.

Mel, Ida, Ruth, and Adi in Leningrad, 1940.

A flowery reception in Kharkov, 1940.

A calm moment in the Caucasus before the command performance for "The Boss," 1941.

*On a concert tour
through Russia.*

After a performance before French troops in Odessa.

Hymie (left) and Adi [sho]w off the medals they [rec]eived for entertaining [S]oviet troops, Minsk, 1944.

Viktor (left) and Erika, about 1945.

[...]tein, the fur trader and [K]osners' alleged contact with the West.

A happy Rosner family, November 5, 1946. The next month would bring arrest and imprisonment.

Viktor, 1948.

Ruth's house in
Kokchetav.

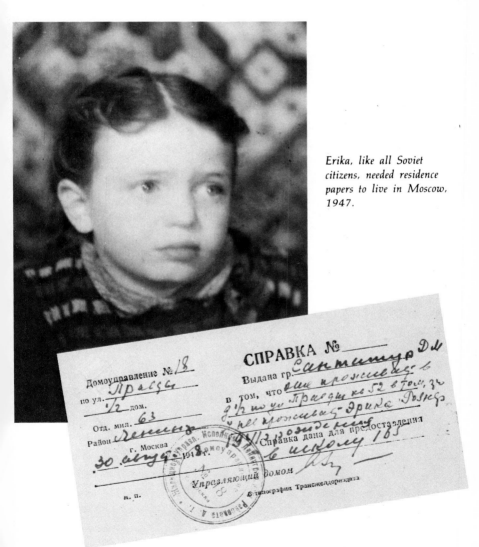

Erika, like all Soviet
citizens, needed residence
papers to live in Moscow,
1947.

Doba Markovna, 1948.

Tono took the picture of Ruth and Erika reunited in Kokchetav.

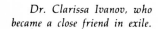

Dr. Clarissa Ivanov, who became a close friend in exile.

Erika (on far right) with playmates in Siberia.

A RZECZPOSPOLITA LUDOWA
ocnik Rządu do Spraw Repatriacji

k t R e p a t r i a c y j n y
Wigrowej k/Warsavy

KARTA REPATRIACYJNA Nr 6990

Ob. *Kamińska Ruth c. Zygmunta*
(nazwisko, imię, imię ojca)

20.7.1919 Kijów
(rok i miejsce urodzenia)

przybył(a) do Polski z *ZSRR*

wraz z *1* nieletnim(i) (do lat 16) dzieckiem(ćmi)
córka Erika Rozner, ur. 1941 r Frunze - ZSRR
(podać nazwisko, imię i wiek dziecka(i))

Dnia *9 lutego* 1955 r.

Obecnie udaje się do *Warszawy, ul. Marszałkowska 55/73 m 57*
(dokładny adres)

   Zgodnie z Uchwałą Prezydium Rządu Nr 739/55 z dnia 10 września 1955 r. Prezydia Rad Narodowych, instytucje państwowe, gospodarcze i społeczne proszone są o udzielenie jak najdalej idącej pomocy okazicielowi niniejszego zaświadczenia.

KIEROWNIK PUNKTU REPATRIACYJNEGO

Wydano dn. *17 grudnia* 1955 r.

U W A G A : Okaziciel niniejszego zaświadczenia obowiązany jest *zameldować się* w ciągu 24 godzin po przybyciu na miejsce zamieszkania.

Ruth's Polish repatriation papers.

With Erika in Warsaw, 1958.

Family reunion in Warsaw: Viktor, Ruth, Erika, Ida.

Ida Kaminska as Mother Courage and Ruth as Katherine in the Jewish State Theatre of Poland's Yiddish-language production.

working on a composition in Russia, 1963.

Ruth in Warsaw, 1957.

Erika and Amaris Kovalick, 1978.

Ida, Mel, and Ruth, New York City, 1978.

the Ukrainians was about forty and the only member of her family who had been arrested. One was my age; her husband, too, was in prison and the children were with their grandparents. Then there was a girl of about nineteen who never spoke. The fourth was a nun with a diseased leg. She had bone tuberculosis and her leg looked dreadful and smelled worse. The four Ukrainians were Banderovites. I was not too happy to have to share their cell.

The fifth woman, the Pole, had been arrested because she was a Jehovah's Witness. A widow named Zosia, she had been a maid in rich homes. Since her arrest her two children had been sent to an orphanage.

When I entered the cell, she motioned me to sit next to her. It was the first cell floor I did not mind sitting on; to keep busy, the five constantly cleaned and polished the floor and all took turns emptying the *parasha*. When my turn came, Zosia tried to take over for me and offered as well to do my cleaning and wash my things. With someone to do things for, she felt she was back to her normal way of life. But I too needed something to do, especially since I was now deprived of my exercise.

Even carrying out the *parasha* was a treat, because the toilet where we emptied it contained a small window from which we could see people coming and going on the street. We never tired of watching them pass. I marveled that there were still people outside and I wondered whether they were aware of our eyes on them.

The Ukrainians kept mostly to themselves; they had in common their language, their peasant background, and their independence movement. Besides, they frequently held prayer sessions in which Zosia and I did not participate.

After being with them for a while I was non-plussed at their being political prisoners. They were illiterate, except for the nun. Their political awareness began and ended with the conviction that the followers of Bandera were the good guys and the rest of humanity the bad guys. They were anti-Semitic, anti-Polish, anti-Russian, but even so I wondered how they could be taken seriously by the Soviet authorities.

Our one consensus involved the food—we agreed it was vile. And we discussed in detail our dreams, which were interpreted by the oldest Ukrainian.

"The best things to dream about," she maintained, "are potatoes and cows." They foretold imminent freedom. I never dreamed about potatoes or cows. Once I dreamed of driving in an open car along a seashore. That meant something terrible would happen to my loved ones, she told me. Next day I announced I had withheld the fact that I was an expert interpreter of dreams and offered my services. The senior Ukrainian said she had just dreamed of picking mushrooms. In my interpretation, I buried her cow and revealed that her husband was having an affair with a neighbor.

She mused for a moment, then said, "It must be Gingerplum Theresa."

"Exactly."

"I knew it!"

Zosia looked at me approvingly.

One dream that recurred constantly, I never shared. It concerned Grandfather Turkow, who used to "visit" me almost nightly, dressed as I remember him, in brown morning jacket, comfortable flannel slippers, and brown sports cap. The cell door would open and there he would be, carrying a basket covered with a gleaming white napkin. Grandfather would sit down near me, wordlessly uncover the basket, remove a fresh loaf of white bread, and divide it among all of us. After we had eaten, he would shake away the crumbs, push the iron cell door, and leave as soundlessly as he had come.

In the morning, the first thing I did was to glance at the floor for crumbs. I liked those quiet visits, which made me wonder if I had been warm enough toward him. I had always rather feared him, as had the rest of the family. He was most religious and conservative and maintained rigid rules in his household.

Those nightly dreams reminded me of a story I had heard about him. It concerned my father, Zigmund. Against Grandfather's wishes, my father had attended drama school, and had been invited to join the Theater Polski, a top repertory theater.

Grandfather, who managed real estate, knew many of the policemen assigned near his properties. One day, he ran into one who had been transferred to a beat near the Polski. The patrolman said, "Do you know, Mr. Turkow, I meet your son quite often when I am on duty near the Theater Polski."

"Oh, yes, yes," my grandfather agreed. "I am sure you do. He works there as an usher." That, to him, was more respectable than acting.

For some time, my cellmates watched me rather obviously and

questioned me crudely to make sure I was not a *siksot* (informer). One day a guard ordered us to put our things together in front of us and stand against the wall, hands behind our backs. The Colonel Inspector would be in directly to ask if we had any complaints.

A few minutes later the guard returned and stood at attention. The inspector marched in behind him with insignia and medals on his chest as if he were about to review an army. He gruffly asked, "Any complaints?"

The nun wanted to see a physician. The youngest spoke up for the first time, shyly asking why she had not received any *piridachas* and news from home. All complained about the food.

The inspector nodded at each complaint but nothing was written down. Then he looked up sharply at me. "And you? No complaints?"

"Me? Oh, no. I am enchanted."

His face reddened and he stalked out. Nothing was ever done about the requests.

About the same time I announced I planned to go on a hunger strike in order to get news of my child. The others protested, afraid they might be accused of appropriating my food, so I abandoned the idea.

After these incidents they became convinced I was straight. They manifested their confidence by pushing away the *parasha* and pointing out a small hole in the wall.

"In the next cell, there are seven men. But since the last man came in and you came in, we have not tried to contact each other. Yesterday they banged on the pipe to let us know everything was okay. So now if you would like to find out if they know something about your husband, we can do it. What is your husband's name?"

"Just ask them if anybody knows about Erika's father," I said. While one woman pretended to use the *parasha*, another bent to the hole, cupped her mouth with her hands, and whistled low. Then she spoke quickly in Ukrainian. Every few moments she turned to us to share her news. The new man had become ill and had been taken away. No, nobody knows anything about Erika's father. Then she said, "I told them about you. They ask if you have another wish."

"I am dying for a cigarette," I said, "but what's the use?"

She spoke again near the hole and then said, "Wait till evening; they'll send it by special messenger."

After *ad'boi* the parasha was again moved and the woman whistled. A frightened mouse poked its head out of the hole and then, pushed from behind, ran into our cell with two cigarettes tied to its tail. The young girl caught the mouse and, as a reward for our neighbors, we shipped back a small package of sugar.

One night in June we were awakened by the sound of many feet tramping through the corridors and of trucks apparently being driven in and out of the courtyard. We tried to see out the window by standing on cellmates' shoulders, but the window's muzzle did not permit even a glimpse. Perhaps they were shipping people away, but where and why?

The oldest woman guessed—perhaps war had come again. "If so, they will take us someplace and shoot us—they would never evacuate people inland from a jail." It seemed possible; in prison any idea becomes plausible.

The women prayed and cried. I could only hope that the orphanages would be relocated.

Suddenly a banging on our door and a shout, "Prepare with belongings!" A few moments later, the door opened. With shouts of *Bistro, bistro, davay vychoditz!* "Hurry, hurry, go out!", we were invited to leave what suddenly seemed a cozy haven.

In the corridor on the way to the staircase there were thunderous footsteps, and rhythmical bangings in all the corridors and stairways. It was incredible that they had maintained such quiet up to now when the place contained so many people.

In solitary I had felt I was alone in the prison—except for those screams, real or imagined. Later, placed with other people, I realized the Soviet Union was not running a jail just for my benefit, but even then, it seemed to exist only for me and those I was with. Walks in the yard were only with cellmates. I never felt part of a large group. Now, the whole place was alive.

At the staircase we were ordered to stop. We saw, on the landing half a flight below, the backs of male inmates facing the wall. The men were waiting their turn to descend. Could Adi be among them? He was not. Then I saw a faded green coat. Hymie?

I whispered the name. The figure in the green coat slowly turned. Hymie! He looked at me for a moment in silence before he recognized me. Then he lamented in whispered Yiddish, *Vais mere! Rutele! Ida's tochter! Esther Rachel's ainicle!* "Woe is me! Ruth! Ida's daughter! Esther Rachel's grandchild!"

At that moment we were ordered to move. I passed Hymie's

trembling back. In the courtyard, we were told to sit with our backs to the wall. The place was filled with prisoners sitting the same way. I searched with my eyes all around and under the trucks as each was loaded. Adi was not there. As soon as a truck was filled, it drove through the courtyard gate, guarded by men holding guns.

Hymie's group came along, and was placed close to us. Slowly shifting places, we managed to sit near one another. We could hardly talk and there was so much to say, to ask.

Hymie knew no more about Erika than I did—he had been arrested two days after I failed to return home. But he had first phoned Doba Markovna that my husband's disease was contagious and that I now had it also.

He learned from Doba that Mama and her family had reached Warsaw, and Doba promised to notify Mama about my "illness." So Mama knew! I was happy she had my little brother. Perhaps he would ease her suffering because of me. But I hardly knew what to say to Hymie—he, too, could have been safe in Warsaw had he not elected to leave with us.

At the same moment, Hymie and I found ourselves saying, "Lucky that Mama cannot imagine what it really looks like here."

We shared a piece of bread and a bit of sugar that I had in my pocket and Hymie gave me a scrap of old newspaper and some tobacco to make a cigarette. We discussed our situation.

"To tell the truth," I said, "I wouldn't even mind being shot if I only knew Erika was safe." We considered the possibilities of escape: there were none and if there were, where could we hide? In the Soviet Union you could go nowhere without papers.

chapter 16

Hunger Strike
Summer, 1947

Our turn came to climb into the truck. We were encouraged by sharp blows on our backs with the butts of the guards' guns. Hymie's group was jammed in with mine. The number of people on each truck was governed by the guards' ability to close the tailgate.

At each corner of the truck stood a guard with a machine gun pointed at us. Sitting on the floor, we could not see where we were being taken, but soon the truck stopped and the tailgate opened. Machine guns still aimed at us, we were told to jump down and crouch like racers ready to run. But at least we could look about us. We were at a railroad station. Then they did not intend to shoot us, because they would have taken us to an isolated spot, rather than to the depot.

They separated women from men and loaded us onto a train. We were counted twice—each time by a bang on the back with a gun butt—once by the guard who brought us and then by the guard who received us.

Climbing the train's high steps, I dropped my treasures, including my soap, to grasp the handrail. In spite of the heat, I was wearing my mink. I had had no chance to take it off and it was easier to keep it on than to hold it. We filled the compartment; I could not even stretch my arms. The gate closed behind us.

Some inmates screamed that they were suffocating. Some screamed from the pain of the gun-butt counting. Worse came in a few minutes when lice and bedbugs attacked. During the nearly eighteen hours we remained in the compartment, I was convinced I would be eaten to death by bugs. We begged the guard to take some people out so the rest could scratch. We got nowhere. Our physiological needs had to be met as we were and where we were.

About midnight we arrived at Zolotchov, a distance normally covered by the slowest train in an hour and a half. How the train had kept moving all that time without getting there hours ago I could not imagine. We were unloaded into a field, amidst guards with pointed machine guns. Hymie's group debarked near us.

The first thing we did was attempt to rid ourselves of the lice and bugs—without soap, water, or brushes. Jumping up and down, covered with welts and blood, we must have looked like victims of some horrible disease.

Then we were formed into lines, five people in a row. The armed Zolotchov guards, accompanied by German shepherd dogs, took over. For the first time I heard the words which were to accompany me whenever I moved anywhere, "Three steps forward, three steps back will be considered an attempt to escape and you'll be shot without warning."

At that, we summoned strength enough to walk, mostly uphill, to a distant building that looked like a castle. A priest in Hymie's group told us it had been the mansion of the Polish King Sobieski's mistress, Marishenka. At the gate we were ordered to sit on the ground. Our new prison was not ready for such an influx of guests.

Hymie and I sat close. We tried to console one another but neither of us believed a word we said. Ahead of where we sat was an iron gate. Behind it we could see guards and a number of tables piled high with file folders; the tables spread on both sides of an entrance archway, under lights. Were they planning to work through the night? We were in no hurry. We prized any moment different from those in our cells.

Our stomachs yearned for our missed meals, however dreadful they were. Then we saw civilians—or perhaps prisoners—carrying large baskets and we smelled freshly baked bread, pieces of which were handed to us through the bars of the gate. The smell was better than the taste, but for the first time I ate my entire bread ration at once.

By the time they opened the gate, it was dawn. We had to pass by the tables giving our full names and the charges against us. When the formalities had been completed, the sun was hot and I started to take off my coat. Hymie whispered, "Don't. They might take it away from you. And don't mention how valuable it is. Just consider it something to keep you warm."

"In June?"

"The way you look, you can use it in June. Besides, there will be winters ahead."

Then we had to go separate ways. Before we parted, Hymie said,

"Rutele, you have to be brave. Remember, you have your family waiting for you, people who love you!" No family waited for Hymie.

We were led to a *sanobrabodka*, a sanitizing treatment. We had to undress and hand over all of our things to be put through a disinfecting machine. I hesitated about my coat, but Hymie's warning not to draw attention to it was still fresh. Besides, what good would it be full of bugs?

The mink came through unharmed, with the bugs gone, and despite the disinfectant, the coat still smelled of perfume. I remembered the day that Adi had bought the scent for me. He had gone to a *komis* for luggage before we left Moscow and the *komis* manager had told him, "I have something your wife will be delighted with, real French perfume. I got it from a French lady." After paying an outlandish price, Adi presented me with a small vial of Guerlain.

I had just had a shower with caustic soda provided by an attendant, since I no longer had soap of my own. I recalled that when I was a child in Warsaw, our housekeeper would tell the laundress, "Don't put caustic soda in the wash, it will make holes in the clothes." Now, I was glad to have it for cleansing myself, and I saved some for my next bath, whenever that would be. When I finished, it felt good to wrap myself up in my sweet-smelling fur coat.

The rest of that day and night I spent in a sort of catacomb. Chains hung from the rough stone walls, the floor was paved with stones like those of the wall, and the whole place was dark and dank. I was happy to have my coat. I was utterly exhausted, and I slept despite the darting rats.

Next day I was transferred to a new cell. For the first time there would be something to sleep on—slats hammered onto wooden supports. But after so many months of sleeping on bare floors, I knew this planking, covered with my coat, would be luxurious. There was also a massive table with a can of drinking water on it, and in the corner the *parasha*.

Three women were in the cell, each occupying a "bed." The bed nearest the *parasha* was free—that was mine.

When we began to talk, I learned the women's stories. One of the women was a Mrs. Teitlebaum, a Jewish mother of ten who had worked with her husband in a knit goods factory. Her husband had been accused of stealing garments. The charge was false; the militia had searched the house and found no stolen goods. But they did find the woman's Sabbath cloth for the Friday night bread and her silver candlesticks.

That was evidence enough on which to arrest her husband. The woman explained that the cloth and the candlesticks had nothing to do with her husband—they were things she used. Rather than return without a prisoner, they arrested her instead. Now she was awaiting sentence on a charge of Zionism. Deeply religious, she ate only kosher food, but she was afraid to admit to such a crime, so her husband obtained a doctor's certificate prescribing a diet for an intestinal illness from which she actually suffered. Armed with the certificate, her husband brought kosher food to her from Lvov every few days.

Unlike the Lvov prison which held only political prisoners, Zolotchov mixed common criminals and "politicals." Vera, another cellmate, was in for theft, and Anna, a rough-looking character whose bed was nearest mine, for armed robbery.

In order for Mrs. Teitlebaum's kosher food to be separated from Vera's, which was sent by her mother, Vera's was always placed on one side of the water can on the table and Mrs. Teitlebaum's on the other.

Anna got no parcels, but treated herself to whatever she wanted, with a "May I?" first and a "Thank you" afterward as she wiped her greasy mouth. She held her bread or meat with three fingers on her strong mannish hand, and curled the other two, their nails filthy, in a caricature of a lady drinking tea in a salon. She would whisper to me with a wink that the others had no idea what good manners were. Occasionally she invited me, with the flair of a movie waiter, to dine on the contents of the others' parcels. I declined.

After I had been there several days, Vera and Mrs. Teitlebaum received large food parcels which they arrayed as usual, on the sides of the water can. Anna rubbed her hands. That evening two skinny girls were brought into our cell. There were no more beds so they slept on the floor. In the morning the table was empty. The girls had consumed everything—including Vera's large piece of salt pork, Mrs. Teitlebaum's roast goose, bread, and preserves, and five pounds of sugar.

Mrs. Teitlebaum was upset because she would have nothing to eat until her husband returned, but Vera was furious at the blow to her professional pride. The idea of anybody stealing from her! Anna muttered, "Imagine, not even to have the manners to say 'May I?'" I burst into laughter at my mental picture of this woman robber asking her victims "May I?" as she held a gun to their heads.

Criminal inmates like Vera and Anna knew the penal code and knew pretty much what to expect in any criminal prisoner's case. But in political cases, they could only guess. They surmised that Mrs. Teitlebaum, as the mother of ten children, would be freed as soon as she had "learned a good lesson." So for days, I rehearsed with her Doba Markovna's address in Moscow; she promised me *bai allem Heiligin* (by everything holy) that as soon as she reached home she would get word to Doba about me.

I had thought that now, since I was no longer under interrogation, they might tell me about Erika. So every time the head guard, whom we descriptively named "The Red Ape," came near, I asked him to let me see someone in authority. Once or twice he made some notes but nothing ever came of it.

Then the great day arrived for Mrs. Teitlebaum. "On the letter T—and with belongings!"

She gathered her things, wished all of us short sentences and left her last *piridacha* for us to enjoy in good health. She reassured me with a blink and a nod that she would keep her promise. It was the first time I had seen her smile. I counted the hours now until I might hear from Doba Markovna.

Near the end of June I was cleaning the small smelly fish that was our most frequent meal, Vera was standing guard near the peephole, and Anna—on the shoulders of the other two girls—was looking out the window. It was the time when already sentenced inmates walked in the yard, and Anna always looked for someone she knew. Suddenly she exclaimed, *"Pani!"* Polish for Madame, it was her name for me. "Pani, come here. Look who's there!"

Walking with the sentenced prisoners was Mrs. Teitlebaum. She was gazing at our window and when the guard turned his back she held up ten fingers.

"Mrs. Teitlebaum got ten years for her own candlesticks!" shouted Anna. I was shattered—with her tragedy went also my last hope of communicating with Doba Markovna.

At that point I told my cellmates I had made up my mind. The only way I could obtain word about my child was to go on a hunger strike. Like my cellmates in Lvov, they objected that they might be accused of stealing my rations. "Do it legally," they suggested.

"How?"

"Tell the guard you have some information. You will see how soon they will bring you a piece of paper and a pen. This is the only way to acknowledge in a legal way what you plan to do." Soon enough the Red Ape presented me with paper, pen, and ink. And so I declared,

"From the first of July 1947, I won't accept any food until I receive official notification from the authorities in Lvov concerning my child, Erika Rosner, born in Frunze, Kirghizstan, where she is and how she is. Signed, *ZeKa* (Prisoner) Ruth Zigmundovna Rosner Kaminska Turkow, charged by 16-80, Prison Zolotchov."

The Red Ape shouted that perhaps I did not realize where I was. "You are in a Soviet prison and in a Soviet prison such behavior is outrageous!"

I refused breakfast. At that I was transferred to a vacant cell. I spread my things out on a wooden couch. From then on, I was an outlaw even in prison—I was beyond the regulations and could lie down in the daytime.

I did. In the seven months I had been in prison, a tremendous amount of vitality had been sapped, but if I did not move around too much, perhaps I could endure lack of food longer. That first day, when food was offered to me, I said I would not take any. The second day I just shook my head. The third day I did not hear them come in. Instead I heard bells, thousands of them, high-pitched bells, deep, booming bells. I was not hungry, just a little chilled.

But then I felt something happening to me. Everything was black; I could not see, perhaps because I was just too tired to open my eyes. My limbs tingled and after a while, my whole body seemed to be pierced by pins and needles. In a flash of light, I saw myself seated on a chair with a needle in my arm. People in white coats surrounded me, and I was not in my cell. Then everything went dark again. Moments later the light seemed to return.

The Red Ape was shouting at me. I did not hear what he said; I heard only the bells clanging. A few moments more and I realized that Red Ape was pointing at a paper and trying to put a pen in my hand. I wanted to say no, but could not. Besides, I could not hold a pen. In a minute I became aware that the needle in my arm was attached to something. I felt wet. I wondered if I had fainted and been doused with water. Then I understood I was perspiring—streaming with water. When I was able to focus my eyes, I saw my perspiration was yellow.

One "white coat" tried to open my mouth by squeezing my cheeks, but my jaws were pressed together so tightly he could not pry them loose. He took a flat metal tongue depressor, the kind used in the throat examination, and tried to get it between my teeth. There was a terrific explosion in my head and blood spurted on his hand. He had broken out a tooth, but still could not open my mouth. They pushed a rubber tube into my nose. I felt the pain of that. Then for a while—nothing. I must have blacked out again.

The next thing I was aware of was a hunger pang. I could see they were pouring something through the rubber tube. I heard voices. Red Ape's face was right before me, but his voice came from a vast distance. He was shouting, "Don't be stubborn! You won't survive it. Sign this and everything will be finished. You will get more milk. You want to taste milk, don't you?" With the rubber in my nose, I could only gurgle. I meant no.

Then I started to shiver because everything I was wearing was wet from sweat, from blood, and from spilled milk. Finally Red Ape dragged me by the collar of my dress through the corridor. I was inert and my body bounced like a rag doll on the stone pavement, rubbing off the meager layer of flesh over my spine. The Red Ape threw my sore bones on the cot and I managed to turn over onto my stomach.

This became everyday procedure. Sometimes I woke in my cell; other times I found myself among the white coats, who were pushing a needle in my arm or a tube in my nose. Most of the time I hovered between awareness and oblivion. Sometimes I was brought to consciousness by a pain in my back, so sharp that it seared like a flame. When I was placed in a chair with my back touching the back of the chair, I would moan and lean forward. Finally one doctor looked for the reason. He put something soothing on my back and I was picked up by one of the white coats. It seemed strange to be carried so easily by so small a man.

Instead of being dumped back in the isolation cell, I was returned to my former cell. I tried to object but the Red Ape waved a piece of paper in front of me. He read it to me but I could not hear what he said and could not see well enough to read it. My coat was spread on my bed, and Anna gently laid me down on my stomach.

My cellmates told me that had my things not been brought in, they would not have recognized me. I had been away a week. I had lost an incredible amount of weight and my skin had a blue tinge. The women's friendly concern relaxed me and I fell into a deep sleep. The first thing I was aware of when I awoke was their whispering. I could hear! Then I opened my eyes and saw my cellmates sitting on their cots, watching me.

Anna jumped up. "Shall I read the paper to you?" I could only signal with my eyes that I wished her to. It was the paper the Red Ape had left. Anna told me it had been signed by the Lvov MGB—it said only that my child had been taken by an older woman and remained with her. In addition, a note signed by a doctor said I was entitled to a special diet with white bread, one egg daily, and milk.

A day passed. No white bread, no egg, no milk.

My cellmates asked for them.

"Where does she think she is?" Red Ape replied. "Sure, she is entitled to them, if someone brings them to her. This is a jail, not a sanatorium."

And so my cellmates began to feed me with whatever they had, a little at a time. Vera even asked her mother to include milk for me in her next food parcel. After a week, I began to recover but I got a shock every time I looked at my legs. I resembled an inmate of a Nazi concentration camp.

Toward the end of July, I was called to the office. A guard helped me walk there.

An unimpressive piece of paper, the size of a bill and dated July 7, informed me I had been sentenced by the Troika of the Supreme Soviet to five years of exile in Kokchetav. I had only to sign it. What if I refused to sign? It would make no difference.

No trial, then. Just a few pieces of paper had gone back and forth, making decisions about my life! I had been sentenced July 7, the day my hunger strike ended. I was getting superstitious about sevens. My birthday was in the seventh month, July. I had been arrested on December 7. Now I had been sentenced on the seventh day of the seventh month. In prison it is easy to become superstitious about that kind of thing.

When I returned to my cell, I was not able to repeat the name of the place to which I would have to go.

chapter 17

Camp at Lvov
Summer and Autumn, 1947

All recently sentenced prisoners were gathered in the courtyard at the end of August. No sign of Hymie. Outside the gate new arrivals were sitting as we had sat a few months earlier. We were moving on. Once again we filed by the officials sitting at tables beneath the arch. Now when I identified myself I had to add "sentenced to five years of exile under Article 16-80 of the Ukrainian criminal code." The official looked up. "You must be mistaken about your article, because 16-80 is an administrative punishment which usually carries six months imprisonment."

I murmured that possibly my connections with people in high places had enabled me to have myself sentenced by the Supreme Soviet to five years in exile for an administrative matter. He did not reply.

Red Ape shouted, "Move! Move!" and pushed me along. As always when one group of prisoners passed another, we searched hungrily for someone we knew. Guards, guns, and dogs accompanied us to the railroad station. We were going to Lvov. The bugs on the train, although fed so recently, greeted us enthusiastically and the trip to Lvov was as long as the trip from Lvov had been. This time we were led afoot through the dark streets and stopped in front of a gate. Some of the prisoners recognized it as the deportation concentration camp on Pelczynska Street, where most prisoners were held only until they could be shipped out—in days, weeks, or months. What we saw was a wooden fence with a huge gate. When the gate closed behind us, we found ourselves in a narrow passage bounded by barbed wire. Ahead was another fence, its gate closed. The area absorbed all of us, together with guards and dogs. On each side of this "no man's land" were towers with searchlights and guards on patrol.

For hours we sat in the dirt, total darkness alternating with blinding light as the searchlights roved. The inner gate finally opened at dawn. The *sanobrabodka* again. As I was led in I noticed everyone looking curiously at me, which should not have surprised me since I was wearing my mink coat on a hot summer day.

Even here, I was a sight. But all of the clientele looked picaresque. People were dressed in what had been priestly garb, civilian clothing, uniforms—all rags now. Despite my mink, my feet were bare, my tattered dress hung unevenly in a dozen places and my two braids were bound with different colored threads. The showers were not working. Instead we were to use water from barrels scattered in the area. Around each barrel clustered women, some with apparently syphilitic sores, all washing with the same water. I refused to bathe. My head throbbed. I felt faint and I must have looked the way I felt because I was taken immediately to the hospital. This was an unexpected stroke of luck because of the prospect of a good bath.

Before long I was in a huge laundry tub, where a woman poured warm water over me and gave me a piece of soap. She remarked to another standing nearby, "She wasn't diseased, just filthy." She handed me a hospital gown that gaped open because its strings were missing, and I was put into a bed which I shared feet to head with another woman. I hoped her illness was not contagious.

For two or three days, I felt too ill to notice what went on around me, but finally I saw I was in a large dormitory filled with beds, most occupied by two people each. My bedmate was a young Austrian, Mimi, who was delighted that I spoke German because she had been unable until then to talk to anybody. She had been taken here from Vienna, and she told me, with torrents of words, she was not the only one from Vienna; there were also Hungarians and people from other countries.

Mimi first had been in the regular barracks—this camp had no cells—but because of severe pains she had been sent to the hospital, Barrack 13. That was a lucky number, she said, because Barrack 14 was for seriously ill people.

"While I was in the quarters barracks, I could see that from Barrack 14, most of them went to 15."

"What's 15?"

"Fifteen? It's a hole with chloride of lime. That's where the patients from 14 usually end up. You can smell it from the quarters barracks."

Mimi appeared to be over thirty. She was so swollen that I was certain she was pregnant. Her face and body were covered with brown patches, and one could see her scalp through her sparse, pale hair. She lacked some front teeth.

When I asked her what had got her into this place, she told me her story. At the war's end, she married "a wonderful young man," an electrician, and moved into his apartment. They felt lucky because the apartment was in Vienna's allied zone; she had lived with her mother in the Russian zone.

After she gave birth to a son she regained her strength slowly and they needed her mother to help her. But to obtain a transfer from the Russian zone was complicated, so they skipped the technicalities.

One night Mimi slipped over the line, but on the way back with her mother she was stopped. She imagined that her mother escaped because she did not see her again.

"They took me to the commandant of the Soviet zone," she said. "It was the picture of my grandfather, who was in Emperor Franz Josef's army, that caused the trouble. I told my mother not to take that picture but she wouldn't listen, and the Soviet soldiers were sure the man in the picture was one of Hitler's generals. They insisted that I knew his hiding place and that I was a spy.

"I tried to explain that even his uniform would indicate that I was telling the truth, but they wouldn't believe me. They beat me so long that I finally confessed that my grandfather—who had been dead for twenty years—was indeed Hitler's general. That was when I lost my teeth, and since then I have had terrible pains in my back. But I did manage to save something—I have a picture of my husband, my child, and myself. Would you like to see it?"

She took a picture from a tiny sack hanging from her neck. It showed a young, handsome man, his arm around a pretty, laughing girl with a head full of silky, curling hair. They were holding an infant.

"We had that picture taken a few months ago, just a short while before I was arrested. My boy was three months old. By now he must be a big boy."

I buried my head in my pillow.

Every few days a young doctor visited us; we heard him giving orders to older doctors. He was free; the others, who took his orders meekly, might once have been distinguished professors but now were prisoners.

One day an older Polish doctor, a Dr. Malinovsky, approached me. He told me that he, too, came from Lvov, knew who I was, and would do his best to restore my health. He had been sentenced to ten years in the concentration camp in Kolima, but was being kept here on the grounds that he was tubercular. "The other good reason they keep me here," he confided, "is the money my family slips them. I may live long enough to ruin my family financially."

Since he had contacts outside, I asked him to help me let Doba Markovna know where I was. He promised.

I was sure it was not Dr. Malinovsky who spread the word of my presence, but I soon had a parade of inmates passing the window near my bed though visiting was forbidden. Most knew Mama from the stage or had seen me with Adi at concerts. Each one exclaimed, "My God, look at her!"

Mimi had an occasional visit at the window from a young Viennese named Johann who had been a drama student taking private lessons from a teacher in the Soviet sector. The young man had been stopped while returning from lessons. He had with him scripts of plays he was studying. Having papers in his possession was enough to lay him open to suspicion, and the commandant, who knew no German, arrested him to be on the safe side. The commandant's suspicions no doubt would have been aroused, I thought, even by "To be or not to be."

When Johann learned I knew both Russian and German, he asked me to write a petition to Herr Stalin because he was sure Herr Stalin would order him freed. "Herr Stalin probably has no idea what is going on." I wrote one petition for him and another for Mimi. They needed hope.

Some time later, Dr. Malinovsky told me he had sent word to Doba Markovna. He also warned me not to take food from the visitors at the window, as I must be careful about what I ate. His warning came too late. Once I began to feel better I was always hungry and devoured anything offered—fruits, onions, tomatoes, cake, anything.

Soon enough, I was transferred to Barrack 14 with the bloody dysentery, as they called it. Two male prisoners—nurses—carried me on a stretcher. To make a place for me, they took a patient out of a bed and dragged her by the legs into the corridor to wait for darkness, when she would be dumped into Barrack 15. I wondered how soon my turn would come.

Dr. Malinovsky was the only one who attended patients in Barrack 14. If he saw a chance that someone might survive, he administered from his meager supply of serum. We patients were all attached to intravenous feeders. We talked to each other from time to time, but sometimes someone would stop in the middle of a sentence and his nearest neighbor would announce, "Gone!"

Our greatest fear was that we might be dragged out while alive, so we cooperated in hiding information about anyone who was dying. In a period of a week, three of us among sixteen survived; after some time, we were transferred back to Barrack 13, but to a room where we had beds to ourselves.

When a nurse began to help me walk around I looked for Mimi. Dr. Malinovsky told me to stop looking. She had gone to 15.

As long as I remained in the hospital I felt sure I would not be ordered shipped out, and some of the doctors tried to arrange for me to stay as a nurse until I gained strength. But the sanction had to come from the free doctor.

Meanwhile I began to walk a little, holding on to the walls. I enjoyed sitting on the steps outside the hospital building, soaking up the waning warmth of autumn. One day while I was sitting there with a group of hospital workers, a guard approached.

"Who is Rosner?"

In camps people were not summoned by the letter. I was pointed out.

"You have a visitor." I had to hold onto a railing. When I caught my breath, I asked him to wait a few minutes.

I put my torn but clean dress over my hospital gown, braided my hair and followed the guard to the administration building. It was my first real walk in weeks and the guard had to steady me. As I entered the small room for visitors, there was Doba Markovna.

A guard was cutting into little pieces the contents of a basket of food she had brought. At first, she did not recognize me. But after I addressed her she burst into tears. Then she took me in her arms murmuring, "You poor martyr. Poor martyr." I bit my lips.

We were permitted twenty minutes. Erika was well. She was with Doba and constantly asked when her parents would be back from their tour.

"Adi is in a concentration camp, sentenced to ten years under Article 54 as a traitor to the homeland," Doba told me.

Mama and the family were well in Poland. They phoned her every few days, hoping for news of me. As soon as Doba had been called by relatives of Dr. Malinovsky, she had phoned Mama to tell her she would visit me soon. I asked her not to reveal my true situation to Mama and to tell her I hoped to write.

Doba had permission to see me again in two days. We decided that next time I would wear my fur coat and exchange it for her coat. I was afraid to keep mine any longer; I had heard stories about the inmates of barracks and on the *etap* (transfer train); my coat could endanger my life. (In the hospital an attendant took care of it.)

Before Doba left, she gave me my baby's most recent photograph, on which Erika had written, "To my dearest mother—Erika." She could write! How changed she looked—so grown up! I kissed the picture a thousand times. The face was so solemn and sad. Perhaps she just happened to look that way at the moment the photograph was taken. . . .

Now, feelings that had been deadened reawakened within me. My illnesses had obscured my major suffering. My longings and yearnings revived with such vigor that I felt I could not cope with them. My whole female being yearned for a man—not any man—but my man. A child within me cried out for my mother. As a mother myself, I longed for my baby. The pain of that was the worst. I had failed as a mother. I had left my child an orphan in a hostile world. That evening in bed I wept as I had not wept in years. But I would be damned if I would let them send me to Barrack 15.

Next day I received permission to remain at the hospital a bit longer as a nurse. I had no desire to stay because I felt that once I reached my place of exile, no matter how rugged it might be, I would have Erika sent to me. I must find the strength for what lay ahead. In the hospital, paper and pen were available. I prepared two letters to give to Doba, one for Adi and one for Mama.

When I was escorted to see Doba Markovna the second time, I looked better—a scrap of news, a bit of hope had worked wonders. Doba had been instructed, no doubt, by Dr. Malinovsky's family, on whom to handle and how. So no one seemed to notice that I entered the visiting room in my fur coat and left it in a much too long, much too wide, much too worn cloth coat. Doba had put on weight since our first meeting in Moscow.

I need not worry about Adi, Doba told me. He was well and leading a big band in his concentration camp. He had even managed to have musicians transferred from other camps to enlarge and improve his orchestra. They occasionally traveled—in cattle trains and under guard—to other camps to entertain guards and officials, and in reward, he got good food and good quarters. When he traveled, he managed to mail letters. He only asked, in letters to Doba that were meant for Mama, for a suit, warm sweaters, and a new embouchure for his trumpet. These items were on their way.

At Doba's news that I was fine, Mama had cried with happiness. She had been approached by a lawyer from Lvov who had promised to do his best to help me, and she had sent him money.

Erika was sweet, pretty, and intelligent, Doba assured me. What more could I ask? And she promised that as soon as I was settled wherever I was sent, she would visit again. Then the guard parted us.

When I returned to the hospital barracks, I prepared a treat for my friends from the parcel Doba had brought. Several of the inmate doctors and nurses met in a small washroom which was the one place we could smoke—and one always had an excuse for being there.

Barrack 14 inmate workers included a kind of high society. Mrs. Blanca, a Pole, had been a famous designer and milliner who lived in Lvov but before the war had spent much of her time in Paris and Vienna. She was charged, naturally, with espionage, but her family managed to have her kept on here as a nurse. Besides Dr. Malinovsky, we had a famous Jewish professor from Leningrad and a surgeon from Kiev, both in for high treason. The aristocracy was represented by Count Pokropov. He was a nurse, but as soon as a shipment out was rumored, he became a patient, sometimes by injecting himself with nicotine, sometimes by contriving a small accident. He was bent on staying in Lvov until he could get word from his wife who had been shipped out. Since mail was not forwarded for outlaws, he feared he might lose track of her.

The count, born in Russia, had lived in Paris after the revolution. He was very much in love with his Austrian wife, many years his junior. When the war ended, his wife wanted to visit her family in Vienna's Soviet zone. The count and his wife were sure their French citizenship would protect them. But the gifts they took to their relatives resulted in a charge of smuggling, later changed to espionage. As the Russians say, "Try to prove that you are not a camel."

The attire in our washroom club was informal. The women

nurses wore robes, too short and wide, that they kept closed by tying in various places, and the doctors had similar robes over their underwear. But Count Pokropov who was very tall and skinny and whom the nurses' robes did not fit, appeared in his long johns. Attending our gatherings he always apologized to *mesdames* because he was not wearing a tie or had not shaved.

Our unwritten law was that we must behave like normal, free human beings—no talk of sentences, fears, or Barrack 15.

Instead we talked of politics, of international affairs, of the prospects of new scientific achievements. But we had all been isolated so long we had little idea of what was going on in the world. Sometimes we enlivened our chats with drinks served in test tubes provided by the doctors. The *aperitifs* were medicines rich in alcohol, or, on occasion eau de cologne; we preferred *Zelezndorozhny* (Railroaders) brand because it was less scented than Chypre.

As a nurse, I was assigned to a male ward. Most of my patients were Hungarian, and I understood no Hungarian, but few were in condition to speak anyway. They, too, were victims of the bloody dysentery, but they seemed to have even less resistance than the women: none survived during my time in that ward. There was little I could do for them; the most important thing was to make their last hours a bit easier by showing them that somebody cared. While I fluffed their pillows I would whisper in German, which I believe many of them understood, *"Keine ankst nicht 15."* What I really meant was, "Not so long as you are warm."

Sometimes I thought I detected gratitude in their dark, suffering eyes. Their eyes died first. One moment they would be glittering and expressive, even if only of suffering, and the next they would be open and staring.

One of my patients named Kovacs—I had several, since it is a common Hungarian name—looked like a retarded child and insisted on always keeping his trousers on. Other patients could not get out of bed and had to be cleaned and changed constantly because they could not control their excretions. But you could meet Kovacs in the corridor any time, either going to the toilet or coming from the toilet, holding up his pants, which now were vastly too big for him. He had been a physicist until he had been beaten into idiocy during interrogation. He died sitting on the toilet.

I learned his story from a young Hungarian inmate who spoke German and who worked as a gardener for an official living on the camp grounds. The gardener had been a track champion in Hungary, and had known Kovacs. The gardener used to sneak carrots to me, saying, "Eat them; they are full of vitamins."

Other inmates, mostly petty criminals serving short terms, worked in factories or farms outside of the prison area, or built roads. As they marched out each morning and back at night, they sang such songs as "Broad Is My Motherland," the lyrics of which include the words, "I know no other country where people breathe so free."

Still other workers—carpenters, electricians, shoemakers—were employed inside the camp. One carpenter, a graying, full-bearded man of medium height and broad shoulders, wore the uniform of an American army officer. It had been stripped of insignia but there was no mistaking that uniform, which the man kept neat. He spoke to no one, no one spoke to him. He never was allowed out of the camp with work crews.

Because I might be shipped out any time now that I was no longer ill, I thought it would be wise to get shoes. The professor from Kiev told me of a Polish shoemaker who was serving his sentence in this place because he made shoes for officials. For two rations of bread and some butter, which was issued only in the hospital, he promised to make over and fit some left by patients who had gone to Barrack 15.

Mrs. Blanca helped me to make a pair of slacks out of an old blanket. A few days later I was transferred to Barrack 5, which was so crowded that we knew it contained people due for shipment. Many women there were Rumanians, accused of nothing but ordered deported as unreliable. They had been allowed to take many of their belongings, over which they had to keep vigil.

Faced again with sleeping on a bare plank cot, I traded a ration of bread for a large feather pillow belonging to one of the Rumanians. At night it would be a mattress; by day I could drape it over my shoulders for warmth. Doba's cloth coat was no substitute for mink.

My shoes were ready, too. I smeared them with a little butter, as I had been advised to do, and put them near my cot.

That night we were awakened by the sounds of sirens and gunfire and the play of searchlights. We heard screams, but guards with guns at the ready drove us back from doors and windows. Since we had never heard of anyone escaping from a Soviet prison compound, what could the commotion be?

Next morning, friends at the hospital told me. On the other side of the camp were barracks occupied by young delinquents. The youngsters had hacked to pieces a fellow inmate who was a trusty serving as a guard. Several regular guards and a number of the delinquents were killed before the frenzy subsided.

When I returned to my barracks with my story, my shoes had disappeared. So Mrs. Blanca gave me some more pieces of the blanket from which we had made my slacks and suggested I wrap my feet with them. Lined with paper and tied on the outside, they would be boots of a sort, warm in the cold—but worse than useless in rain.

Then the day came, early in November, when we were all told to prepare our belongings and gather in the passageway through which we had entered in the summer. There was no time to notify my friends at the hospital. As we awaited transportation, Dr. Malinovsky appeared on the other side of the barbed wire, handed me his shoes, and passed me a shot of *Zelezndorozhny* eau de cologne.

At dawn we headed for the train.

chapter 18

Kiev
Winter, 1947-1948

Our destination was Kiev. At the railroad station there, we boarded black vans which everyone called Black Crows. How often I had seen such trucks bumping through Kiev's streets and thought nothing of it. Those were the days when I was luxuriating at the Hotel Continental and banqueting with high officials. I craned my neck trying to peer through the tiny window in the van's back door. A companion nudged me: "Hey, you. Have you been here before?"

"I was born here," I said and let it go at that.

The Kiev prison was full and the cell to which I and a number of others were taken—after the usual formality of the *sanobrabodka*—teemed with women. We pushed the number to about three hundred; though large, the room was never meant for so many. Doubledeck bunks of rough planking ran the length of three walls, and beneath the bunks some women lay on the cement floor.

The cell's occupants greeted us with groans and obscenities. At the guards' order they grudgingly made room by crowding even closer. The space left for us was on the floor under the lowest planking: we were so jammed that we could only lie straight, and if we wanted to turn over, we had to turn together. Sawdust and dirt fell on us whenever those above us moved.

I had begun to shiver after putting on clothes still damp from the *sanobrabodka* and I could not keep my teeth from chattering. My nearest neighbors began to shout. "Hey, this one has a high fever. Get her out of here! What if she's contagious?"

People on the upper bunks, who could move more easily, banged on the door. When the guard entered they explained that someone was very sick. I heard everything fuzzily.

The guard left and returned eventually with two other guards. "All right, let's have the sick one!"

They pulled me out by my feet. Again I found myself in a hospital. I was put into bed with another woman. We were feet to head, but I could feel how feverish she was—she seemed hotter than I.

I must have slept for the better part of three days. Acquainted with hospital routine, I realized as I felt better that this would be my only opportunity to send a message to Doba Markovna. Before I went to see the doctor for examination prior to discharge, I got hold of a tiny pencil lead and a minute piece of paper. I knew the desperate risk, but I slipped the paper with Doba's name and address into the doctor's jacket pocket. The doctor, who was "free," saw me do it but said nothing.

When the guard took me back to the cell, he made room for me on the upper level and lifted me up.

I looked for water but saw none. All I could see at the front of the room was a large *parasha*: day and night you could hear it being opened, the sounds of body functions filling it and then the noise of the cover being put back. Every time it was used, there were the same cries, "Close it tight! Put that cover back on!" But the stench was unbearable and I constantly stretched my neck to get nearer to the one window, which was level with the top bunks.

Each morning and evening, we had make rows of five to permit a count, and during each count we were obliged to respond with our full name, charge, and sentence. So I learned that my fellow inmates included both "politicals" and common criminals. The inmates on the cement floor were mostly people under administrative charges. The lower deck of bunks contained the politicals. The upper and most desirable level was occupied by criminals—and me.

The criminals constituted the cell's aristocracy, and those serving the longest sentences exercised the most power. Of these, the three girls to my right, all named Marusia, controlled the cell. We distinguished them as "Red," "Fat," and "Black." Black's dark hair was thick even on her legs. The Marusias were muscular and as lithe as panthers: they sprang rather than climbed down from their top-tier bunks. They wore only brassieres and ragged homemade panties that they never changed and which gave good visibility to the tattooing they all boasted.

The Marusias made the cell rules, under one of which they took food from anyone unable to fight for it. They also divided up any food brought in. They left no doubt that they ranked in importance only below the guards.

The criminals scorned the politicals. The criminals considered themselves practitioners of a trade, and saw no reason to be ashamed of taking something from someone too stupid or too weak to protect it. But the politicals had committed crimes against the motherland, which offended the criminals' intense patriotism.

There was no way to hide one's crime since it had to be stated aloud twice a day. Because my article of conviction sounded like an administrative matter the Marusias did not object to my presence on the top tier. I could not see all of the women, stacked up as we were, but I heard them, I breathed their smells, I heard their bodies function, and I was aware of their bickering and animosities. The Marusias, however, I came to know well.

Several days after my return from the hospital, a guard entered the cell with a paper in his hand.

"On the letter R—"

Groans and curses. Many of us had names that began with R. Those in bunks had to jostle their way down. Those on the floor had to slither out from under the bunks on their backs. I trembled. Could my message have reached Doba? The call was for me. The guard led me to the visiting room.

There was Doba. Despite the nearby guard, she slipped me several photographs at which I barely dared to glance. They were recent snapshots of Erika, and of Mama, Mel, and Viktor.

Doba's messages were terse. Erika sent her love. I was looking better. Mama was exploring every avenue to obtain my release. Adi, who was in a place called Magadan, had sent Doba copies of letters he had written to high officials requesting that his accumulated record royalties be spent to send me along with a private guard when I was shipped out, for he feared I would not survive on a prison train. Doba would visit me as soon as I was settled permanently.

In addition to her news, Doba had brought a package. The guards, as usual, had cut everything into small pieces. The package contained nothing I would have given second notice to outside, but here, oh—wonderful onions, heavenly garlic, luscious bread, fantastic dried prunes, soap, tobacco. I felt rich.

In my cell, I asked the Marusias to help me divide my gifts. I kept a little for myself and did not care how they split the rest. They took my instructions seriously, muttering all the while how stupid I was to share everything. I knew better. They would have taken what they wanted anyway.

While they were busy, I hungrily studied the pictures. How handsome Viktor was. How tall Erika had grown; she had her hair in pigtails. Even Mama and Mel, despite their worry over me, looked so much better than they had when I saw them last in Moscow.

The door opened and I thrust the pictures away. Once again—"On the letter R—" Again—for me!

I worried that the guard had seen Doba pass the pictures and had reported it. I reviewed every scrap of conversation, but we had kept to safe subjects. All the time I stood there in the visiting room, empty except for myself and the guard, I sensed uneasily that eyes were fixed on me. After some time, an officer came in and asked if I were Ruth Rosner-Kaminska. "There has been a mistake," he said. "You may go back."

It occurred to me that when Doba Markovna had asked to see me, my file had been taken out. The officers must have seen me on the stage or bought my records, and now they were satisfying their curiosity without having to buy a ticket.

Going back, I made up a story about the call. So little ever happened in that place that any minor incident became everybody's business. I returned complaining, "The people running this place are idiots. No wonder they're prison guards. Would you believe they made me go all the way back there to sign a receipt for my parcel?"

I had no desire to set myself apart from the other prisoners—I was safer, if that was the word, as one of them.

And then one day, gruff Red Marusia shattered my veneer. Squatting, her elbows resting on her knees and her hands cupping her face, she peered at me.

"What are you thinking about?" I asked.

"You, in the free. I imagine you standing in front of a big piano with candles on it and you're wearing a long white dress. Like somebody I've seen in the movies. You know, with class. A grand lady."

"You, too, could be a lady," I said, "if you would take care of yourself and watch your language. I think you could be quite pretty if you wanted to."

From then on, almost imperceptibly at first, the Marusias' behavior improved. They tempered their language and even affected mannerisms that I recognized as mine. Once when a woman loosed an obscenity in our hearing, Red Marusia shouted, "Shut up. Can't you see there's a person present?"

They asked if I knew any stories and so I became Scheherazade. The place quieted down and even the coarsest prisoners reacted like children. They cried over sad events and demanded happy endings. I related opera libretti and all the plays I had ever appeared in, giving the characters Russian names: Romeo and Juliet became Roman and Juliana, Tristan and Isolde became Ivan and Olga. After one story, one of the Marusias tried to slip some stolen lard and an onion under me in bed. I demurred. "Take it," she said. "They'll survive. You need it."

By now most of us had enough experience in prison life to know that nothing could be hurried or changed by us. We stood when we were ordered to stand and we slept, ate, and washed by set procedure. In the same way, when the time came, we would be shipped out with nobody asking if we wanted to go.

One day the guard announced that we would have to remain for thirty days more because of an outbreak of typhus. All I could think of was the woman whose bed I had shared in the hospital. How long was the incubation period? Was it contagious before, during, or after the high fever stage? My thoughts must have taken only an instant because before the door closed, three new prisoners were thrust in.

Wrapped in long, thick shawls with peasant skirts down to their shoes, they seemed terrified. I pitied them. They looked like some of the *kolkhoznitzi* we had in our cell—people caught gleaning what the tractors had failed to harvest. (The ancient Jews were forbidden to harvest every bit of their crops; they had to leave some for the poor. But in modern Russia, gleaning was a crime against the state.) Apparently, our Marusias classified the newcomers as thieves rather than politicals and made room for them; if the Marusias accepted a newcomer, the rest did.

But that evening, when the guard came to take his count, the women acted as if they had no idea what their charges or sentences were. They spoke their names and then stood there, cowering. The guard, with a ferocity I had never seen even in a guard, shouted, "What do you mean you don't know the charges? You are charged under article numbers—here came a long list of articles—and you are sentenced to penal servitude for life."

I happened to glance at the three Marusias—they were wild cats ready to pounce—and the moment the door closed behind the guard, they leaped down to beat the three women. The victims bit and scratched in self-defense. The Marusias went for the peasants' throats and others egged them on. The guard returned and the three newcomers fled beneath the lower bunks. The Marusias returned to the top tier, breathing heavily and licking their own wounds. It was a long time before they calmed enough for me to ask them what had caused their fury.

They explained that the combination of charges against the three women applied to a large group of people involved in decoying children with sweets, kidnapping them, and turning them over to butchers who killed them and ground them into wurst and hamburger. Most of the victims were small girls.

That night there was no story.

For hours the women whimpered, hidden as far under the lower bunks as they could push themselves, while the rest of the inmates discussed lynching them. Before morning, however, they were taken away and our lives returned to normal.

Normal meant that each morning, after the count, we were let out in groups of thirty. One group carried the *parasha* to a latrine and emptied it. This latrine consisted of a row of holes without partitions. Spigots on a small pipe near the entrance provided water for washing.

As soon as I entered the place, I would strip and hand my clothes to the person behind me. Then I would wash. The water was cold. A glassless, barred window near the ceiling provided ventilation. It was now winter.

At first the Marusias laughed at me. But after I had talked with Red Marusia about grand ladies and later explained that cleanliness helped prevent illness, the Marusias too washed and made others do so. Sometimes a woman would borrow the scented soap Doba had given me.

Then the Marusias began to make our fellow inmates clean the planks we slept on, and if anyone owned a blanket she had to shake it out the glassless window each morning. Soon the women took to washing the cloths they used for their menstrual flow, drying them at the window near me. (The practice did not improve the appearance of our cell.)

Probably because they all had been locked up together for so long, they had developed a physiological synchronization and nearly all of them had their periods together. At such times the stench overwhelmed that of the *parasha*; guards did not linger when they had duties in our cell.

I did not have that problem. After the hemorrhage in the ice cage, my menstrual flow had stopped.

I continued to tell my stories and the Marusias rewarded me with the thickest part of the soup we got, and with the advice that if I ever ran into trouble anywhere, I should just mention their names to any criminal prisoner. They were still, to my amusement, having trouble with their language, for they had forgotten how to say the simplest things without obscenities.

A whole year had passed since the night I found myself in the cell with the Ukrainian women. It was again the time between the Roman Catholic and the Greek Orthodox Christmases. Everyone made elaborate plans for festivities. The Rumanians and Ukrainians still had some possessions and set to creating costumes. The cell ringleaders knew who had a hidden piece of onion, a bit of garlic, a little salt pork for the feast. If the owner hesitated to contribute voluntarily, the ringleaders covered their own faces with a blanket, beat the recalcitrants, and confiscated their treasures. Because of the blanket, the victims could not identify their attackers—had they dared.

The day came. Starting the festivities, a woman hummed. Others joined in and the humming swelled into song. Someone banged a wooden spoon rhythmically on the *parasha*. The rest of us clapped hands to the beat. Some of the women left their bunks and went out into the small open area to dance. The Marusias tossed them fragments from their "feast," like participants in a witches' Sabbath. A hypnotic trance was engulfing us.

As the trance deepened, the Rumanians shouted, "Let Paula dance! Paula, dance for us. Dance!"

A Rumanian girl dressed in her national costume, with long, loosely flowing hair, started to move with marvelous grace. Then, a Ukrainian girl named Stefa, who had short-cut hair, was transformed before our eyes into a boy. Her companions thrust her legs into the sleeves of a blouse and tied a sash around her waist so that she seemed to be wearing short pants. Paula and Stefa began to dance together.

At first, they swayed slowly, tentatively. Then the women sang louder and faster. The dancers increased their tempo. The rest of us clapped faster, faster. Stefa and Paula took one another's hands. Their eyes became fixed on one another. Stefa drew Paula closer and closer.

Paula started to tremble in Stefa's arms, her eyes glowing, her face flushed. Stefa had paled and her dark eyes stared intently at Paula. The rhythmic sounds, the dance, the excitement overwhelmed their inhibitions. They were oblivious to the rest of us.

Tormented by their own unfulfilled yearnings, some of the women whimpered like kittens, others wept uncontrollably, still others uttered violent obscenities. The three Marusias sat in awed silence.

I could stand it no longer. I took out a cigarette and banged on the door to get a light from the guard. I had a long wait—apparently the guards were having their own celebration.

Finally the peephole opened. "You want fire, eh? Come close to the peephole, you will get some." When I approached the peephole with my cigarette, the guard put his own lighted cigarette in my eye. I fell back screaming. My lashes were burned and the lid pained horribly where a piece of burning cigarette had stuck.

When the Marusias realized what had happened, they exploded in rage. They shouted and banged on the door and commanded the rest to do so. The uproar verged on the volcanic. A high official and a guard appeared to demand what was going on. When the official learned what had set us off, he peremptorily replaced the offending guard.

But the bedlam persisted. That night, nobody ordered us to sleep.

The night ended with Paula in Stefa's arms, crying, "Why have they done this to me? Why am I in jail? I am so young." Stefa comforted her. "Don't cry, Paula. From now on we will always be together. I will follow you wherever you go, and I will protect you. I love you."

The cell never returned to normal. Every word, every act, sparked bitter quarrels, complaints, and curses. I sensed violence lurking just beneath the surface. So we were relieved when one day a guard read off a long list of names, including mine, and told us to "Prepare with belongings."

chapter 19

Kharkov
Winter, 1947-1948

We found ourselves in the prison courtyard. What a relief to leave this place! Joined by inmates of other cells, we became a sizable crowd. A new group of convicts waited to be admitted. Crouching like runners, as usual, and surrounded by guards and dogs, some wore leg chains. Their blue faces and their flapping arms indicated they had been waiting a long time in the cold.

More newcomers were descending from black vans and as the vans emptied we were packed into them. Looking at the hordes being shunted around, I mused that the only free people left in the country must be the guards.

This train ride was shorter; we went nonstop to Kharkov. As the train halted on a siding, our guards shouted to their colleagues waiting below, "Hey, receive your guests!" Gales of laughter.

I remembered vividly the enormous reception our band had had at this very Kharkov terminal. City officials had showered us with flowers and were eager to be photographed with us. It had been a warm, sunny day; but now, in the early half-light of a cold morning, thick snowflakes showered down on us.

I was glad I had my pillow. I put it on my back, under Doba's coat, and by tightening the belt I kept it from falling. I looked like a hunchback, but the pillow kept me warm and protected me from the blows administered in the counting.

We were led to the Kharkov prison. In spite of the cold it felt good to walk. It had been a long time since I had breathed fresh air.

After the showers and the *sanobrabodka* I felt feverish and began to shiver violently. My temperature was taken and I was sent to the hospital. I had all the symptoms of "flu" but by now I suspected that my recurring illnesses were caused by nervousness resulting from change of place and routine. I was delighted, though, to go to any place that was not a prison cell. For one thing, only from a hospital could I hope to make contact with Doba again.

The hospital occupied the entire wing of a large building from czarist times and was better equipped than the others I had been in. In my room, ten beds were lined up around three walls; some beds had two occupants, some only one. The linen looked clean. Almost in the room's center, two wooden pillars rose from floor to ceiling and on one, near the ceiling, was a lamp. A small table used by the floor nurse stood against that pillar, and between the table and the light was a hook on which patients attached string sacks containing food sent from outside.

A Rumanian woman from Kishinev shared a bed with me and almost immediately began her story. She had been rich before the war. After the Soviets took over the area, she maintained her living standard by smuggling people out of the country. She acquired a Soviet military official for a lover so she could operate safely. But they were caught; her lover was court-martialed and she was sentenced to fifteen years in the concentration camp at Vorkuta.

I had such a headache that I was glad when the nurse announced *ad'boi* and silenced her. I was asleep when my bedmate kicked me in the back. I was about to demand an explanation when she put her finger to her lips and pointed above my head. On the table three huge rats were jumping toward the food. I was about to scream but no one else seemed to share my horror. From a bed opposite I heard a whisper, "You see, I told you you hang them too high! They have to be able to touch them with their noses."

Another whisper: "I bet half of the morning bread ration that Short Tail will manage. Any takers?" From the left corner, a weak voice: "If you add sugar, I will."

Finally the nurse said, "Well, that's enough for tonight." She banged her shoe on the floor and the rats scampered off. Then she moved the table to the opposite pillar, and patients, content as after an evening at the theater, made themselves comfortable for the night.

I was convinced the rats would climb all over me if I closed my eyes. My bedfellow reassured me. "This happens every night. They never come back."

After twenty-four hours my bedfellow was discharged, and the doctor who discharged her approached me with his nurse assistant. A Dr. Darsky, he recognized me and examined me carefully. I was sure I would be able to send a message to Doba through him. Then I learned he was a prisoner, too.

That night, while taking my pulse, he mentioned he had seen me on the stage often. When I asked him the charge against him he said brusquely that he preferred not to talk about it. However, the next time I saw him, he apologized, saying a prison was no place to try to keep one's charge secret. His crime, to his great shame, he told me, was murder in a fit of passion.

Because of his reputation, he had been sentenced to only five years and had been allowed to remain in Kharkov, his home town. He received visits from his children and other relatives nearly every day, was allowed to eat the homecooked meals they brought, and was permitted to work alone on my floor.

Within a day of my meeting him, Kharkov was whispering that Ruth Kaminska, wife of Adi Rosner, was in the Kharkov prison. I learned this three days later when I had unexpected visitors, two well-known actors on tour. They risked a great deal, for consorting with a prisoner could lead to serious trouble. (For Doba Markovna it was another matter. She was my child's guardian and, anyway, had no position to lose.) Their visit gave me more of a lift than almost anything I could imagine. Upon learning of my arrest, they had offered to care for Erika and had remained in touch with Doba.

When I returned from the visiting room, Dr. Darsky promised to try to keep me in the hospital as long as possible. Then he whispered, "Beware of the nurse. She's serving a long term as a political but she manages to stay here because she is a *siksot*—an informer and denunciator." When I took my *piridacha* to my room, I treated my roommates and the nurse to the sweets my visitors had brought and contributed a bit to the hook for the evening's entertainment.

From then on I felt fine, but to remain in the hospital I warmed the thermometer by rubbing it, coughed whenever the nurse passed, and simulated weakness by walking a little bent, holding on to the walls. On one of my corridor walks, I met two elderly men who reminded me of my Grandfather Turkow. They had the same way of walking with hands behind them, the same old-fashioned slippers, even the same caps with visors. As they passed, I heard them speaking Yiddish, and I said, "*Sholem Aleichem.*" They spun around. "*Aleichem Sholom.* You speak Yiddish?"

"As you see."

"Solomon, you hear? A girl who speaks Yiddish! The Messiah's time is approaching!"

They had been arrested and sentenced to ten years because they had refused to work on Yom Kippur. I doubted if they would see freedom before they died.

The next morning, walking in the corridor, I sensed unusual activity in the TB patients' room. At the door, I encountered a roommate, holding a pat of butter on a piece of paper. When I asked what she was doing with it, she pushed me away. "I know what I am doing."

I followed her to our room. Suddenly she ran to the toilet. I waited to help her back into bed. "What's this all about?" I asked.

"I am sentenced to twenty years at Kolima. I cannot survive any more cattle trains or prisons, and I can't stand to be so far from my family. Here I see them occasionally."

"And?"

"Some of the patients in this ward have been taking their butter to the patients in the TB ward to trade it for spit, mouth to mouth. I tried too, but I couldn't take it. I vomited. Do you think I vomited all the germs out? Do you think some may have remained in me?"

"These germs are very vigorous," I said. "It probably will take."

New Year's Eve was approaching, my second New Year's in prison. I had not heard from Doba. Perhaps Erika was ill and she did not want to tell me. Perhaps Doba herself was ill. Perhaps she had received bad news from Warsaw. I begged Dr. Darsky to ask his family to try to find out what was wrong.

For New Year's Eve, Dr. Darsky invited me to his room for a party with the nurse and some doctors from other floors. On a surgery table sat a large cake, in the center of which was a card, "Happy New Year to you, my dearest child—Your mother, Mel, and Viktor," and underneath, "And from me, your daughter Erika, and Doba."

We drank that night to endure and to celebrate the next New Year's Eve "in the free."

I put the card under my pillow and in the darkness I felt I could still read the words with my fingers.

Next morning Doba showed up, and her visit this time was a real one—Dr. Darsky had her taken to his room, where we met without a guard. I talked freely, until she became upset when I described some of my experiences. "Well, I survived," I said, and changed the subject. We agreed that so long as I was in prison, she should not bring Erika to see me. I had to content myself with Doba's tales about her—she was six now, but sounded so grown-up. Once I settled in wherever I was sent, Doba would bring Erika to me.

Doba had brought a *piridacha* and three hundred rubles Mama had sent. A dozen times she repeated, "Remember to hide the money. At least you will have something to start with." She had sewn a tiny cloth money bag to put around my neck. Not wanting to spare even a minute from talking to her, I merely glanced at the other gifts.

Finally we had to part. Doba had been invited to stay overnight with Dr. Darsky's family and had to return to Moscow the next day because Erika was going to a children's New Year's party in the Hall of Columns.

After Doba left, I examined the parcel. Mama had sent me silk embroidered lingerie. My mother!

I told Dr. Darsky I would not mind now if I were shipped out. "I feel much better," I told him, "and I'm anxious to go because I'll be able to have my daughter with me after I get there." I felt bad, though, about leaving Kharkov. For the first time since I had gone to prison I had had real human contacts. And the conditions here were better than anywhere else. But the possibility of seeing Erika outweighed creature comfort.

My transportation orders came through a few days later.

I went around to say my good-byes. The nurse had tears in her eyes and gave me a sack for my belongings. Dr. Darsky slipped me bandages and ointments and some red and white streptocyd—the most popular drug in Russia—in case I became ill.

At the railroad station, as I waited in the usual crouching prisoner position, a train with a *mezhdunarodnyi* first class car chugged by. In the comparative freedom of the hospital I must have lost my prison mentality, for when I thought I recognized the famous actor Raykin at a window of the car, I stood for a better look. A bang on my head by a guard reminded me who and where I was.

"Hey, you!" he shouted. "That is a train for people. You would like to ride on that one, wouldn't you?"

Soon enough, the prison train was ready. Destination Kokchetav! I had no idea how far that was from Kharkov.

chapter 20

En Route to Kokchetav
Winter, 1948

Adi's efforts to have me sent out with a private guard had failed. As soon as the iron gate was pulled shut on our compartment, my nine companions, shouting in Ukrainian, Rumanian, and Russian, began fighting over seats. Before a guard quelled the near-riot by threatening to pour water on the lot of us, I clambered over the combatants to a narrow luggage rack and arranged my pillow behind my spine and my sack of belongings under my head.

When our rations were dragged in—bread and the dreadfully smelly little fish known as *komsa*, which were packed in salt and grease—we were told they must last for five days.

Twice a day, we were given water. When nobody was watching I had my evening cup of water with a dried prune from Doba's last *piridacha*. What a treat! Twice a day we were marched to the toilet. Always the same, the obscenities of the male prisoners we passed seemed not to shock even the priests among them.

The only break in the routine occurred when someone begged to be taken to the toilet "off hours." If the guard walking the corridor was not in a good mood, the petitioner had to use whatever she could and dispose of it later.

One night our train stopped and our car was shunted to a siding. Through the gate and the small, dirty corridor window I could see a very large city. I sensed it was Moscow and asked the guard but he did not reply. I pressed my face against the bars.

From afar, I could make out lights on tall buildings. We *were* in Moscow! If Doba Markovna only knew, maybe she would pass by the railroad yard with my Erika! Moscow! Moscow with its concert halls vibrating to thunderous applause. Moscow with luxurious apartment 704. Flowers. Friends. And here on a railway siding I was hungry, cold, and frightened, while my baby slept nearby. Why we were in Moscow, I could not fathom, since my destination lay in another direction. But a few prisoners were taken off and new ones loaded on; they included men, and I searched for Adi and Hymie.

As the train finally moved on again, my greatest concern was the lack of washing facilities. Time in the privy was limited and the next in line, after banging on the unlocked door, sometimes barged in and threw out the occupant. That always evoked uproarious laughter.

Once while I was in the privy, a lurch of the train threw me against the door so hard that I fell into the corridor, scraping my knee. I asked the woman next in line to let me go back in to wash the laceration, but she shouted, "Look at the princess!" and pushed past me. Next day my leg hurt more than it should have and through my slacks I felt my knee was hot. I crushed a pill of Dr. Darsky's streptocyd, sprinkled the contents on the skinned flesh, and bandaged my knee. That night my knee throbbed so badly I could not sleep.

In the morning I asked a guard distributing the water to report that I had to have my knee treated. He returned later to tell me there was nothing they could do so long as we were in transit, but at the next stop I could get help. Hoarding bandage, I turned each dressing several times, putting a clean spot over the wound and discarding the gauze only when all of it was wet and discolored. Finally I had no more bandage and no more clean spots.

After two more days during which I suffered continual pain, we arrived at a town somewhere in the northern Urals. I could not see its name because the train stopped far from the station. The guards had difficulty prying open the frozen doors. Wind attacked so violently that the guards had to hold their fur caps on with both hands. Once the doors were open, the guards could not close them again because the wind had driven so much snow inside. Dogs barked and new guards shouted impatiently.

I put my pillow on my back under my coat, and hung my sack from my neck. I rejoiced that Doba had given me warm gloves.

I jumped down from the train on one leg, but how to walk? The slightest movement of the infected leg caused agony, and my slacks had stuck to the wound. While we waited for all the others to get off the train, I saw that this entire section of the station was filled with prison trains. Everyone's lashes, eyebrows, and whatever hair escaped from scarves, hoods, and caps was coated with ice, but I was perspiring. I could not keep up despite "Three steps forward or three steps backward, and we shoot!" Other prisoners passed the word to go slow, but the guards, anxious to reach warmth, hurried everybody along. The rear guards were finally directly behind me and I sensed their dogs baring their teeth and straining at me, perhaps because they smelled the leg wound.

The snow was so deep that even two-legged people found it difficult to walk. With the wind blowing and the guards shoving, I wondered if it would not be better just to lie down and have them shoot me.

But was this the time to give up—now, when I might soon see my daughter? So part of the way, I dragged myself on my arms and my good knee, my sack of belongings pressing against my throat and making it hard to breathe. Suddenly, I felt with my arms that the snow seemed less deep. We were approaching a town.

Our column was moving down the left side of the road, which was flanked by a wood. On the right side I saw wooden huts, then brick houses in which some of the windows were brightly lit. I began to imagine the normal family lives behind those windows—people making love, people cherishing their children. I wanted to shout "Enjoy! Enjoy your warmth! Your illusion of safety! Perhaps tomorrow, you, too, will be out in the cold."

That was when I noticed the flowers. Flowers? Here? Now? On trees? Out in the snow? I began to worry. Is this how insanity begins? Just then, the most important thing in the world seemed to be to find a rational explanation for those flowers. Perhaps a truck carrying cotton had its cargo loaded so high that the cotton reached the tree branches.

We were ordered to move faster.

"Quickly. Quickly! Walk to the right of the road!" And then it passed us. Wonderful, beautiful truck—carrying cotton! I was all right. In my elation, I moved faster and the slacks broke away from my knee. After that, it was easier to walk.

The cold accelerated the admittance procedure, and we were led to primitive wooden barracks surrounding a large courtyard, in the center of which stood the guards' lookout tower. The barracks looked like stables and perhaps had been once. They were of rough planking and divided into cubicles; hay covered the floor.

I reported ill and was told the nurse would come to see me. No hospital. In a tiny cubicle, three women huddled in a corner, shivering.

Forty of us were shoved in to join them. The three said a large group had been removed shortly before and they were happy to be crowded again as a protection against freezing.

I was pushed against the planks that divided us from the next cell, and through the space between the boards, I saw a room full of men. They, too, were clinging together for warmth, rubbing ears and faces and looking each other over for the white spots that betray frostbite.

Suddenly they were laughing. I asked through the boards what could be so funny. Still laughing, one man moved close to the wall. "It's a fantastic story this fellow just told us. You think you have troubles? Listen to this. We just came in from the train."

"I know. I was in the same party. I was the one who had trouble walking."

"Ah? We tried to slow down, but the guards and the dogs kept snapping at our heels. How do you feel now?"

"Well, I am still in pain but they promised a nurse would be along. But tell me, what were you laughing about?"

"Well, when we came in, we found one frozen Kazakh in the corner. We asked him where he was from and the poor fellow said, 'From a village near Tashkent.' You can imagine how he feels the cold. But when we asked him how long he had been in prison he told us, 'Long. Long. Don't remember. Not know anymore.' So we asked him how long he had to serve and he told us, 'They tell me know no way to let me out. Everything, the rat, he eat.'"

And then the man, who was in rags that had been a priest's habit, laughed again. "Can you imagine! A rat ate his papers. So cheer up and don't complain. It can always be worse."

"What are they doing with the poor man?" I asked.

"No prison can admit him without papers, but neither can anyone release him. Who would take the responsibility? So they just ship him from place to place."

No nurse came to see me and I think that only Dr. Darsky's streptocyd prevented the inflammation from growing worse. After a sleepless night I enjoyed the nearly hot water we got for breakfast. Then the barracks doors opened and all inmates were ordered to gather around the tower. Some guards with dogs and guns took positions behind us, others stationed themselves in front of us with their backs to the tower. After a while, the commandant appeared with a huge stack of file folders. He stepped onto the first level of the tower, and guards placed a table in front of him and a coal burning stove on the table near him.

I feared it would take days to get through all those files. I wondered when I would have a chance again to report my problem, but I had seen prisoners obviously in worse condition than I dragged out by their cellmates and laid out in the snow. There was no point in making a fuss.

The commandant had some difficulty pronouncing names, which made him irritable, but after only three hours, we were divided into four groups. Each group had some sick members lying in front of it, and a number of them looked as though they had already reached their final destination. The rest were jumping, flapping their arms, standing with one foot on top of the other, anything to keep circulation moving—which was difficult for me as I could only stand on one foot and the toe of the other.

Before he left the platform, after giving the files to four guards, the commandant ordered all sick prisoners to step forward. A male nurse, wearing a white coat over a sheepskin—which made him resemble a barrel—scrutinized us. Those lying in the snow were carried inside the barracks. Those walking, including me, followed him to a small, but warm infirmary in which there was a woman nurse or doctor.

My leg was throbbing so painfully that I feared to let anyone touch it, but I expected no gentleness. Indeed, when I had difficulty removing my slacks, they were pulled off roughly and I fainted. When I came to, my knee had been dressed, and my file now showed that the leg required further treatment. Then I was sent to rejoin my group. Darkness was falling when trucks took us back to the station.

As soon as I found myself squashed into the train compartment and the gate was locked behind us, I looked up, hoping to install myself again on the luggage rack. Nobody put bundles on it because nobody dared to leave her treasures out of reach. But three women had squeezed onto it and I ended up on the floor with my back to the gate and my legs under the lower bench, between two other pairs of legs.

The three women fell several times before resigning their perch. To make room for them in the mass on the floor, I volunteered to take their place aloft.

The corridor remained packed with as yet undistributed prisoners. Suddenly I froze. One male group was talking, cursing, shouting—in German. From my rack I could see through the gate that they were German soldiers in their green-gray uniforms—in 1948! Their looks, mood, and spirits were far better than mine.

Later, on my way to the toilet, I found them occupying three compartments from which they shouted obscenities at us. I never betrayed that I understood them.

Our route lay through cold emptiness. After two or three days of relentlessly unchanging landscape, the train stopped in the midst of the nothingness. A military guard emerged out of nowhere, the Germans were disembarked, and we changed guard crews. The moment the train had stopped, the exit doors on both sides of the car had been opened and the cold wind howled down the length of the train. The women wrapped their shawls tightly around them and huddled closer. Finally the outside doors closed.

At that moment, a guard opened our gate and shoved in a newcomer. It was pitch dark, for when the train was not moving even the dim bulb in the corridor went out. The newcomer stood with her back against the gate. We knew it had to be a "she" or she would not have been placed in our compartment, but when a guard passed with a flashlight, I began to doubt. This form did not look female and was much bigger than an average man's. Then a guard opened our gate and shoved the newcomer aside. Checking prisoners, he addressed the form first.

No doubt about it, the newcomer was classified as a female, by the name of Yevdokiya Stepanovna. I did not catch the last name. Her legs were chained. She had been sentenced to hard labor for life, for murders, robbery, and breaking out of concentration camp. The Soviet penal code has no provision for a death sentence. The Soviet system has ways to get rid of the inconvenient without formality, but as far as Yevdokiya was concerned, she had received the maximum penalty and had no more to lose. I had heard of the danger of attack from fellow prisoners like her.

While she answered the guard's queries in a hoarse voice, she dropped her short-fingered strong hand with which she had been shielding her eyes from the flashlight. She had small, wrinkled eyes, a narrow forehead surrounded by wild reddish hair, and a strong jaw. Dr. Lombroso would have pronounced her a perfect criminal type.

I wondered what would happen to us once the guard left us tête-à-tête with Yevdokiya. She seemed to be growing more and more angry as she responded to the guard's questions, and some she refused to answer. Once she shouted, "I'll kill all of you!" Then she loosed a string of sophisticated obscenities that made the three Marusias sound like nuns.

She complained that the bracelets around her ankles were too tight. The new commandant, whom I could not see because he remained out in the corridor with our files, ordered two guards to take her out and check her chains. If the commandant was concerned about Yevdokiya's comfort, I had reason to hope that he might act on the note in my file that I needed medical attention.

I was checked next. After I spelled my names and destination, I detected a slight change in the commandant's voice as he told me, "At the next stop, I will see to it that you are treated."

The train started to move, and the bulb in the corridor twinkled.

While the rest of the women were being checked, Yevdokiya was brought back in, her hands chained instead of her legs. Before, in the dreadful cold, I had not noticed her stench. Now it was unbearable.

After the guards had finished with us and closed the gate, Yevdokiya stood as before, back to the gate. In a hoarse whisper, she demanded that we hand over our possessions. If we did not—she raised her chained hands.

I thought of the money I had sewn into the little bag that I wore; I would need it for getting in touch again with Doba, Erika, my family. Besides, the necessities it would buy could mean the difference between life and death in the forbidding future I faced. Despite the cold, my hands were clammy and a cold sweat crept between my shoulder blades. Once these other women gave in to Yevdokiya, I should lose my money to her.

I was sure Yevdokiya had not spotted me on my rack and she had been in the corridor when I was questioned. In a split second, I applied the maxim that the best defense is attack. I reached down, seized her lapels with all my remaining strength, and flung myself down from the rack. Because of my stiff leg, my body was rigid and seemed heavier.

I had counted on diverting her long enough for the other women to pounce. Instead, surprise and my weight, little as it was, knocked her down. For the first time in my life I used all the obscenities I had ever heard—and many I never knew I had heard. I was the one to be obeyed. I made the rules. If she tried anything I would let her have it between the ribs with my "shiv."

"From now on," I snarled at her, "your place is under the bench!" I had not acted in a long time, but I must have been convincing. The rest of the cast supported me well. When I climbed back to my perch, I was soaking wet and quivering like custard. For a time I had her beaten. But for how long?

All night, whenever Yevdokiya tried just to poke her head out, her neighbors lustily kicked her and someone watched her every movement, ready to warn, "She's moving!" Once daylight came, I could not stand up to my role. But at dawn, the train stopped and a special escort boarded to pick up Yevdokiya. I remember their faces when she meekly crawled out from under the bench.

After those hours on alert, we all slept until the guards with the water rations awakened us. A guard on the other side of the gate was peering in. When he spotted me he said, "Are you Rosner?"

"Yes."

"The commandant wants to see you."

The summons filled me with dread. Anything out of the routine created panic among prisoners. What could it be?

Yevdokiya would not have complained about me, because her reputation would be ruined if she ever mentioned the happenings of the night before.

The emotion, the dread, and the infected leg made me so weak that the guard had to help me down from the rack. I was taken in the direction of the guard's quarters from which the stench of alcohol emanated. It was a tedious journey for the guards too, and since I was among the youngest of the women prisoners I feared I had been chosen to provide my keepers with entertainment.

I must have shown my apprehension when the commandant ordered my escort to return to his duties. "Don't be afraid," he said. "Perhaps you'd care for some vodka." The words were those of an approach, but the manner was not.

"I'm afraid I am much too weak to drink."

"Then have some tea. Do you smoke?"

While I enjoyed a cup of real tea with sugar, and smoked a real cigarette, he looked through my file. He was quite young but something in his manner inspired my confidence.

After a long silence, he spoke quietly, almost haltingly.

"The last time I saw you was in Moscow. In Tchaikovsky Hall. My parents took me to your concert. You were wearing a pink-purple dress and you sang a very touching song about Paris. You seemed to me like a goddess, and now— Why? What happened?"

"You have my file."

"But I can't understand."

"I don't think anybody can."

"But is there anything I can do for you? Of course, I know about your leg and as soon as we reach Petropavlovsk, I will take you to the doctor. But are you hungry? Stupid question. Of course you are! Would you dine with me?"

Wouldn't he be risking too much?

He told me not to worry. As a student of criminology, he interviewed cases from time to time.

"There is something I want more than food. If I could wash . . ."

At the next stop they would take on hot water and he would let me into the guards' washroom.

We dined. He shared a fresh piece of bread with me, the tastiest sausage I ever ate, and a cucumber. But he gave me much, much more—a short visit with humanity.

Late that night the train halted, and the commandant kept his promise. I washed my hair and scrubbed myself with Doba's fragrant soap, using a woolen glove for a washcloth. I sprinkled myself with the eau de cologne Doba had given me. I washed my clothes. I felt born anew.

For the next two days, I did not see the commandant. In spite of his reassurances, I suspected he preferred to remain on the safe side. But the morning the train reached Petropavlovsk, he sent for me to take me to the doctor at the *Med Punkt* which, with its red cross, was a familiar sight at most rail stations.

The commandant walked ahead, I in the center, and a guard behind me. I knew my leg was in trouble. I was not prepared, though, to hear the doctor say it might be best to amputate it. But he promised to do all he could to save it. For more than half an hour, he worked on the wound. I got nothing to ease the pain and several times I cried out, but for the most part I bit my lips and my hands.

When he finished, he handed me a sip of vodka and said, "Well done! Quite a girl!" Then he gave me some pills and told me I would need crutches for some time. I was practically carried back to the train by my guard, one leg stiff with packing, the other shaky.

Once I was up the high steps and in the train corridor where nobody could see us, the commandant pressed my hand and wished me luck. Then he told the other women in my compartment they must make room for me to lie down.

I never saw the commandant again. I never asked his name. And I will never forget him.

The train moved. For so long I had been living in pain. Now the pain was gone and a tremendous weariness took its place. I must have slept most of that day. Hungry, I reached for my bread. Tomorrow I would be on my own. The moment I had longed for, the end of bars and transports, was at hand. And I was frightened. After jails and concentration camps, exile was a kind of freedom, but what sort of freedom when there was no return? Would I have to live alone or with others? Would everyone I met be an exile, too? How would I support myself? Most of all, would I be able to correspond freely, to reach Doba and my baby? Mama?

The system had succeeded. I had been conditioned to fear change—even a change for good. I had become used to doing as I was bidden. Could I become me again? We were given our daily water ration, but there was no bread for me. The authorities in Petropavlovsk had decided I had been fed by the government long enough.

The train ground to a stop. A guard shouted, "Rosner—prepare with belongings!" My companions helped me to stand up and put on my coat over my sack and my pillow. We wished each other luck. I was ready. But Kokchetav was not ready for me. Not a soul had showed up to receive me, as the rules demanded.

The guards grew angrier and angrier because the cold was unbearable. They could not get in touch with anybody; this was not a regular station, just a stop on the way. Until now, an hour, a day, a week had been of no importance to me. Now—every moment was an eternity.

Suddenly I heard a banging on the outside door and an impatient, "Let's go!"

More quick good-byes. At the exit door stood a man in an enormous fur cap and a huge sheepskin coat, wrapped in a woman's heavy shawl. His coat was so long one could only guess if he had legs. He was thrusting my file inside his coat. Looking down from the door, I realized I could not manage the steps and the embankment. Way below I could see a sled with a horse, the only sign of life in the vast white desert. They looked like toys.

My escort bounced down the steps and slid the rest of the way in the snow. The guards put a strong rope under my arms and lowered me. My escort helped me to the sled, the floor of which was covered with straw. While he was turning the sled, waving the reins, and cursing the horse and its mother, the train pulled away. It was the only dark thing in this whole white world.

My companion was a talker, but difficult to understand. I asked his nationality and he told me, "Ingush." He volunteered that he worked for the MGB. He told me where I would register and learn the requirements of my new status. I wanted to know much more, but I had grown used to not asking questions, and my escort's line of work served as a conversation stopper.

I recalled that during the war, the Ingush and their neighbors the Chechens were among the peoples banished from the homes in the Caucasus as undependable. The authorities had loaded them onto trucks and deported them to the "deep rear." Remembering the mountain greenery of the Caucasus, I could only wonder how the deportees were enjoying the flat, white, frozen Siberian wasteland. So my companion was one of them—and working for the MGB.

He told me we were thirteen kilometers from Kokchetav. The wind practically blew his words back into his mouth. He suggested I turn around in the sled and sit with my back against his. "You will be more protected against the wind, and perhaps you will manage to take a breath from time to time." I was not sure—the wind made breathing seem impossible, no matter how one faced.

Once he stopped the sled to help me get the pillow out from under my coat to cover my stiff leg. He advised me to rub my face with snow to prevent frostbite. But when we at last reached the MGB Building, I was numb all over.

Sitting with my back to my escort's, I had not noticed the settlement.* In my landscape, there had been no lights, no buildings, and nothing had changed along the way except that the heavens had turned black.

The MGB chief's office, on the building's only floor, contained a desk and a pair of chairs. One wall was covered with photographs which I assumed were of people wanted for crimes. But after I pulled the icicles from my eyelashes, I realized the pictures were of Father Stalin and members of the Politburo.

The chief, relaxed and friendly, began to peruse my file as soon as my companion took it from under his coat. "For the first six months," he informed me, "you will have to report to this office twice a week. After that, only once."

*An obscure and virtually unknown town when I had to live there, Kokchetav has since become the center of agricultural development projects entrusted to Komsomol, the Communist youth organization.

I was not to leave Kokchetav. I could not vote. Otherwise I was free and allowed to work at my profession.

"And what is your profession?" he asked.

"I am an actress and a singer."

"Well, well, We don't have any theater here. But there is some talk about organizing amateur activity in a former church building. So you might come in handy." He would take it up with the head of the Department of Culture. Meantime, if I were in need, I could work with building construction crews.

"This fellow," said the official, pointing to my escort, "whom you already know—we call him Mitya. He might help you in finding a room or a place to sleep. He knows everybody here. Right, Mitya?"

Mitya showed all his strong white teeth in contentment. His master's voice made him happy. As we left the MGB he said: "You must be very hungry. We have here a fine dining place with good beer."

"Splendid."

Mitya helped me walk and carried my sack, this time with the pillow inside. Free, I did not want to look like a hunchback.

On our way, he told me there was a clinic where I could have my leg examined. The dining place nearby was on the first floor of an archaic wooden building, quite large, with windows on all sides, and wood pillars. For me, everything was a revelation. The smell of food. The sight of other people. The fact that one could enter and leave at will. The possibility of sitting down at a table, on a real chair and of choosing what I wanted. Everything seemed like a sequence in my familiar dreams about freedom. I feared it would end again with the banging on the door.

The few patrons, in soiled work clothes, quieted as we entered and I felt they had recognized me as an outlaw just released from prison. But one look at Mitya and I realized it was his presence that had dampened their spirits. Unasked, the waitress put a bottle of beer in front of him, compliments of the house. He was no longer Mitya the pet. Here people feared him. Pouring the beer, he glanced at me to see if I was impressed.

The waitress took our orders. I had dreamed of this moment for a long, long time, and I had had only a piece of bread this whole long day and nothing the day before. But when food came, I could not touch it. Mitya ate my share after finishing his.

When I felt sure his appetite had been satisfied I asked him, casually, the question uppermost in my mind.

"Is there a long distance telephone anywhere?"

"Yes, sure. At the post office which we'll pass on the way."

I paid the check and left a large tip for the waitress. Mitya told me it was not good to spoil people and pocketed the money. (He used the word "people" pejoratively to underline their low status.)

Outside, I could not see a thing in the inky darkness. But Mitya skirted places where the snow had drifted high and other places guarded by barking watchdogs. Suddenly there it was. A hut. The post office.

The office consisted of one room, divided by a counter behind which sat a young girl. Mitya shook hands with her and then sat at a table.

"You go on," he told me. "I must have a nap. It's been a tiring day." (He did not mention the beers he had consumed.)

Hardly able to get the words out, I asked the girl if she could connect me by phone with Moscow.

"Moscow? Let's see. Do you have the number?"

My hand shook as I wrote down Doba's number. The girl told me to sit down. At first I was sure Mitya was pretending to sleep; perhaps he was curious to know whom I was trying to reach. But he was snoring open-mouthed.

I could hear the girl speaking to an operator but the words did not come through to me. My heart beat as though I were awaiting a verdict. Perhaps long distance calls could be placed only at certain times. Perhaps I should have sent a telegram.

I felt clammy and cold, but the postal clerk seemed warm enough; her sheepskin coat hung on the wall behind her.

I heard her say, "Go in the booth; I have Moscow on the line."

I staggered to the booth, my legs numb, and picked up the receiver.

"Moscow? Moscow? Kokchetav calling."

I heard Doba say, "Erika, Erika, your mother is calling you."

And then I heard a voice I did not recognize, the voice of my daughter.

"Mama? Mama? My mommy?"

With the tears running down my cheeks and my throat tight, I listened to the music of that voice.

An operator broke in.

"Kokchetav! Kokchetav! Why don't you answer?"

I wanted to beg her to give me a moment to pull myself together. Words did not come.

I heard Doba's voice again and then Erika's "Mama?" A click.

The postal clerk was shouting, "Are you crazy? What's the matter with you? I get Moscow for you and then you don't talk! Hang up at least!"

I found myself sitting on the floor of the booth, my stiff leg outside. I was clutching the receiver and whispering, "My baby. My girl."

It must have been a dream. But Mitya was still there snoring.

chapter 21

Kokchetav
Winter-Summer, 1948

I told the girl I had developed a sudden, severe pain in my bandaged leg. Actually I did not know how I had come to be on the floor. I had not blacked out; I remembered every word spoken and I still held the receiver.

I said I hoped to return tomorrow. The girl told me that I could telephone Moscow only between 7 and 9 p.m. and had been lucky to have the call go through at the last moment.

The phone call had cut into my cash, but that was what money was for. Ever since I got it from Doba I had been awaiting the moment when I could hear my child's voice; the thought of that had given me the courage to defend the money against Yevdokiya, even at risk of my life.

I had to shake Mitya well before rousing him again. When we went out, the cold was so intense I could not catch my breath. Mitya, impressed that I had connections in Moscow, told me my clothing might be suitable for Moscow but would never stand up to the Kokchetav winter. Every few steps I had to stop and turn against the wind. My face hurt as though a thousand needles were pricking it. I saw no houses but Mitya said we had passed quite a few.

"They are covered with snow and their lights are hidden by shutters. You will get used to finding them by the chimney smoke. The place we are going is near the lake."

"A lake?"

"It's very convenient. You can get water out of an ice hole." Mitya prattled on. "The owners of the place are old-timers and their two daughters are very intelligent. The younger one is a teacher and the older one is a cashier on the railroad. The last time I saw her—I mean the older one, Vera—she told me they had a spare room."

I wondered by what sense Mitya was led. I could not see or smell a thing. We met no one. The only sound was the occasional yelping of a dog.

"Everyone has dogs—to protect their cows from wolves."

The dog's yelping grew loud and excited. Mitya said we had arrived, and he knocked on a door. A bundled up figure, carrying a miner's lantern, emerged. Shortening the dog's chain, the figure led us through a combination of passage and cow-woodshed to a small porch and into a room filled with the odors of kerosene, sauerkraut, and unwashed bodies. The bundled up usher proved to be Vera, who had short, dark, wavy hair and gray-black eyes. The younger woman, Natasha, an ash blonde with her hair in braids wound about her head, looked up from the exercise books on which she was working. The dining table was covered with them and I tried to calculate the awesome number of children her class must contain. Natasha cleared the books away, pulled up two more chairs, and set the table for tea, putting out cups for the guests and jars for her sister and herself.

I murmured something about not wishing to cause them any trouble.

"Please don't offend us by refusing," Vera interrupted. "Our stove is always hot and tea is always ready. So please, eat it up with us."

It was the first time I heard the Siberian expression for drinking tea.

The stove resembled one I had seen in Ludmilla's home in Alma-Ata. It took up a good part of the room and had a large, obviously occupied sleeping space on top.

I apologized for disturbing the sleepers but Natasha laughed. "Nothing can disturb our parents' sleep. They go to bed and get up with the chickens."

After our first cup of tea—which we sweetened with a strange-looking gray paste we held in our mouths—Mitya told the girls why we had come. They were sorry; the room had been rented but I could stay for the night.

Mitya reminded me to register in three days and shook hands all around. I reinforced my squeeze with five rubles.

When the girls learned I came from Poland, they decided to invite one of their tenants, a Mrs. Durach. "She always sews until very late— she's a dressmaker. Oh, she was quite a lady in Poland. But now, they have it hard. As a matter of fact, she might let you stay with them if you share expenses. We could provide a bed."

Mrs. Durach was overwhelmed to find a compatriot. She must once have been a very attractive woman; now in her forties, she looked much older when her face was serious.

She readily agreed to have me stay with them temporarily and suggested that since they were three, I should pay one fourth of the rent—and of the cost of food if I wished. When I asked if her family would object, Mrs. Durach merely raised her eyebrows.

Imperiously, she woke her husband and teen-age son and had them clamber down from the stove to help install my bed in line with hers, against the wall, facing the stove. Her bed and a mirror between the windows were the room's only luxuries.

Fortunately I had my pillow. There was no bedding to spare. A piece of old carpet would serve as mattress and my coat as blanket.

Mrs. Durach sent her son for firewood, made a quick soup out of flour, onions, and water, and ordered Mr. Durach to "bring in the you know what."

A few moments later, we were imbibing a home brew; the alcohol raised our spirits and loosened our tongues, so I soon heard the Durachs' story.

When the Soviets took over the Polish border areas, they sent Mr. Durach, mayor of a small town, to a concentration camp. Mrs. Durach and her son stayed behind until the Germans invaded. As the wife of a Polish official, she found herself on the Germans "wanted" list, so she fled to the Russian interior. There, she too was arrested. Mr. Durach had been released from camp because of a disability, and it was in Kokchetav that they were reunited. Both still had time to serve in exile.

In the morning, while straightening up the room, Mrs. Durach told me that in ancient times Kokchetav had been a crossroads where Siberian tribes met and spread their *yurtas*, which looked like American Indians' wigwams. Later, czarist authorities sent criminals and political offenders to Kokchetav, and the present natives descended from such people. Most of the population was either "law breaker" or "law enforcer." The exceptions were young doctors and engineers assigned to serve internships, and specialists at a factory built during the war to produce weighing and measuring equipment. The lake had been dug in czarist times by prisoners to create a reservoir and was named Lake Kopa (Lake Dig). Administratively, Kokchetav belonged to the Kazakh Republic; geographically, it was Siberia.

The settlement itself was small—one could circumnavigate it on foot in an hour. But it was in the center of a large area that extended from the railroad to the bald hills and from the lake, near which I lived, to the Polyclinic hospital and the school. That was more space for me to move around in than I had known for a long time.

Houses were privately owned huts. Many were of logs, but wood had become scarce, and new houses were made of blocks fashioned from cow dung mixed with straw and lime, and called *kisiac*. (The manufacture of *kisiac*, which I witnessed later, reminded me somewhat of winemaking. The ingredients were tossed into a hole in the ground and mashed with bare feet, which were not necessarily washed afterward. Then the mixture was shaped into blocks or bricks which were laid out to dry in the sun.)

Ingush families, the most numerous occupants of the stretch between the railroad and the settlement's center, lived in holes roofed with whatever they could find.

After my briefing by Mrs. Durach I ventured out to explore. It was a cold, clear day, and as I walked I took the deep breaths that I had promised myself back in the crowded, stinking cells, would be my first free act. But it was not the joy I had imagined—the cold was too biting. So I contented myself with the thought that I could see as much land and sky as I chose and I could make my steps take me this way and that, without gun butts or dogs to keep me from straying.

In the town square stood a building that obviously had been a Russian Orthodox church. Traces of paint remained on its walls and tower. On one side of the square, facing the church, was the municipal building, a two-story baroque, stone building that had been a bank in pre-revolutionary days. On the other side was MGB headquarters. Also flanking the square were the post office and some white-plastered brick shops containing little to sell. Kokchetav boasted, too, a marketplace, a slaughterhouse, and a bathhouse.

Kokchetavians made pilgrimages to the bathhouse before holidays or family celebrations. They took clean clothes with them and did not emerge until the entire family, beginning with the eldest, had washed in one tub of water. Then the soiled clothing was washed in the same water, for seldom could a family pay for more than one tubful.

The result of their standards of hygiene I saw on my first visit to the Polyclinic for treatment of my knee. As I awaited the doctor, I watched several nurses busy themselves with a teen-age girl. I thought she was being prepared for a head operation, for they shaved her hair. Then they shoveled the hair into a stove. After that the nurses used pinchers to pluck out worms from pus-filled holes about the girl's ears and neck.

My knee was better, the young Armenian doctor who attended me said. I would need perhaps only two more changes of dressing.

All day I waited for evening, worrying that this time the call would not get through to Moscow. I was sure that Doba had managed to inform Mama that I had arrived in Kokchetav and Mama would be impatient for news of me.

By six o'clock, dinner over, I was on my way to the post office. How would I explain to Erika why I did not go to her, why I had abandoned her? Earlier, Doba had told her I was sick. But now? Would I be able to tell her how much I loved her, how much I cared? And should I? I must not break her heart.

At the post office I chatted away to the girl at the counter to mask my nervousness. My knee was better. I found it hard to get used to the cold. Where did she live? She had been reading a book and no doubt wanted to return to it, but I felt if I stopped talking I would break down again.

Erika's first words were those I had been dreading, "Mommy, when will you come?"

As calmly as I could, I told her that I was working in Kokchetav and that she would visit me before I joined her in Moscow. How big was she? Did she remember me?

Then, because I was weeping, I told her to put Doba back on.

I begged Doba to sell whatever she had left of my things and to bring Erika to me. The operator interrupted us after three minutes and after six minutes. I asked for ten.

Outside, I realized how difficult it would be to achieve, but the desire to see and touch my child and have her with me was so strong that I felt sure I could make it happen. Mama would find ways to send money or parcels. I could make and sell sweaters. If necessary, I could work on a construction crew. Oh, God, nothing would be too difficult, if only I could see my daughter.

Blinded by tears, I was lost from the moment I left the post office. I avoided most of the ditches, but once I missed and fell into deep snow. It covered me to my neck and still my feet did not touch solid ground. I flailed frantically, but the more I thrashed, the deeper I went. My cries for help were too muffled to be heard and I was sure I would not be found until the spring thaw. Had I come through so much, to drown in snow? Then I felt a stone under one foot and got the footing with which to reach the edge of the ditch. When I dragged myself out of the snowbank and stood on hard ground, everything I wore had frozen solid.

The adventure resulted in a severe bladder irritation. Under the circumstances, such an illness was disastrous. For toilets, Kokchetavians used the ground behind their houses. For the better part of a week, I did not undress because I was constantly on my way outdoors. At the Polyclinic they advised, "You should have a warm toilet." They knew the advice was unrealistic but I suppose it was in the book. They gave me some pills, the only discernible effect of which was to turn the snow behind our hut a strange green.

When I showed up at the MGB office, they presented me with a registration card with all my names on it and in quotes, my title "Exile." On my return to the hut, Natasha, her face red with excitement, was waiting outside, waving something. "It's for you! It says here 'For Ruth Zigmundovna Kaminska Rosner'—five hundred rubles from the Polish embassy!"

Mama's efforts were bearing fruit and I was delighted. But Natasha was overwhelmed. I could not understand why until a day later, while I was melting snow with which to wash my things. All blushes and giggles, Natasha came into the woodshed and asked if she could help me. She was awed and fascinated by my silk underclothes, which Mama had sent. Then in a low, embarrassed voice she said she knew I probably had never done my own washing, and she would be happy to do it for me.

I tried to convince her that I did not mind what I was doing, but the more I tried, the more insistent Natasha became. Then she said, "Don't be afraid. I will keep your secret! But I know. I guessed it the moment I saw you. I knew somehow, that there is a mystery about you. But then when you got the check from the embassy, that made me sure I was right."

I asked what she meant.

"Shh, we shouldn't speak so loud. The others might not understand. But I am a teacher and I know the Polish King's name is Zigmund, and I guessed at once that you are his daughter. You are an exiled Polish princess aren't you?"

Poland had not been a kingdom for hundreds of years, and this girl was a teacher! I searched for words but the longer I remained silent, the more convinced she became that her surmise was correct.

She forced me away from the washbasin and I sat on the edge of my bed, holding my head in my hands in disbelief.

Mrs. Durach asked what was wrong. I shook my head. To talk about this—a Soviet teacher who admired royalty—would endanger her career and even her freedom.

On my next visit to the MGB I was told to get in touch with the Department of Culture. The department occupied one small room in the municipal building and consisted of one man.

I guessed he was a MGB official with artistic aspirations, and Kokchetav was probably the only place where he could have functioned in charge of culture. He wanted me to put on a "fine, patriotic show," but I was more interested in the money I would get than in discussing art. When he named the amount I tried to seem offhand—I would receive fifteen hundred rubles, five hundred payable in advance. He was not being voluntarily generous; that was the figure in the budget he had been handed.

Next day, in the old church—the odor of which betrayed it had most recently been used as a stable—I found actors constructing a stage and actresses shoveling the straw on the floor toward the walls. The Cultural Department clapped his hands, and the crew stopped work and sat down on benches and piles of straw.

The chief introduced me as a professional who had been sent from Moscow to create a theater in Kokchetav. They showed no enthusiasm—they looked stupified—but I soon discovered that they intended no slur at me; they were munching sunflower seeds of which they all seemed to have pockets full.

Some of my performers could not read or write, but all could sing. I had suggested to the chief that we start with a program of colorful songs, dramatized and using easily created scenery and costumes. "It will be patriotic enough," I told him, "and entertaining as well." I would write the text to hold the songs together.

chapter **22**

Reunion in Kokchetav
Spring, 1949

When Erika and Doba arrived, I would need new quarters. I learned of a widow who lived in a hut at the far end of Lenina Street—the main street—who had a room to rent because her son was serving time. We came to quick agreement after I promised that when she went to visit her son, I would take care of her cow and calf.

The room was whitewashed clean, but empty of everything except a round stove that rose to the ceiling. That was just as well—furniture in most huts was infested with bedbugs. I slept on a pile of rags on the bare floor until a telegram from Doba foretold her arrival with Erika on April 11, about a month away.

I decided to use my five hundred ruble advance for furnishings. I still had part of the five hundred rubles sent through the Polish embassy. At the market, I got two new bamboo cots, and to cover them some freshly sheared wool bought from a Kazakh. It was dark brown, dirty, and smelly, but the price was right.

It made an enormous bundle to lug. I boiled it, spread it all over the floor, and kept turning it to dry. As it dried I kept pulling it apart and the pile of wool soon reached the ceiling. I was at work on the wool when there was a knock on the window.

Zosia, who had been with me in the Lvov prison, was peering in. She had heard I had been sent to Kokchetav and all the way there she had been hoping to see me. She was laboring at a construction site, but strong as she was, the toil was so demanding that she spent most of her time in the infirmary. So she had set out to find me; it had not taken long to learn that there was a Polish actress in town.

She was in rags, frozen and hungry, and begged to stay with me, promising to cook, do the wash, anything. It was a bit strange to keep a maid in my position, but of course she could share what I had.

I usually bought the cheapest leftovers from a butcher and made soup or stew. Zosia's first treat was a bowl of hot soup. Then she was down on the floor with me pulling wool. I could not help comparing my situation with that of Robinson Crusoe and Friday.

Zosia and I fashioned mattresses by putting the wool into large bags which we made of gauze and sewed to simulate tufting. From bandages, the only material available at the stores, we sewed bed sheets, drapes, tablecloths. I knew that Doba probably would bring pots and pans, so I spent almost all the money I had on things she would never think of, such as water pails and a tank for drinking and bathing water and a wooden tub for washing clothes and bathing.

For a few nights before the great day, I could not sleep and I hardly noticed that all the food we had in the house were potato peelings which my landlady divided between us and her animals.

The train was due at 3 a.m., but it was a six-day journey and the train was always late. I did not want to go to the station at 3 a.m. anyway because one had to pass the homes of the Ingush, who robbed or murdered someone almost every time a train came in.

For protection, we borrowed our landlady's small black dog Tusik, which guarded her cows from wolves, and set out for the station in the dark. Tusik was fond of me, but we had to keep feeding him to make him stay with us. In the midst of the Ingush area, we ran out of food and Tusik turned and raced for home. But we made it to the station, where we flailed our arms to keep from freezing and worried about how we would carry the luggage Doba and Erika would bring. Then sparks from the train's locomotive lit the dark in the distance. The train stopped. The embankment was high and we ran back and forth below. Two or three people got off. No Erika. No Doba. They could still be asleep. Zosia and I ran the length of the train calling, "Doba, Erika,—Doba, Erika!" The train huffed and puffed and moved away.

For three nights we repeated the trip to the station—without Tusik and, surprisingly, without trouble from the Ingushes.

The third night we turned back to the hut with my face frozen with tears. A wildly biting wind hurled snow at us. We could hardly breathe or keep our eyes open. If I had three rubles, I could send a telegram: "What happened?" But I did not have three rubles any longer.

As we approached the settlement I thought about begging the

post office girl to send the message on a promise of payment later. I would leave her my MGB document. But I knew that "rules are rules." We reached the post office undecided—should we bother to go in?

Over the post office a lamp swung wildly. Suddenly, in its light, we saw something besides snow fall at our feet. I bent to pick up whatever it was. It was a new three-ruble note, carefully folded into four parts.

Neither of us said a word. I gave the girl the message "What happened?" When we left, Zosia asked me, "Now you will believe?"

"I always have," I told her.

That evening we received a telegram, "Everything okay. Coming the 17th as scheduled." The first telegram had contained a transmission error. I borrowed ten rubles from my landlady. Some went for bread, and I spent the rest for peroxide to bleach my hair so my daughter would see me as she had remembered me—if she remembered me.

This time they arrived. First I saw Doba, dealing with the conductor to help unload her luggage—valises, bundles, with pots and pans attached. Then, as in a spotlight in the darkness, my daughter's face. I called, "Doba, Erika, Doba, Erika! Erusinka!" (my pet name for Erika).

Erika called out, "Mamotchka!" I do not know how I climbed the embankment but suddenly she was in my arms.

I clung to her as though afraid that even now somebody would take her from me. She tried to calm me, "Mamotchka, I am with you. I am with you." She wiped the tears from my eyes. "Don't cry, Mamotchka. I am here with you."

Doba, too, was in tears. Thank God for Zosia, who set about gathering up the luggage which the conductor was still throwing off as the train started away.

Our luck held. A man in a jeep called out to ask if we could use his help. In all the time I had been in Kokchetav I had never seen a motor vehicle. I did not even ask the driver what he was doing there. Later I realized he had probably accompanied someone from the factory to the train.

I do not remember unpacking. The cries of joy from Zosia and Doba's chatter seemed to come from afar. My attention focused on Erika. I undressed her. I bathed her, kissed her from toes to eyebrows. Seven years old now, she seemed so plump and grown up, with cheeks like apples from the cold weather. Her talk was interspersed with giggles. When she fell asleep in my arms and I put her into bed, I noticed only then that the beds were covered with real, clean sheets. Doba had brought them. Long after I had tucked Erika in, I knelt beside her bed.

At last, I turned to Doba. It was hard to begin. There were letters from Mama, pictures of my family, a million things to tell one another. "You probably know that since Mikhoels' death they have shut down the Jewish theater and the GITIS," said Doba. GITIS was the Jewish Acting School.

"What do you mean, since his death?"

Mikhoels had died in an accident in Minsk in January 1948, Doba said. There had been an imposing funeral with speeches by top government personalities.

Was Doba sure his death had been accidental? She responded in agitation. "What do you mean? What are you insinuating? In this accident there also died an innocent non-Jewish journalist."

Innocent—non-Jewish—if he had been Jewish he would have been guilty?

Doba's agitation indicated to me that the official version of Mikhoels' death had not convinced everyone, for good reason. As a prisoner I had met people accused of being Zionists, but I knew better. The term meant all Jews, whatever their political persuasions. Mikhoels, for example, was not a Zionist, but he was identified with the Jewish culture and Jewish national pride. If the authorities had a purge of Jews in mind, they would begin by striking at those who were embarrassingly influential.* There was no point, though, to telling Doba what I sensed. I myself presented enough of a problem to her.

We slept through the entire next day, Doba on one cot, Zosia on the landlady's trunk in her kitchen, and I with Erika in my arms. When we woke, we treated ourselves to delicacies Doba had brought. And

*On January 13, 1948, Mikhoels was in Minsk on business concerning the State Committee for Theater Prizes, and died there that day. The Soviet government attributed his death to "hooligans" and an automobile accident. The unofficial but reliable version says that he was assassinated by the MGB. He was being interviewed in a Minsk restaurant when a limousine arrived to take him to the offices where he had an appointment. He had been expected to ride alone, but the interviewer, a journalist, asked to go along to continue the conversation. On the way, the limousine was stopped and both men were shot. Their bodies were then thrown to the road and deliberately run over to simulate an accident. At Mikhoels' elaborate funeral, his body lay in state but mourners were not permitted to approach it closely. Stalin's daughter Svetlana has written that her father was personally involved in covering up the murders.

then we slept again. It was only on the day after that I took them proudly for a walk, and visited every acquaintance to show off my daughter.

Erika and Doba remained through the summer and Erika shared the lives of the neighbors' children. Days began at dawn, when the cows went to pasture and we walked together toward the hills, delighted when we found wild flowers. The children gathered droppings for *kisiac* and Erika claimed to have picked up more than anyone else.

Land on the outskirts was divided up for gardening and I had my patch. I planted potatoes. I bought two geese. Erika delighted in playing with them. (Erika never knew she ate them. The geese had wandered off once and when they disappeared into the oven, Erika assumed they had got lost again.)

In July heat struck with the force of the winter's cold. It was bearable only when we bathed in the lake. One day I took off Erika's swimsuit and put it on a fence to dry. While I was wiping her, I heard her cry in horror: a cow was finishing her swimsuit and the two straps were sticking out of its mouth.

Once when we were walking back from the lake, Erika asked me to carry her. I realized she must be sick. As soon as we arrived home, she vomited and complained of a terrible headache. I ran for the Armenian doctor who had treated my leg. On the way to our hut I asked him frantically, "Could it be meningitis?" It could. "Or could it be appendicitis?" "Maybe." "Or sunstroke?" "Perhaps." Examining Erika, he remained baffled and suggested I try another doctor, a woman exile new in town. I found her washing her hair, but she grabbed her bag and followed me. She looked at Erika and asked what she had eaten. Erika described a flower bud. The doctor reached into her bag. In an hour, Erika's temperature was down and she was sleeping quietly.

But what if—? If there had not been an exiled doctor? If she had not been at home? If she had not recognized the flower bud as poisonous? If she had not had the antidote?

When Doba had to return to Moscow, we decided that Erika would stay with me and start school in Kokchetav. I could not part with her.

Parcels were arriving with fine clothes from Mama in Poland and from friends and relatives in America, and I was confident I could keep Erika from suffering from the winter cold.

I looked for an apartment large enough for the three of us. I found it in an old house on Lenina Street—one room and kitchen with its own private entrance. The house had been built of good round logs and seemed well protected from the cold, but it sagged on both sides and we joked that if anything fell we would only have to look for it downhill.

For cooking, the kitchen had only an oven and I wanted a stove atop which I could put pots. So I dismantled the sleeping stove, which occupied much of our one room, used some of its firebrick to make a cook stove, and rebuilt the sleeping stove into a heating stove. As the operation left bare earth where the sleeping stove had been, we scrounged cement from construction crews to pave the floor. I bought glass for the windows and got putty from the construction workers. We painted the walls in colors. (In Kokchetav nobody had ever heard of colored walls.)

To achieve that I mixed whitewash with red ink and milk; the milk prevented smearing and produced a nice pink. We scrubbed the wooden floor with sand until it whitened, then we waxed it. I made shelves for the kitchen, bookshelves and a wardrobe for the other room. I stained our bamboo cots with permanganate crystals, a disinfectant that made them look like mahogany. Out of an old blouse I made a lampshade. We had a radio that Doba had brought—but the only station it could get was Radio Kokchetav. Best of all, we had electricity because we were downtown.

People came from all over Kokchetav just to look at our apartment, and some of them said that only in the czar's time had anyone lived like that. Our biggest job lay ahead though. It was to build a toilet. To the puzzlement of our neighbors, Zosia and I dug a deep hole in our backyard. Over it we constructed a hut of packing cases, which we covered with roofing paper wangled from construction crews; we secured the paper with *kisiac*. We lined the inside with layers of paper. Two raised boards made a seat, and a hook held a kerosene lamp. We put a lock on the door, but it proved unnecessary—our neighbors did not dare enter such a contraption.

Our house was ready for winter, except for fuel. I learned that when the train came from Karaganda, a major source of coal, trainmen would drop off coal for a price. But one never knew who was an informer. After a discreet approach I made a deal with the engineer and his fireman.

My coal proved to be a great mound of huge chunks of anthracite.

I had never expected so much for my money. How to carry it home? A fearful but money-hungry driver agreed to take his truck to a spot I designated, leave it, and return after it had been loaded and the load covered—so that he could claim ignorance. I would have to load the coal myself—I could not leave Erika without Zosia. I went out at night with a shovel and buckets. The coal was on the high embankment, the truck below. All night, I climbed the embankment, loaded the buckets, jumped down the embankment, put the coal on the truck, and went back up for more coal. At the house, the driver and Zosia helped me put the coal in the basement. Then, using branches, we swept traces of coal from the snow. We were rich! We had coal.

We still needed wood to start the fire. Even poor people, if there was no man in the house, hired woodcutters. We borrowed saws and cut our own.

We also needed a food supply, because there would be weeks when we would be snowed in. At the market I bought a huge barrel cheap, because it stank of the sheep fat it had held. It could be cleaned, I learned, by heating stones in the fire until they glowed, dropping them into the barrel—outdoors—and pouring water over them. Repeating the process several times and rinsing with lake water, I got the barrel clean and odorless.

The barrel was for sauerkraut; you could not get through the winter without it. So I bought one hundred kilos of cabbages, and borrowing from all the recipes offered to us, we produced what I was willing to bet was the best sauerkraut in Kokchetav.

As soon as it got really cold we bought meat—whatever we could get for little money—and hung it on the porch. We had already harvested our potatoes and stored them alongside the coal. We bought a sack of flour. We were ready for the Kokchetav winter.

Meanwhile I made sweaters. I had obtained wool cheaply by buying sweaters so drab that even in Kokchetav nobody would purchase them from the store. I ripped them apart and washed and colored the wool. The stores had dye because people seldom could afford new clothes and had to dye old ones. I exchanged some of my sweaters for milk, bread, and butter and sold some for cash. Then the MGB said I would have to take a job, since private enterprise was forbidden.

What could they offer me? The theater venture, after several successful shows, had collapsed because the old church had been torn down. (I never got the promised one thousand rubles.) I had inquired at the school about teaching German, French, or English. The school needed an English teacher because the teacher assigned to Kokchetav had not shown up. (Kokchetav was not considered a great place to work.) But it hesitated to hire me because of my status.

Reluctantly, the MGB gave me permission to teach English. Besides, I served as a consultant for other languages taught in the school. I was paid less than the other teachers, but I made up my mind to look like a teacher, act like a teacher, and be the best teacher I could. I was in for a hard time. Some of my pupils were Ingushes who spoke Russian poorly and had no interest in learning any language. A number were taller than I and had mustaches; if I had met them in an alley, I would have run and even in class I feared them. The books were dull, and lessons had to foster belief in "Comrade Stalin, our leaders, and our party."

The rooms were cold, the ink froze, and the pupils sat in class in coats and hoods. When I entered the room, I greeted the students. When I asked a question, I required the pupil answering to stand up, and I thanked him for his answer. When I left the room at the lesson's end, I said good-bye. That was the way it was done in my *gymnasium* (high school) in Warsaw, and the only way I knew. But I inspired mockery.

I had had enough. I was passing through the corridor when I found myself surrounded by some of the most ferocious-looking boys of my class. They said they had some questions to ask. I told them that if they wished to talk to me, they should take off their hoods. They laughed.

I said calmly, "I am polite with you and I expect politeness from you. I am a teacher and a woman, and you have to mind your manners."

Another peal of laughter. Suddenly I changed from teacher to actress playing the role of teacher. In a low voice, I commanded, "Take off your hoods immediately." They took off their hoods.

After that the school director made me the official teacher of that class—not merely the language teacher—and from then on, my class was the best disciplined in the school.

When Erika was home from school, I would tell her about our family, show her the pictures which Mama had sent, talk about her father, and try to make her feel part of the world away from this wasteland. She did not ask many questions but I could sense she was troubled. Once she said, "I know you weren't sick when you went away from me. And I know my father isn't sick." But how can you explain to a child that you can walk the street, go to work, come home and cook—and are, nevertheless, under arrest? Little lies come easier, but one incident made me realize how careful one must be of every word one says to a child. Erika had been naughty and I found myself saying, "My goodness, they surely must have switched children while I was away. This bad little girl can't be my daughter Erika."

She said nothing then, but several days later she showed me the scar on her arm. "Do you remember the time I was burned?"

"How could I forget?"

"Well, if I weren't your child, I wouldn't have this, would I?"

I vowed then to myself to tell her the truth, or as much of it as she could understand.

But I never really could. In school she was learning songs about Father Stalin, and how just and good he was and how he cared for all of his people. Yet he punished her father and mother. Either we were bad or Father Stalin was bad.

The incident of Erika's poisoning resulted in a friendship with the doctor who treated her, Dr. Clarissa Ivanov, and her husband. She was Jewish, he a Volga German who had changed his name. A quiet man and an engineer by profession, he worked as an electrician at the hospital where his wife was on the staff. They never volunteered why they were in exile.

It was at the Ivanovs' home that I met Piotr Pietrovich, a strikingly handsome, intelligent, well-read doctor serving an indeterminate term in exile. We called him Pieta. I was attracted to him and he, I sensed, to me. We met again and again but almost from the beginning we tried to avoid seeing one another alone. Pieta had awakened in me all the yearnings and desires I had tried to suppress. But Pieta had a wife who was expecting a child and who would visit him as soon as the baby was born; she might remain with him in Kokchetav. Furthermore, any breach of morals would probably become known quickly to the authorities. Pieta lived in a small room adjoining the laboratory; I daydreamed of visiting him there, but I did not dare.

One day Pieta told me he had recently encountered the most interesting personality he had ever known, a man named Tono who worked in the weights and measures factory but had been assigned to help him install laboratory equipment in the hospital. Tono wanted to meet me and since a revolutionary holiday was approaching, I had two good reasons for giving a party. I invited the Ivanovs, a Mrs. Pavlovska (a Polish accountant who was rather mysterious but engaging), and Pieta, who would bring Tono.

I could afford a feast. At the market the parents of my pupils always offered "Comrade Teacher" bargains and gifts that I could not refuse without offending them. All day long, before the party, Zosia and Erika and I worked to prepare a Siberian banquet. The pièce de résistance was a huge mound of *pelmeni*, bite-sized dumplings whose dough encased several kinds of ground meat and lots of garlic, salt, and pepper. (Erika helped press down the dough's edges.) We put them out in the snow—our freezer—until it was time for them to be dropped briefly in boiling salted water and then dipped in separate bowls of melted butter and diluted vinegar.

We decked the table with a white cloth and matching napkins, shining plates, and shining silverware. The hut was warm and cozy when our guests arrived, bringing their own liquor—99 proof from the hospital (I suspect), which they transformed into aperitifs.

I was unprepared for Tono's appearance, though I had seen people who resembled him dying in prison hospitals. His face seemed to consist only of skin covering the skull; he was almost bald and he had a bushy mustache. He looked pathetically like a fledgling eagle that had been ejected from the nest as too frail to survive. He wore a cap, a filthy, oil-stained jacket, and far-too-big pants tucked into far-too-big boots. Only his shirt was clean. He was shy and softspoken, and it took time to become aware that he was a man of knowledge, warmth, and skills.

Tono had been born in a Slovakian mountain village, and his parents had sent him to a monastery to become a monk. But he renounced the religious life, married and fathered children, studied engineering, learned several languages, mastered the violin, and became a pilot in the Czechoslovakian air force. When the Nazis invaded his homeland, he flew his plane toward the Soviet Union. The Russians shot him down at the border. He had been in concentration camps until his exile in Kokchetav but he was soon to be free.

We three—Pieta, Tono, and I—spent many long cold evenings playing cards and, even better, talking. For the first time since I had come to Russia, I found myself discussing politics. How could this system function without riots or protests? Pieta explained that the history and heritage of the Russian people had made them intensely patriotic, and the Communist regime had identified the party with the motherland. Criticism of the system represented treason to Mother Russia.

Our evening threesomes were disrupted by the arrival of Pieta's wife and baby. But Tono still came. He brought me stunted, fishy-tasting ducks he had shot with a homemade rifle. He dug my potatoes and harvested my cabbages, and gave me his share of those distributed at the factory. When I lost my job as a teacher—the administrators said they were most satisfied with my work but that a "qualified teacher" was arriving—Tono taught me the fundamentals of photographic laboratory work and his factory hired me as a technician. (We used the lab to run an "underground" studio where I retouched photos of my subjects to their satisfaction.)

Pieta's wife stayed only two weeks—the cold was too much for the baby. The day after she left, Pieta came back. I had guests, including Tono, and I went out of the hut to get wood. Pieta followed to help me carry it. He embraced me passionately. Now he was sure, he said, that he loved and wanted only me. I broke free and told him to go into the hut. I needed time to think. I rubbed my burning face with snow.

I was a young and vital woman. I had rights and natural human cravings. I would not hold off Pieta any longer. That night Pieta returned and tapped on my window. I joined him in the snow. Later, alone in my bed, I did not sleep. For the first time since my imprisonment I was happy. Now it would be easier to survive Siberia.

The next day was Sunday and I waited for Pieta. It was the first Sunday that nobody came.

At dawn Monday, Tono's roommate, a young "free" engineer, rapped at my window. While Tono was visiting me Saturday night, he said, the MGB had searched Tono's room. They had found his homemade rifle, a radio he had constructed, and the camera with which he had taken some of the photographs we developed in the lab. They were damning evidence and Tono had been arrested.

But what had motivated the MGB search? I expected that at any moment I, too, would be re-arrested. Nothing happened. But the waiting and the uncertainty were terrifying.

Pieta slipped a note under my door. I was not to worry—everything would turn out well and as soon as "it was over" he would come. What would be over? Fear engulfed me—the fear that explained how the Russians could be controlled, why they accepted the life their government ordained.

The cold now was at its worst. The house was buried in snow almost to the chimney top. Schools were closed, daylight a memory. There was no reason to leave the house.

After nearly a week, we forced the door open to bring in snow for water. The cold had lessened, the wind had died. Zosia announced she would go for bread and to the Ivanovs for a cold remedy; these were excuses to seek news. She was gone several hours—an eternity in which I feared she too had been arrested, though the MGB could have picked her up at the hut anytime. On her way home, she had met Tono's roommate. Darting his eyes about to make sure they were unobserved, he told Zosia hurriedly he had been interrogated and confronted with a transcript of purported conversations in our house. He had been released, but he had learned that Tono had admitted his guilt—guilt in expressing opinions about matters on which nobody was supposed to have opinions. That was treason. The engineer was so upset that he had asked to be transferred from Kokchetav.

How could the conversations have been recorded? I searched the hut in vain for microphones.

When it developed that Tono was in the local prison, Zosia took parcels to him from time to time, but could not see him. Recurring cold interrupted those errands. When the weather moderated, she went again. She returned with the parcel in hand. Tono had been sentenced to ten years and transferred to Petropavlovsk prison. Zosia and I sat in silence. We wondered why we had not been questioned. Perhaps unconsciously we suspected one another; the Soviets were making us think their way.

I had to see Pieta. But I could not just go looking for him—not in the Soviet Union. I was sure he was avoiding us because he had been questioned and did not want to endanger us.

Zosia and I sat long in the darkness. Then we lit the kerosene lamp and Zosia unpacked her meager parcel. We heard the squeak of the door.

There was Pieta, covered with snow and icicles. He did not want to come in to spoil our floors, he said, and he had no time to remove his boots, but he had to share his good news with us. He had been pardoned by the Supreme Soviet and would be going home. I could see the smile on his lips but there was no way to look into his eyes. All the time he stood there he hid them, using his handkerchief as though to wipe the melting ice from his eyebrows and lashes.

I was happy for him. I was about to say how happy Tono would have been to hear his news, when I realized I should not mention that name. Not to Pieta. For a long time I tried to convince myself that it was only coincidence that Tono, who had been on the verge of release from exile, had been sentenced again, while Pieta, who had had an indeterminate sentence, had been pardoned.

chapter 23

Last Days in Kokchetav
Summer-Fall, 1949

Nothing was the same after that. Zosia found a job as housekeeper in the richest house in town, that of the Secretary of the General County Committee. My landlady told me her daughter was planning to marry and would need my quarters. (I suspected she wanted to be rid of me after Tono's arrest.) Erika was ailing and Clarissa Ivanova said the climate was too much for the child and urged me to send her back to Moscow.

Each time I thought about it, I felt the pain of parting. How long would it be until I could have Erika with me again? After what had happened to Tono, I doubted I ever would be free.

Since Tono's arrest, I had not returned to the laboratory. I could not, nor did anybody ask me to. Whenever I went to register at the MGB, the authorities acted as if nothing had happened. I knew that Karaganda, the largest center in North Kazakhstan, had theaters and a branch of the Philharmonia, a managing organization for the performing arts. Karaganda was also a place of exile. So I decided to write to the central MGB in Moscow to request transfer to Karaganda, where I might find work in my profession. I did not expect a positive answer, or any answer. It was like buying a lottery ticket—something to pin my hopes on for a while.

It was still cold when I found another home, farther from the center of town, with a young couple who had uncounted children (which was rare in Russia) and spoke almost no Russian. I never learned their nationality—I suspected they were gypsies—or why they chose to live in Kokchetav. They owned two houses connected by a sort of barn, and had one of the houses for rent. It was new, looked clean, and had lots of windows. Little by little, we moved our belongings by sled; without Zosia's help, the biggest job was transporting my coal.

Erika, in school, had her own problem. She was the only child in her class who had not been admitted to the Pioneers. She had been told it was because she was too young. I comforted her by assuring her that next winter in Moscow she would surely be accepted, and it would be much more exciting than in Kokchetav. I did not tell her that I could not care less that my baby at age seven had not become a party member.

I soon enough had other things to worry about. Come spring, the walls of the house swelled, and so did I. Shelves and everything else fell down and my house and my landlords' began to look as though they had been created of sponge. The houses had been constructed of *kisiac* and my landlords, foreign to the region, had not cured it sufficiently to withstand thawing after freezing. As for me, I began to suffer excruciating headaches and started to resemble the houses: first my joints and then the rest of me bulged so that I appeared to have elephantiasis; my skin reddened and itched intolerably. What if it was contagious? And fatal? What would happen to Erika if I died? Suppose she caught the disease from me? Even Dr. Ivanova could not help me. I had to get better on my own.

Whoever knew of my ailment and of Erika's proneness to illness recommended that we drink *kumis*, a fermented mare's milk that is a traditional cure-all among Kazakhs and Tartars. The best *kumis* was sold twice a week at the market by tribesmen who came to town and traded their *kumis* for tea. *Kumis* has a sharp, sparkling taste, and makes imbibers drowsy. Though I cannot say how much it contributed to our health, Erika and I both loved it.

So I visited the market frequently. That was the best place to find out about a new house for us—or anything else.

Once when we had joined a crowd around a fire, sipping *kumis* from our bowls, my butcher suggested that I see Old Nikita because he had recently built a house for his son. He had expected him back from the army but had received word that he was missing.

One cold morning, after I had seen Erika off to school, I went to visit Old Nikita. As in most Kokchetav buildings, I had to enter through a combination barn and woodshed. As I went in, I heard whining; what seemed to be a huge shepherd puppy was chained to a wooden pillar. The animal was begging for attention.

I liked dogs (when they were not working for MGB) and I petted the animal, which put its head on my knees. Its hair was matted and filthy and it looked utterly pitiable. A door opened behind me and I heard Old Nikita muttering, "God have mercy. Back up slowly, whoever you are."

His eyes were wide with fear. He wiped his forehead and neck with a dirty kerchief. His voice trembling, he said to his wife, "Yevdokia, she petted and played with the beast."

They crossed themselves. They explained that the animal was a wolf. A truckdriver friend of Nikita and several companions had been attacked by wolves in a wood. They had killed some and one cub remained by its mother's body.

On impulse, they took the cub along and persuaded Nikita to keep it as a watchdog. But Nikita and his wife had never been able to tame it, and Yevdokia, who had fed it with a baby's bottle, had been bitten by it. They did not know what to do with it, fearing to turn it loose.

Only after we had "eaten up tea" together did I explain the purpose of my visit. "Of course, if you don't mind," I told them. I had no need to add, and I did not, that I would understand if they did not want to have me because of Tono's arrest.

Nikita banged the table with a fist. "No, I don't mind at all! And I don't believe my son is missing. They have him somewhere! He saw too much! He learned too much during the war!" He started to shout. Yevdokia patted his arm. "Enough, Nikitushka. Enough." He showed me the house he had prepared for his son. It was a room with a kitchen, and I could smell the new wood and fresh paint.

Then Nikita said excitedly, "You know what? Take the beast—I mean the dog! You can keep it outside and nobody will ever come near you. You are the first one he ever allowed to touch him. You couldn't ask for a better watchdog, could you?"

So we came to terms, with the wolf as a bonus, and I moved my coal again. The beast was a "she." Erika was delighted and the beast proved—despite my initial fears—gentle with her. Erika even played with her. We called her Venera.

We kept Venera chained to the outside wall of our new house. Old Nikita did it most professionally: the chain had to be long enough for her to move around freely, short enough not to endanger passersby. Not too many people passed by. But those who did, including our new landlord and the mailman, announced their presence from afar.

Nikita further enriched our household with an owl with a damaged wing. The same truckdriver had found it and Old Nikita brought it to me. I had my reservations but could not resist my daughter's begging eyes.

A big black cat, Vashka, soon joined us. I found him on the roof, terrified of Venera. I would have Erika with me for only a few months more and I wanted to do everything to make her stay with me as memorable as possible. But how do you feed a wolf? My butcher solved my problem. I had to go to the slaughterhouse very early, and he would fill my sack with a horrid mess.

Venera soon attained the size of a full grown wolf; she was a perfect guard and a loving pet, though she sometimes knocked me down in play.

The owl lived in the woodshed and graciously accepted small pieces of raw meat. Vashka resented both of them and when he wanted to take a walk, he jumped on my arm for protection.

Then Doba arrived. It was not easy to make her accept Venera, but we assured her we had the situation well in hand.

At last I again had somebody to talk to, to share my thoughts with, and to look after me. Doba brought with her all the news. Mama was going to Paris as a delegate to the anti-Fascist committee. There she would meet her brother, Josef, the concertmaster of the Israeli Philharmonic orchestra, and my cousin from London. The news seemed to come from another world. I was happy that Mama was having a full life—success as an actress, a devoted husband, my sweet baby brother.

But I did not know what I myself could hope for. I dared not dream that I would ever be reunited with my family. If the impossible did happen, would I be able ever to enjoy life again? The news shattered all of the protection I had placed around myself. Until now, I had not tried to reach too far. Shelter. Food. Warmth. Someone to talk to, to care for or care about. What else was there?

What I found difficult to accept was perfectly understandable to Doba. She had grown up in Soviet Russia—people disappeared all the time. One learned to live with it, she said. Only when she saw me with a yoke on my shoulders, carrying buckets of water, was she shocked. Arrests, imprisonment, exile she could accept; but manual labor for me was beyond her comprehension.

Our owl's wing had healed and the bird grew strong and aggressive. I could hardly wait to release it in a wood. But one night, before that opportunity presented itself, the owl got out of the woodshed. At dawn I was asleep with Erika on a cot in the kitchen. Doba was in the room. The outside door was wide open because of the heat. At first the bird stood on the threshold, wings widespread. I had not known owls could be so big. Then the owl flew into the kitchen, wings beating wildly.

I covered Erika with a blanket and closed the door to Doba's room. I picked up my bathrobe and began to chase the bird. It seemed to fill the room. Erika was crying from under the blanket not to hurt our owl. Doba was screaming in terror. The owl jumped from pot to pot. Finally I managed to throw my robe over the creature and took the bundle to old Nikita. I hope he turned the bird loose in the wood, to live as an owl should—free.

Doba and Erika left at the beginning of August so Erika would be ready for school in Moscow in September. All the way back from the train, I cried. Summer was already over in Kokchetav. The day was cold and windy. At home, abandoned, broken toys lay on the floor. I picked up Erika's toy rabbit, the one with the missing ear, and sat in my coat and boots, holding it.

I placed my bed, which Doba had been using, between the window and the stove, and after a time I lit the lamp and decided to light the stove for the first time that season. Whatever I did, I did as in a daze. I had a bottle of good Moscow vodka and I sipped from the bottle and grew sadder and sadder. Finally, I went to bed, the bottle beside me.

I was awakened by turmoil and Venera's howling. Smoke filled my room. My bed had caught fire from the oven. I had not heard Venera's howling at first but the neighbors had. Afraid to pass her to go through the door, they forced my window.

Venera had saved my life. But she was becoming a problem. Her appetite had been growing every day and she had become extremely restless, pacing back and forth on the end of the chain, howling all night.

One morning an unusual quiet awakened me. I was afraid Venera had broken her chain and escaped. But she was licking a puppy. I had never suspected her pregnancy and attributed her recent heaviness to her appetite.

I ran back and put a large pot of water to boil on the stove—it was the first thing that came to my mind, because it was always done in movies when a child was delivered at home. When I rushed back, there were two more puppies and then two more. One of the puppies looked exactly like Venera, and the other four took after their father, whoever he was. I realized the hot water was not needed. Instead, I gave Venera a huge bowl of food and ran with the news to Old Nikita. He said he knew people who would take the puppies, and I decided to keep the one that looked like its mother. I could not deprive Venera altogether of her motherhood.

The puppy was also named Venera. She ate out of the same bowl as Vashka, who played with her, licked her, and encouraged her to eat, until even big Venera tolerated him.

Venera's puppies and the fact that she had saved my life made her a celebrity in Kokchetav. The fire had taught me I must not live alone. Soon afterward, on a visit to MGB to report—and to find out whether or not they had word on my request for a transfer—I met a new exile, a beautiful woman artist named Talia Maximovna. We communicated our loneliness to one another, and she suggested I move in with her. She had a large attractive room, and her landlords were parents of one of my former pupils. They would be happy to have me—for an increased rent, of course, and my coal. But what would they think of Venera? I would not part with Venera and I did not broach the subject. By the time I was ready to move, though, Venera was so famous that my new landlords welcomed her. Simultaneously, I persuaded a railway conductor—twenty rubles worth of persuasion—to take little Venera to Erika in Moscow on his return trip. (Doba eventually told her son to turn Venera loose in a wood. Erika was heartbroken.)

Talia Maximovna had been married to a painter who had asked for annulment of the marriage upon her arrest. She had had a good life, I gathered, and a large circle of bohemian friends. Now she received letters only from her mother in Dnepropetrovsk. The reason for her arrest? I did not ask, but I had my suspicions, based on things she let drop in conversations. When the Allies opened the second front during the war, the Soviet Union encouraged fraternization with foreigners. But people who took the encouragement too seriously found themselves in trouble. It was no crime to go to bed with a Soviet citizen, but a pretty woman like Talia who was even seen frequently with an alien was likely to be arrested on a charge of intimacy with foreigners.

Talia and I spent hours talking about what had happened to us. Could we ever achieve contentment with the remnants of our lives? The Germans had robbed me of my past; the Russians were robbing me of my present. I felt as though I were constantly missing trains,

trains that kept passing me by without stopping. From time to time we discussed suicide, the only decision we could make on our own. One night, a faulty oven almost made the decision for us. We were partly overcome by carbon monoxide and dragged out by an emergency doctor. From afar, I could hear Talia crying, "Save her, she has a child." And I remember saying, "I don't want to live, but she does." Thereafter, we talked no more of suicide.

About that time I received a letter directly from Adi instead of through Doba. He had mailed it between prison camps while traveling with his orchestra. I read excepts to Talia Maximovna. "Whatever may happen, whatever will be, we have to survive! If I have to crawl to go back, I will!" He begged me to believe that we would be back together, that we would be able to pick up where we had left off. I had my doubts.

A few weeks later, I jumped out of bed shortly after we had put out the light. It seemed to me I heard Erika calling me, "Mama. Mamotchka!" I had not been asleep. In the early morning I telephoned Moscow.

Doba seemed to be crying. "How is it that you called?" Erika had just been taken to a hospital. "My baby was calling me," I said. That evening I received a telegram from Erika's doctor: "Your child, Erika Rosner, is in intensive care with acute hepatitis; mother's presence requested."

Next morning I asked the MGB for a leave of absence to be with my child for one week.

"There are no leaves of absence from a sentence," the official told me.

I pleaded.

"Nothing can get you out before your time." With a wink he added, "And sometimes longer—you should know." It was an allusion to Tono.

Daily I waited at the post office for Doba's call, until finally it was Erika's voice on the phone. By the time Erika was back in school, my petition for transfer to Karaganda had been granted.

I wanted to give away the possessions I could not take with me, but Talia Maximovna was more practical; she sold anything I could do without in Karaganda. I could use every ruble.

Only Venera was left, and I could not travel with a wolf. But the whole village had grown fond of her; she would be cared for.

I purchased the cheapest ticket—which did not provide a seat. But who cared? An eighteen-hour trip in a normal train seemed like an adventure. I had one valise with my clothing secured with a heavy rope, and a sack with my bedding and household utensils. I said my good-byes and found myself boarding the train which I had met so many times before. This time I was on it.

chapter 24

Karaganda
Autumn, 1951

We arrived in Karaganda in the evening. It was dark and cold. The station seemed very busy and it frightened me. I was used to crowds in prison trains, but those were quiet, orderly, and sullen. Here—how to move around on my own, among so many other people? Bewildered, I spent the night in the train station sleeping among scores of people bundled up on the waiting room floor, clutching their belongings as I was. I slept soundly, but when I awoke I felt awful. Unable to change clothes or wash, I associated the episode with my not so distant past. Again the dehumanizing feeling. But now, I could do something about it.

I took the first bus to the center of town where, I was sure, the main MGB would be. It was still dark and very cold. The bus traveled a sort of elevated highway on both sides of which rose hills of coal slag glowing from the fires of trapped gas. The air around the fires shimmered.

The hills vanished, and in the dawning day—a city! It looked to me like a world capital. No buildings rose more than five or six stories, but after Kokchetav they all seemed to be skyscrapers.

From the bus I peered into store windows; I stared at posters announcing theatrical events and concerts. In Kokchetav I used to dream that I was in a large department store of the kind I remembered from my childhood visits to Paris. But I had little money and only a half hour. I rushed to the children's department. What should I buy? Ribbons for Erika's braids? Or the cute little panties? Or maybe nice, warm boots? Suddenly, the bell announced closing time and I had bought nothing. I would wake up angry—why hadn't I decided sooner? I would have to do better in my next dream.

So now I was afraid I would hear the ring of a bell or wake in Kokchetav.

The second stop of the bus was in front of the MGB building. I was almost in love with the MGB for letting me come here. It was still very early, but a crowd waited at the bus stop, some people were hurrying along the sidewalks, and some were already at work shoveling snow.

I had no other place to go, so I entered the MGB building. Only cleaning women were on the job, and I washed up and changed clothes in the ladies room. I felt great. By the time I finished, clerks were arriving and one directed me to a door to await a supervisor. The supervisor arrived relaxed and smelling of Chypre. How I loved Chypre now! The supervisor looked over my "credentials" and told me to report once a week to a clerk on the main floor.

"How do you like Karaganda, after Kokchetav?" he asked.

I loved it. Then, surprisingly, he told me a joke: "Someone was asked what was his favorite city. 'Karaganda,' he replied. 'And what is your favorite song?' 'Farewell, My Favorite City.'"

The song was a current hit. We both laughed, I almost to the point of tears.

After asking if I had a place to stay, he wrote a letter of introduction to the woman manager of a hotel several blocks away. The manager was sympathetic but warned me not to expect privacy. I could sleep in a room with six beds, only one of which was occupied. Most of my luggage would have to go to a storage room.

The storage keeper was a sad-looking, petite woman in a white coat without buttons and ill fitting, poorly made clothes. From her accent I was sure her native language was German and, looking around to make sure nobody would hear, I asked her in German, "You are not from the Volga Germans, are you?"

Her face lit up and she replied in the melodic tones of an Austrian, "No. I am from Vienna. My name is Else."

Else helped me unpack my dresses. Some Doba had salvaged from my former landlady in Lvov; some were new evening dresses Mama had sent when she learned I was going to Karaganda, in case I got work as a singer. Else fondled them one by one.

"So, this dress will need to be ironed," she said, talking as though I were not there. "This I will just sprinkle a little with plain water and it will come alive by hanging. Oh, this one, its hem needs mending. She probably stepped on it with a heel." Else behaved like a child suddenly showered with toys.

"Madam, I will be right back." In a moment she reappeared with a clean rug and some white paper, cleaned my night table, put away my cosmetics and accessories. Among them was a box of Leichner theatrical makeup, courtesy of Mama. Else exclaimed, "Leichner! That is what we used also. May I smell it?"

Else was in heaven. Then she was summoned to the storeroom.

I stretched out on my bed. All my bones complained about the night on the terminal floor and the luggage they had carried. But I could not get Else out of my mind. Who was she?

She returned with a pot of coffee and told me about herself. For years she had worked in Vienna for Lili Darvash, the Austro-Hungarian movie and stage star who had been married to Ferenc Molnar, the Hungarian playwright. (I had appeared in some of his plays.) But Else had fallen in love with an idealistic Polish Communist, a refugee in Vienna whose dream was to reach the "promised land," Soviet Russia. Else followed him to Russia. I finished the story for her. "He was shot as a spy sent by the 'imperialistic government.'"

"Yes," she said quietly. "We had only two years together. And since then I've been kept in refugee camps for undesirable foreigners, and for five years I have been in exile in Karaganda. The only charge against me is 'undesirable foreigner.' But I have not been able to get in touch with relatives or friends. They just don't know what happened to me. Tell me, please. Will I ever be able to return?" She answered herself. "No use. Nobody's place is nowhere."

Else had to leave my room. We had spent too much time together. (Two aliens talking together alone—what an incriminating act!)

In twenty days it would be Erika's birthday. I had to send something. I went to a department store and saw a beautiful baby doll. That was it! The price was high. But I could not take my eyes from its face. I told the saleswoman that if she could put the doll away for me, I would be back with the money in two days. Reluctantly, she took a deposit. I had no idea how to get the rest of the money.

When I returned to the hotel room it was dark. I lit the lamp and was overwhelmed by a torrent of Russian and Georgian reproaches. My roommate was Aunt Gurya, as she wished to be called. I apologized, fled to take my bath—it had been scheduled for 10 p.m. and had been paid for in advance—and crept into bed silently in the dark. Aunt Gurya was gone when I awoke.

I dressed carefully to impress the Philharmonia people whom I was going to see. The day was sunny but as I entered the new, small Philharmonia building, I trembled. "You are an idiot. Those people once would have been happy to become acquainted with you." Then, "That's true. But now? The only thing that means anything here is the MGB."

The head of the Philharmonia, Comrade Beloborodov, was on the phone. As soon as he finished his call to Moscow, his secretary would tell him somebody was here to see him. "What's your name and what is it about?" I wrote my name on a piece of paper.

After a while, Comrade Beloborodov approached with hands outstretched. "I know. I know. I have already heard that you are here. Glad to see you. Last time I saw you, you were singing a marvelous French song. And you look just fine, prettier than ever. "Dasha," he called his secretary, "give us some tea. Do you smoke? Let me call my wife. She will be so glad to meet you. She is a pianist." I knew what it meant. It meant he had nothing to say and was embarrassed. He wanted his wife to come because he needed reinforcement.

I drank the tea, sitting comfortably, smoking a Kazbek cigarette. But whenever I tried to say a word, he carried on again. "You know whom I met not so long ago—a very good friend of yours? Raykin. Yes. Arkasha Raykin! (Raykin was one of Russia's most famous actors.) He told me he wanted to take your child . . . when . . . when . . ." He blushed and gulped his tea. His reinforcement burst in and I doubted if he had ever greeted his wife so enthusiastically before.

"Natasha, Natashinka, please meet my wife, Natalia Pavlovna." He settled into his chair and Natalia Pavlovna took over.

"Dov, you know whom I should call? I have to call the Levines and tell them the good news."

I still had not opened my mouth.

Covering the phone mouthpiece, she enlightened me. Leonid Moyesevitch Levine had been director of the Minsk Jewish Theater—now he was director of the Kazakh opera. "We have a fabulous opera here." All in one breath. Then, "Hello, Leonid Moyesevitch. This is Natalia Pavlovna. Guess who is now with us? You will never guess. Ruth Sigmundovna Kaminska. The wife of Adi Rosner, yes. So help me God. I mean, I swear." She winked, covered the phone again, and handed it to me. "He wants to talk to you."

I heard a warm "Sholem Aleichem." I responded, "Aleichem Sholom," a lump in my throat. Then the voice said, "I would like very much for you to come to us for dinner. Of course, if you have nothing better to do. We will be happy to have you."

I had nothing better to do.

I was to be there at four o'clock. Then Comrade Beloborodov, elated, exclaimed, "So, everything seems to be arranged. I am so glad. I knew Natasha would come up with something." At last I found myself able to say, "I, too, am glad, but I came here to talk to you about a job for me. You see—"

Comrade Beloborodov put his arm around me and told me again how happy he was, and as to the job, if I could come next week, he would think about it. Yes, they certainly would think about it, "Isn't it so, Natasha?" He led me to the door. I was sure he needed time to get in touch with the MGB to ask what if anything, he ought to do for me.

The sun was not shining so brightly any longer. It was windy and cold. Very cold.

I could guess Comrade Beloborodov's words after I left, "Natasha, you are a wizard, as usual. That you came up with that Jew!" I was also happy that she had come up with that Jew. His warm "Sholem Aleichem" rang in my ears. How long had it been since anybody had greeted me so?

But no advance. No promise of a job. How would I manage? And what about the doll? Should I ask Leonid for money? I could not.

Four o'clock found me knocking at the door of a third floor apartment. Young and pretty, Mrs. Levine answered the door. Leonid Moyesevitch came to greet me. They ushered me into their dining room. The building was new (five stories, no elevator), the apartment was elegant, with a study full of books and good paintings on the walls. Most important—they were normal, cordial hosts. They knew everything from the moment Adi had been arrested. They could imagine what I had gone through. When they heard of our arrest, they had tried to get in touch with anybody who knew what had happened next. Had I seen Erika? Was I in touch with Adi? How was my wonderful mother?

Leonid Moyesevitch told me he had lost his job not only in the theater but also in the GITIS. The only place he could find work was in Karaganda.

No, Mikhoels' death had not been accidental. But let's better have another cognac.

When I returned to the hotel, Aunt Gurya was asleep. I undressed in the dark.

Next morning I did not feel like getting out of bed. No plans. Nothing to do. No money. I looked around and met Aunt Gurya's eyes. "Well, thank God—I was sure you would never wake up," she said. "Where were you yesterday?"

I told her of my disappointment at not getting a job. She asked me if I was married, if I had a child, if I had pictures of my family. She loved pictures. Aunt Gurya was sitting up in bed, wearing an old-fashioned flannel nightgown with ruching around her neck and at the wrists. Her once black hair was partly covered by a matching nightcap. Over her nightgown she wore a short sleeveless rabbit fur jacket. She was skinny, old, with dark wrinkled skin. Her hands were crippled by rheumatism and she wore fingerless woolen gloves. But her eyes were sharp.

"I knew right away that you were not Russian. You are an exile, aren't you? Of course. They will soon have the whole country behind bars. Why not? They need slaves. Have you ever been to Georgia?"

I nodded. I was afraid to talk. I suspected she had been planted.

"What a country we have! They grabbed it! They destroyed it! Destroyed its beauty! Robbed it! Our best people are in prison. They stole our vineyards. They made whores out of our daughters. All because of that bastard, Dzhugashvili [Stalin's real name]. He betrayed us and sold us into slavery.

She wept silently but hysterically. I got her some water. She took it thankfully and swallowed some pills. After a while she calmed down. "Don't mind me. And don't worry. There will come a time for you. You will return. You will reunite with your lovely family. And when it happens, remember Aunt Gurya told you." She was not feeling well and had decided to remain in bed.

Aunt Gurya regarded me as a remnant of a vanished world, the last position left for her to defend. Every day I had to report to her what I did, what I intended to do.

She demanded the phone number of the Levines. If I planned to spend an evening with them, she would call Leonid Moyesevitch and order him to accompany me home. Often she waited up for me with food prepared by Else which Aunt Gurya kept warm under her pillow. Sometimes it was the only food I had had that day.

It was time to report at the MGB again and I encountered other exiles who talked of the difficulty of finding jobs. No wonder. People from all the concentration camps around were doing the work. The Dolinka camp inmates were chained together and taken to construction sites in open trucks in the early morning. Then the guards removed the main chain but the prisoners' legs remained chained. That contributed to the enormous accident rate at the job.

"But who cares? They have enough of them," one man among the waiting exiles volunteered.

"I remember," said a red-bearded elder, "how they put the captive Japs to work to build the summer theater. The one in the park, you know. Even their engineers were chained together. They were funny, tiny people, but the skills they had!

"Some of our artisans wanted to watch them work, but nobody was allowed. They died like flies. I didn't care much for them. They were too strange a breed for me. People should look like people. But I used to throw bread over the fence for them. Many people did. Well, you would feed an animal if you saw it starving, wouldn't you? I heard they didn't even care for bread. They are raised on rice, like the Chinese. Strange people. I don't think any of them survived. But the theater they built—it is a beauty!" (The theater was indeed a beauty. Its tall, tapering columns, which oddly but successfully wedded Grecian and Oriental design, were contrived of molded slats. Multicolored lights inside the columns glowed through the interstices: the theater was the swansong of a great and innovative artist, doomed to eternal anonymity. Less impressive was the production of *An American Tragedy* that I saw at the theater. The women in the cast all wore red wigs and riding breeches and carried riding crops, and the male actors were decked out in checkered suits too loud for even a racetrack tout. Everyone perched on high bar stools.)

The red-bearded elder stuffed his mouth with crumbs of bread taken from his pocket with a fingerless palm. With the fingers of his other hand, he picked the crumbs out of his beard and put them back into his mouth.

They all seemed to know each other, and gave each other tips about jobs.

"Listen, go to mine number 22. They need people there—guards, because of the thievery. They wouldn't take me—they told me I was too old. 'I have fifteen more years to serve,' I told them. 'So you have a guarantee that I will live that long. Therefore I must be young enough.' Yes. Fifteen years to go."

The other exiles laughed uproariously. I wanted to scream.

He continued, "But they might take you. You're young. If you are not afraid—they say there are deadly fumes around there."

Another said, "Well, today's the day. As long as there is blood in my veins, I can get some money and good food."

"What are you talking about, Papasha?" I asked.

"They need blood. What they are sucking out of our bodies and souls, they don't pay for. But in the Polyclinic, they have a place for blood donors. First they check the type of your blood, whether you are free of venereal diseases, if you are not an alcoholic—the hell they know—they took mine anyway! And if the blood is good, I mean, if it has enough of what they want, they'll take it. If you need money badly, go. They pay well. But before you go, eat some big, black radishes. It does miracles in raising whatever they need from your blood."

I went to the Polyclinic. They paid well, by the amount of blood taken. I had decided I could spare two hundred fifty grams. I registered and was told to return about noon for tests. I went to a vegetable stand, bought a black-skinned radish—about all I still could afford—and ate it on my way.

By noon I was back in the Polyclinic. After they took a sample, I had to wait a while. Then I was asked to spit on my wrist, and with a chemical pencil they wrote a number on it.

The radio in the waiting room was on full blast, transmitting news. The same news was on all the front pages of the newspapers: now, after the war effort, it was time to think about the well-being of the people. Industry must be more people-oriented in the manufacture of clothing. There would be more consumer goods. Then came a list of which products were to rise in price and which would go down. Bread, fuel, and some necessities were going up. Tractors and earth movers were going down. One woman remarked, deadpan, "Now I know what I shall buy for my hungry children for the holidays—an earth mover! They can have a party!"

From time to time a white-coated girl emerged.

"Number five, get ready. Number six, next time. Number seven, get ready. Number eight and number nine, no good. Number nine, go and see the doctor on the third floor. Number ten—" That was me—"Get ready."

After giving my blood I rested on a cot, then received a coupon to be cashed for money and a coupon for a meal. The meal was plentiful—bread, hot bean soup, meat, a cup of tea, a piece of sugar. As soon as I cashed the money coupon, I went to the department store. I hoped the saleswoman had not sold my doll. I had checked almost every day, telling her I was sure that by tomorrow I would have the money. She had got used to me and only shaken her head.

This time I had come to buy. But by now I was sure the doll would never get to Moscow by mail in time for Erika's birthday. I would have to put it on the train to Moscow.

"I only hope that when your daughter grows up," said Aunt Gurya, "she will repay every drop of blood."

I took an early bus to the station. They made up the train for Moscow in Karaganda, so people arrived early to settle in. I could look up a train crew member, but I was not handing out tips from my blood money. So I walked back and forth in front of the sleeping cars, on the theory that sleeping car passengers would be more reliable. Several times my eyes rested on a middle-aged woman sitting close to the window.

She called to me, "You are looking for somebody?"

I told her I was looking for somebody I might know who was going to Moscow to whom I could entrust my package.

"And what is it?"

"My daughter's birthday is going to be on the fifth of November. But with the holiday rush the mail might not deliver it on time. And I would like my baby to get the doll in time for her birthday."

She hesitated.

"If you take it, you'll have nothing to worry about. They live not far from the terminal. I will phone them and give them the number of the car and the number of your seat and they will meet you. There will be no trouble to you. You'll see. Please."

She agreed at last and took Doba's phone number in case of a slipup.

The blood money had come most opportunely. Besides the doll, I had to pay for the hotel room again. I also had to call Doba to tell her to meet the train, and I had to find out if she had managed to sell anything.

I had asked Doba in a letter to sell my mink coat and suggested whom she should approach. I counted especially on one famous folk-singer who had made me promise many times that if I ever thought of selling the coat, I should see her first. "You have so many others," she had said, "and I will pay any price."

I went to see Beloborodov again about a job and he said he would do his best, but it would not be easy. The Philharmonia sponsored many "concert brigades" but they traveled a lot and I could not leave the area. But he could probably arrange two or three concerts for me during the holidays. His wife would accompany me on the piano. He hoped I realized I should not use any of my husband's songs.

The hotel was in turmoil when I returned. A high MVD official had arrived with his wife and three small children. Their luggage—and people to keep an eye on it—filled the lobby. The cars to transport them to their new home had not arrived; they had been taken to our room, and we were not to disturb them because they had to feed the children.

Aunt Gurya sat in the lobby, cursing under her breath in Georgian. I sat next to her. She recited loudly the slogans posted all over the walls—slogans such as "Long Live the Great October Revolution." "Long Live Comrade Stalin." "Long Live our Politburo." I pulled her arm. "Long live . . . " "Long live . . . " "Thank you for our happy childhood." (This was the slogan near a huge portrait of Stalin with a baby in his arms.)

A plainclothesman guarding the luggage stood in front of us, his behind almost touching Aunt Gurya's knees. From time to time she shoved him away, but he kept moving back.

Suddenly she spoke too quickly for me to shut her up. "Thank you for our happy childhood!" she proclaimed loudly. And then she pulled the guard's sleeve. Innocently, she confided to him, "By the way, Comrade, this reminds me, this young lady had to sell her blood in order to send a doll to her daughter."

With that I almost dragged her out of the lobby for a walk around the block. No sense to have years added to my sentence. By the time we returned, they were loading the luggage and we were allowed back in our room. Under the beds were empty bottles which had not contained formula. The odor of liquor hung in the air. Egg shells, paper, the remains of herring—the babies had been well fed.

The official and his wife, both red-faced, hovered over their screaming children. A plainclothesman was stuffing bags with wet panties, leftover food, and bottles. They rewarded the cleaning woman handsomely; she had been obsequious to them.

After they left, Aunt Gurya and I sat on our beds and I noticed something under one of them. I picked up two one hundred ruble bills. I was about to run after the party. Aunt Gurya leaped up and blocked the door. "Are you out of your mind? You want to give it back to *them*? What they drank and ate just now would be enough for entire families for a week. Don't be a fool!"

While I was trying to get free of her restraining hands, the cleaning woman returned to change the bedding which the MVD babies had soiled.

"*Those* were guests. *Those I understand*," she said, looking at us icily.

Aunt Gurya giggled, let my hand go, and said, "It's too late now, anyhow."

She refused to share in the money, so I decided to invite her and Else to a meal. I bought delicacies I would not have dreamed of purchasing otherwise, and Aunt Gurya took out of her storage a bottle of Georgian wine. She was very proud of it—she had made it herself.

I still did not know much about Aunt Gurya. I was aware of her hatred of the regime and the bastard traitor Dzhugashvili and of her strong nationalistic feelings. But what she was doing in Karaganda, nobody knew. She would vanish for hours. Other times she would sit in the lobby awaiting visitors. After such incidents, she would remain in bed, sometimes praying and sometimes cursing when (I suspected) praying had not helped.

One night I returned from a rehearsal for a concert with Natalia Pavlovna who was, I had to admit, an excellent accompanist. (Beloborodov had kept a promise.) I was humming one of my old songs—not one of Adi's—that I planned to include in the program. The room was dark and as I had not expected Aunt Gurya to be in, I turned on the light. She was in bed, wearing her rabbit jacket, and she was in a vile mood.

I asked her if she would mind if I kept the light on a bit longer as it was still quite early and I wanted to read.

In a weak voice, she told me I could do whatever I wished. "I can't sleep anyhow. I don't feel well." She murmured her prayers and I read.

Shortly after I got into bed the door opened and Else's head appeared. "MGB men are checking the registration books," she whispered.

With lightning speed, Aunt Gurya jumped out of bed. From under it she pulled a valise, hidden by an overhanging bedspread. She opened the valise and scurried back and forth, pushing packages of money, around me, under me. Then she covered me carefully, hopped back into bed, and resumed weakly murmuring her prayers.

A knock. Two MGB men entered. They wanted a word with Comrade . . . and they pronounced a long name that did not sound like Aunt Gurya. In spite of her insistence that she was very weak, they asked her to get up as they wanted her to help while they checked her luggage.

One man asked what was the matter with me. I told him I was tired after rehearsing. I must have caught a cold and because of the concert I had to be particularly careful of my health. He said he could see I must have a fever as my face was very red and perspiring.

He noticed the book at my night table. "And what is it that you are reading?" he asked, taking my book. His eyebrows went up and his look changed to admiration.

The book was from the university library where I had been spending much of my spare time. Because I lacked the necessary documents, I could not matriculate, but I was allowed to attend lectures. One lecture, announced on a bulletin board, was to be by a famous professor on the latest work of Comrade Stalin on linguistics. I skipped the lecture but took the book out of the library. It had an enthusiastic introduction by the President of the Soviet Academy of Science, but I had to be careful not to laugh aloud when I read the book in public. So I got my laughs in bed. With that book beside me I was obviously a loyal Soviet citizen, and the MGB man did not question me.

The two left with Aunt Gurya. I lay there motionless. They might return in a moment, and any move might reveal hundreds of rubles and make me an accomplice to whatever it was.

They had to return because Aunt Gurya had left her clothes on the bed. But what if they would not give her time to dress? Suppose she did not return? What would I do with the money? What kind of money was it? To whom did it belong? I heard footsteps approaching. I could not change my position, so I did the only thing I could—I closed my eyes. My heart pounded. What if Aunt Gurya had confessed to whatever she had done? What if they were coming for the money?

The men just ushered her in and reminded her to appear at the MGB at nine o'clock next morning. For a while she stood with her ear to the door, making sure they were gone.

Then she leaped toward me, pulled the covers off my sweating body, moved the valise toward my bed, and removed all the packets of money. Now I jumped to my feet. I had to cool off.

"Rutinka Tsatsinka," she addressed me, in an endearment used to a good small child, "I owe you an explanation."

"About time."

"You see, a very, very great man—I don't mean for the Soviets, but for us Georgians, is in Dolinka. He is a descendant of one of the noblest families in the Caucasus. The Soviets already wiped out nearly all of his relatives. They have nationalized all that this family had, and believe me, they had a lot. They were good and beloved masters, and they were honored even by their enemies. They were godly people. Everybody who passed by was invited to be their guest, and nobody ever left their home empty-handed. The bastard would once have been happy to get a bone from their table.

"After the Soviets destroyed all that, we were sure that their thirst for blood had been satisfied. At that time the man I am speaking about was a student in the theological seminary and we were sure they would overlook him. But three years ago they got him. We received a tip that there was somebody here who could to fix things for him. But he wanted a lot of money. So we collected among people who care, and I was chosen to deliver the money. The people that I have to contact didn't strike me as being too reliable. I wanted to deliver to the top man. They postponed the meeting from day to day. After what happened today, I am afraid I am being swindled. Now I have to bring the money back safely. Oh, they will keep an eye on me, all right. But Aunt Gurya will outfox them. Tomorrow they want me to explain what I am doing here. I have good letters to cover my story. They won't get me or my money! So go to sleep. Tomorrow Aunt Gurya has a lot of things to settle."

Next day when I returned from rehearsal, Else handed me a scribbled note: "Rutinka Tsatsinka, all is well. I will write to you when I reach home."

Aunt Gurya did outfox them because I was soon getting letters from her from home. And her home, she always assured me, was my home.

chapter **25**

Karaganda
Winter, 1951-1952

I gave several concerts accompanied by Natalia Pavlovna, but selling my blood was better business. Comrade Beloborodov said he had no authorization to pay me more than the pittance I was getting. But one day he summoned me. I had an opportunity for a more permanent job—if I did not mind. . . . It was with the circus.

"With *what*?"

"Don't get excited. I am not asking you to fly on the trapeze. Listen, we have some people registered with us who have the same status as you do. There's a Chinese prestidigitator with his wife who is a juggler. There are three Korean brothers who are acrobats. Then there's a Korean cyclist-equilibrist, and there are two trapeze artists. We'll throw in a Kazakh folk singer, and you can be the announcer and do some recitations. What do you say?"

What could I say? I agreed.

"To tell the truth, I have been in the circus business ever since I was arrested," I remarked. "You have to do tricks to survive."

My jest did not please him, but I liked it. So did the Levines. In Yiddish it sounded better.

My circus colleagues were all good, honest, hard-working show business people, but all were woefully undernourished and most had tuberculosis.

Wherever we went they took along a pathetic pack of coughing, scurvy-ridden children. One reason was that the Chinese juggler mother was still breastfeeding her eldest son, who was eight years old. Another was that there were no babysitters. And the best reason of all was that at the mines where we put on most of our shows, the looks of the children occasionally moved our hosts to give us food to take along when we left.

The Chinese man was a magnificent sleight of hand artist but whenever I watched his act, he mumbled under his breath and rudely waved me away. A colleague explained that he feared everybody was trying to learn his secrets.

For a while our "brigade" included an attractive woman with the widest vocal range I had ever heard—from the deepest contralto to the highest soprano notes which she produced in an amazing pianissimo. Her husband accompanied her, and he and his wife loved one another tenderly. They belonged to an Asian tribe that now numbered only a few hundred families. They and the Kazakh folk musician were the only "free" people; the rest, despite their talents, which would have won them places in any circus anywhere, were "undesirable elements."

The most talkative and helpful to me was the cyclist-equilibrist. His father was Korean, his mother Armenian, and they had produced a handsome offspring. His first name, Konstantine, derived from his Armenian background. Kostya, as we called him, was the only one to give me a hand when we had to mount or descend our open truck, and he always managed to be there when drunken miners became too importunate.

Our performances started with loud brass. Then I took the center of the arena, the lights on me. My outfit was an evening dress—one of those my mother had sent and which had so excited Else—worn over quilted pants and high boots. The quilted pants contributed unusual roundness to my figure in certain places, and the male audience loudly approved my appearance in words familiar to me from the three Marusias' dictionary.

I never felt quite at ease in the midst of those wild-looking, woman-hungry crowds. Once, while I was reading a serious dramatic piece, a broad figure weaved uncertainly toward me. Because of the spotlight on me and the darkness enveloping the audience, I did not see him until he was almost upon me. Kostya leaped to my rescue, but the man fell at my feet. He had a knife in his back. Stagehands and militia dragged him away. The manager ordered me to continue, and I finished my piece in a dress stained with blood.

Apart from such incidents the performances were trying enough. All of my being felt humiliated, but for the rest of the "brigade" the shows were the highlights of their lives, and their enthusiasm and professionalism deserved all the respect I could give them; when they started to treat me as a pal, as somebody who belonged, I felt honored.

The worst ordeal was the traveling. The props went on a van, but we artists sat on the straw-covered bed of an open truck, barely protected from the cold by a piece of canvas. We lay huddled together, depending on each other's breath for warmth. That they were tubercular and opposed to washing their bodies made it torture. Sometimes a one-way trip would take three to four hours over bumpy wasteland.

But still, if I had to be in exile, I was happy it was in Karaganda. On days when we had no performances, I could enjoy good friends, and I already knew, at least by sight, some interesting people.

One character I encountered frequently was a son of the poet Yesenin, who always walked around with a long scarf flowing from his sleeve. There was a once-famous mathematician who resembled Albert Einstein. There was a mysterious couple who wore potato sacks tied at the waist with rope and who sang arias from French and Italian operas in cracked voices that had traces of great technique. Though they sang, they never talked to one another or to anybody, and whenever I approached them, they looked at me angrily and murmured unintelligibly.

Such characters, and a host of others, gave Karaganda a special flavor among Soviet cities. There were many people like a Dr. Suchanova whom I met at the Levines, who had come there to be close to incarcerated loved ones. For people who had served a long time, Karaganda was as good as any other place to remain. The free and the exiled mingled unembarrassed.

Dr. Suchanova on first acquaintance struck me as unfriendly, and I was surprised to receive an invitation to her home for New Year's Eve. She had two daughters who were studying in Karaganda, and a son who lived in Leningrad and was present for the holiday.

Dr. Suchanova and her then small children had followed her husband to Karaganda when he was arrested during the Kamenev-Zinoviev purge in the mid-1930s. He was sent to a nearby labor camp and died several years later. Posthumously, he was rehabilitated, but Dr. Suchanova remained in Karaganda. Whatever she had left behind her in Leningrad had been confiscated; in Karaganda she had a comfortable house and was respected for her skills and integrity. (Some years earlier she had saved the life of a high official's son after other doctors had given up.) Her whole family was talented. They made wonderful music, they painted, and they had the largest library—including unique collector's editions—I ever saw in a private house.

When we took our places at the table New Year's Eve, we drank first to a Happy New Year and to peace throughout the world. Then Dr. Suchanova said softly: "This toast I would like to propose to Ruth Zigmundovna. To human virtues that cannot be wiped out by any adversities, virtues that she carries with her as a torch. Let's drink that she may never grow tired holding her torch with pride." My eyes filled with tears.

The hotel was becoming intolerable. New roommates, constantly changing, checked in mostly at night. Some snored loudly, some were repulsively filthy. And I needed a place large enough for Doba and Erika whenever they could come. My search for new lodgings provided me with a better insight into Karaganda.* The city was growing. The bitter cold never stopped construction; camp inmates had no union.

New buildings looked much better from afar than on the inside. None had elevators, despite their height, and few apartments had baths. The occupants were mostly "free" miners and their families, moved from barracks.

One day, after a fruitless search, I stopped on my way home to look at a window display. Reflected in the window was a familiar face. I cried, "Irene!" The face cried, "Ruth!" Irene, a striking beauty, had sung with our orchestra. We had never been close, but now we felt like loving sisters.

Irene, who had been married to a writer when she joined our troupe, had grown up in France. Her parents, members of the nobility, had fled there from the revolution. They died young and penniless while Irene was a child. As far as Irene knew, only she and a female cousin who had joined the revolution had survived of all her large family.

When Irene reached maturity, the Soviet government advised her she had the right to choose her citizenship and could return to Russia.

*Karaganda's population was given officially in 1947 as 220,000 but the figure did not include the thousands of resident exiles, or the thousands of inmates of the concentration camps that surrounded the city. If they all were counted, it has been suggested only partly in jest, Karaganda's population might have approached New York's.

If she did, she would get a free education and the blemish of her family's nobility would not affect her. Raised in poverty, she accepted the offer, which no doubt had resulted from her cousin's influence.

After the first hugs and joyous exclamations, she invited me to her place to talk. If her landlady consented I could move in with her until her husband came. She had arrived at Karaganda the day before and had just registered with the MGB. She was not interested in a job because her husband would provide whatever she needed. I doubted the authorities would permit her to remain idle. "I don't care about their requirements," she insisted. "I have all the rights not to be fit for any job. You see, when I was arrested I was pregnant with my first child. I gave birth to a beautiful girl and I lost her. I will never even know where she is buried." For a while we remained silent. I could not ask her how it happened and she did not say.

I moved in with Irene. Her landlady looked like the housekeeper in someone else's home; she seemed out of place among the furnishings and the study lined with books in many languages. Dr. Suchanova told me her story. The books had belonged to a former German scientist, a Communist who defected to Russia. For a change, he was not disposed of right away but spent many years in a Vorkuta labor camp. When he became too weak to work, he was exiled to Karaganda where he was admitted to a hospital in which the woman was a nurse.

On his discharge from the hospital she took him into her home and provided for him with slavish devotion. As a result he lived longer than expected and earned money writing science fiction novels under an alias. The house reflected his rather than its mistress's personality.

In the privacy of our quarters, Irene and I could talk. I heard that the most popular of the stories that had circulated concerning Adi's and my arrests had it that we had been caught stealing across the border with diamonds and gold.

I learned, too, how Irene had got into trouble. A French newspaper correspondent newly accredited to Moscow had been her schoolmate in Paris and he had phoned her. Irene was aware of the danger of "fraternization" and "cosmopolitanism" but was ashamed to tell her friend she feared to meet him. To avoid endangering her husband, she offered to dine with the Frenchman at his hotel and made some excuse for her husband's absence. Leaving the hotel, she was picked up by the MGB. Though she had been trying to save face for the country, she suffered the same fate as my friend Talia in Kokchetav, as Fyodorova, the movie star who bore a daughter by an American naval officer attached to the United States embassy,* and all the other beautiful women who had been charged with intimacy with foreigners. A crime could always be invented to fit the punishment.

Irene told me too about her family history. Her ancestors had been related to Russia's royal family but had fallen into disfavor. One beautiful and witty aunt, though, had remained much admired at court. Irene was her favorite niece, and Irene idolized her to the point of stealing and treasuring her handkerchief. She showed it to me, yellow with age, with a small crown in one corner, initials, and, still, an aroma of perfume.

The circus performances stopped abruptly. Beloborodov told us we had already been everywhere in range of our travel allowances. But Kostya, the cyclist, told me the Chinese sleight of hand artist had died of tuberculosis, and since he was the main attraction the circus had to disband until it found another like him.

Simultaneously, I received good news. Adi had obtained permission to apply his royalties for records and compositions to monthly allowances for Erika. On my way from the post office, I visited Else to share my delight. "God from heaven has sent you!" she exclaimed. "You are the only person I can tell. I just got word that Brigitta Helm—you remember, the movie star who played in *Alraune?*—is in Dolinka. They took her in Vienna. She is very sick, and I would like to put together a parcel for her. Will you help?"

I would. But when I told Irene she said she would not, and suggested that if I did help I should make sure no one saw me hand money to Else.

To get information about a camp inmate was crime enough. To try to assist one was unpardonable. I took all the precautions.

Else told me the hotel's woman manager wanted to talk to me. What she had to say was that "some people" might have a notion that I should not become too close to Irene and especially not stay with her. I thought I knew who "some people" were, since I had been referred to her hotel by a MGB official.

A World War II love affair between the actress Zoya Fyodorova and the American naval attaché in Moscow, Captain Jackson Tate, led to Fyodorova's imprisonment and Tate's departure from the Soviet Union. Their daughter Viktorya first met her father, now a retired rear admiral living in Florida, when she left Russia in the mid-1970s. An actress like her mother, Viktorya was formally adopted by her father in July 1975. She is married to an American airline pilot, Frederick Pouy.

The warning was not to be disregarded, but obviously I could not say anything about it to Irene. I told the manager that I had been looking for a private room, as I was expecting my daughter and her guardian to visit me. She just happened to have some addresses for me. How could I face Irene? I had promised Irene that I would introduce her to the Levines and Dr. Suchanova. They were expecting to meet her. I would have to invent a lie for their sake and for mine.

Since Tono's arrest I had become more and more aware that the entire society was divided into informers and victims. The oppressed becomes an oppressor. While I walked, I looked at the passersby. Most had good honest faces and I supposed they possessed the ability to love, to be friends. But they had to be hunters or hunted. I knew most of them carried loads similar to mine, with enforced secrecy, unmentionable fears, never daring to share anything with a friend or even a loved one. How easy for a system to twist a mind—my mind! How deeply would I sink into the lies? In order not to harm friends I had to lie and join the system. I had to lie to Irene not to cause harm to myself. Poor Pieta! No wonder liquor was the best business in this country.

When I got home, I told Irene I needed a drink. I wanted to avoid talking to her. But I was lucky. She told me that she had spoken to her husband and that he would arrive shortly. I verged on hysteria and she was touched that I was so happy for her.

I found a room in a private house. When Doba and Erika arrived, we visited all my friends and Erika charmed everybody. Doba said she had had a difficult time trying to sell my mink coat. The star I had recommended had said to Doba, "Yes, then I was willing to pay her any price but now her needs are different." Doba indignantly sold the coat to somebody else for the price the star had finally offered.

Once when we were browsing in a department store, I asked Erika, "Erusha, by the way, you never wrote to me about how you liked the doll I sent to you for your birthday."

"What doll?"

Doba stepped in. "Of course, don't you remember? We went to the terminal to meet the nice lady who gave you the package from your mommy. But you see, shortly after, Erika was invited to a birthday party of a friend—very important people. Remember, Erika? It was Vala's birthday. So we decided not to unpack it but to take it as a gift. You see, Erika was showered with presents for her birthday."

Could I ever tell them how I bought it? I said softly, "It was probably the right thing to do."

The vacation ended all too soon.

On November 27 I was at the Levines with Dr. Suchanova and some of their friends. They were discussing something but I could not concentrate. I took books from shelves, not knowing what I read. Dr. Suchanova asked me brusquely, "What is the matter with you today?"

"I just remembered that I have an anniversary today. It's five years tonight since they took Adi away." Dr. Suchanova gave me a drink, and I told her how I had been arrested December 7.

"So your term will be over in December."

"Will it? Can one be sure?"

"Leave it to me. I will find out."

Not many days later, on a cold December morning, my landlady opened my door. "Dr. Suchanova is here to see you."

Dr. Suchanova pushed the landlady aside and closed the door almost on the landlady's nose. "Come with me. We have an appointment." There was no time for questions. I dashed icy water on my face and dressed in ten minutes.

"We are going to the office of the head of the militia."

"Militia? I never had anything to do with the militia."

"You will see."

She was excited.

She pointed out in the distance a street still unpaved. The militia building, far less imposing than the MGB, was a one-story cottage-style house with a porch. Before we reached the porch a young peasant girl passed in front of us carrying two buckets on a yoke. The scientific Dr. Suchanova said, "Thank God, the buckets are full. That is a good sign."

We entered. In an almost commanding tone, Dr. Suchanova told a young militia officer, "Tell Comrade So-and-So we are here."

Almost simultaneously, we heard the voice of the head of the department. "Come in."

Dr. Suchanova took my hand forcefully, and we walked into the office together.

"This is she. I will wait outside." With one more squeeze of the hand, she left the office.

A broad-shouldered man seated behind a desk told me to sit down.

For a few moments, he did not look up. With his nose in papers, he reminded me of the major years before.

After a while, he pushed his glasses up on his forehead, stared at me without saying a word, then put his glasses on, stared again, shook his head and said, "Very interesting."

I did not ask what was interesting. (Only much later did I recall the official who had told me that the charges against me required only a six-month sentence.)

"Well, as your papers here state—" He paused, put his glasses up on his forehead once more and looked up at me. "So, as I was saying, as the papers here state, you are a free citizen as of now."

Tears ran down my face and I made no effort to control them. I could not speak. I could not move.

After a long time I heard the official saying, "Enough. There are some formalities to be taken care of."

Dr. Suchanova, who had reentered and embraced me, wiped her face, then handed me her handkerchief.

Eventually, I managed to sign some papers and was given one. I could not see what I had signed or what was on the paper handed to me. I shook the official's hand, kissed Dr. Suchanova. Still weeping, I asked the man, "Does it mean I can go to my child? To Moscow? Am I really free to leave whenever I want?"

"Of course you are."

As Dr. Suchanova steered me out, I could hear his voice, "You are free to go whenever you want."

It was a long time before I could read the piece of paper. It said that Ruth Zigmundovna Rosner, also known as Kaminska, also known as Turkow, had been released after serving her sentence. Signed by the MGB authorities and issued by the Militia of Karaganda to serve as her identification.

It did not look like something to be framed and hung on the wall, but it was a ticket to freedom.

I made my train reservation for January 2, 1952, and I purchased a valise—no more sacks over shoulders. Then I went around to say my good-byes, and this time I went to see Irene, whom I had been avoiding. I suppressed my good news for I could see she needed somebody to talk to.

"You know," she said, "you are the only person I can tell what has happened to me—and here you are. Do you remember when I reminisced about my early childhood? My family? My aunt? The one whose handkerchief I still keep?"

I nodded.

"I met her yesterday."

"What? How?"

"I had to go to the post office to call my husband, and they were shoveling and sweeping the sidewalk. It was very icy and I slipped and grabbed the arm of a street cleaner. The street sweeper turned to me in anger, and I realized it was a shrunken old woman. You won't believe this but I recognized my aunt.

"I exclaimed, 'Aunt Natalie!' She looked at me for a moment. Then she pushed me away, dropped her shovel, and ran into a doorway. I picked up her shovel and wanted to follow her, but another woman scraper yelled, 'What have you done to her? Shame on you!'

"I said I wanted to help her. Where could I find her?

"I gave the woman a few rubles and she said that the poor creature helped a janitor at the building into which she ran. Then she made a sign with her fingers that the old lady was crazy.

"'She never talks to anybody,' the woman said. 'We call her Tasha the Mole because whatever she can lay her hands on, she drags to her hole. She never lets anybody in there.'

"I was afraid to follow her. I gave the woman everything I had left—ten rubles—to give to Tasha. Tasha the Mole. Tasha. Natasha. Natalia. I know it is she!"

After a while I told Irene my good news. I did not mention Dr. Suchanova's involvement. In Russia, good deeds must be kept even more secret than bad deeds. They could have worse results.

chapter 26

Return to Moscow
January 1952

And so I found myself sitting on a train, in a sleeping compartment, on my way to Moscow. I asked the conductor for tea and tipped him well. I was buying my way back into society, and I was almost glad I had a long journey ahead. I had to get used to so many things. If somebody knocked at my door, I did not have to jump up. I could respond, lying lazily on my seat, "What is it?"

We were approaching Kokchetav. I asked the conductor if he could buy something there for me to eat. "Oh, no," he answered. "This is just a very small place with a short stop and there is nothing there. Very few people have any business here."

Our route bypassed Petropavlovsk. I wondered if Tono was still there. We stopped unexpectedly at Chelyabinsk. I asked the conductor why. Looking around to make sure nobody was overhearing, he said, "They are hooking on two prison cars."

"Is that so? Do you think we might be endangered by the criminals?"

"Oh, no. Nobody ever escapes."

Erika, Doba, and her children met me at the Moscow terminal. "I told all my friends my mother was coming today," Erika said excitedly.

Doba had prepared a feast. Her children, her closest friends, and neighbors I remembered were there.

Then came the first call to Mama. Phone conversations in Russia, particularly intercountry conversations, remind me of visits with guards standing by. In the short time you are permitted to talk, you find yourself unable to say what you want or to ask what you need to know. The phone is worse than a prison visit. You cannot even look into one another's eyes. This conversation was nearly as bad as my first call to my baby from Kokchetav. We were weeping, all the time reassuring one another that we were just fine and happy. I hardly managed to say hello to Mel and Viktor and it was over.

Next day Doba and I agreed I needed a few days of rest. After that I would try to get in touch with the most reliable of my friends, seek their advice, and decide what I must do. Doba told me she had to report to the building management that I was staying with her—just a formality, but nobody was allowed to stay anyplace or change addresses without reporting to the militia.

I was just going into the kitchen with an armful of dishes from last night's party when the doorbell rang. Doba opened the door and two men entered. Leather coats, plain hats, but MGB pants. They said they had come to check the electrical wiring, and they made small talk. They were sorry to have interrupted us. They could see we had had a party. Then they asked how many people lived in the apartment. Still with their eyes on the wiring, they asked if everybody who lived here had reported according to law. I put the dishes down.

Doba was white-faced. Finally the men asked for the documents of all the apartment's occupants. Doba, in a coquettish way that I never expected of her, suggested that while she was getting hers, perhaps they would have a bite and something with it. They helped themselves.

Meanwhile I told them I had just arrived and had had no time to report but my child had lived here for years. Doba came in with her documents. While I was getting mine I heard her assuring them she intended to go right down to the management.

Then I handed them my documents. They studied them, stood up, wiped their greasy mouths, told Doba that she was an excellent cook, and told me that in twenty-four hours I must be out of Moscow.

I gasped. "Why? I was told in Karaganda by the head of the militia who signed here on this document, that I was allowed to go to Moscow. My baby is here. I have no other place to go! And I am very tired."

They treated themselves again to vodka and said that that was the trouble with local officials. They forgot the rules. "Moscow is a restricted city and people who don't have any business in Moscow are not allowed to stay in Moscow. Especially people with the kind of document you have. You are not allowed to stay within one hundred kilometers of Moscow or any large industrial city. It's the rule. The vodka was very good. So was the fish." Tomorrow at the same time they would check whether I was still here.

Maybe we should go to the militia. To the MGB. Apply somewhere. But we did not have time. Tomorrow I should not be here anymore. Where to go?

My trip to Moscow and Doba's preparations for my arrival had left us nearly without money. At any moment Erika would be back from school. She must not know what had happened. Finally I told Doba to calm down—I knew what I had to do. I would go to Minsk. It too was a restricted city, but Adi had been a "meritorious artist" of Byelorussia, we had many friends there, and I knew all the top echelon of the Byelorussian government that had sponsored Adi's band.

Meanwhile Doba would have time to find out how to obtain a permit for residence in Moscow. It remained for me to find a convincing reason to present to Erika. She would be home soon. I put on my prettiest dress and combed my hair. The doorbell rang wildly. It was Erika with a crowd of schoolmates. She flung herself into my arms; she was proving to her friends that she had a real mommy. While I held her I felt like Abraham about to sacrifice Isaac. But there was no angel to stop me. The wound I was about to inflict might never heal. I pressed her close, suppressed my tears, and treated the children to cookies and cake that were still on the table.

After the children had gone I did not know how to begin. Doba came to my rescue. In a cheerful voice she said, "You know, Erika, while you were at school, we had some wonderful news." Erika stopped talking and looked at us with wide eyes, lit with expectation. It struck me she must be thinking that her father was also about to come. I wanted to say something to prevent her disillusionment, but Doba went on.

"They have learned in Minsk that your mother is in Moscow. They phoned soon after you left this morning that they want her to come and perform in Minsk right away. Isn't that wonderful? She will be leaving tomorrow morning."

Erika's eyes remained wide, but they looked as if somebody was switching off the lights one by one. After a long silence she said coldly, "I suppose you are going alone again, without me."

"Well, as soon as I know exactly how long I will be in Minsk, you will join me."

She did not believe a word I was saying.

"I will tell my teacher that you won't be able to come to school tomorrow." She left the room without looking at me. A moment later I saw her lying on her bed with a book.

Doba left to get me a train ticket to Minsk and to telegraph a good friend of ours there, Samuel Abramovich. He was bright and he had managed to maneuver his way up in the culture and art business without getting into trouble.

There were other people I could count on, too. It would be better to notify them by telegraph, specifying the time of my arrival, and avoid giving details by telephone. I packed one valise and tried to talk to Erika.

"I know, darling, you are disappointed. It was unexpected for me, too. I was sure I would be able to work here, but I have learned that it would be hard to get anything in the middle of the season. In Minsk my chances are much better. What else can I do?"

She did not take her eyes from her book. After a long while she said, "I don't think we would starve if you didn't start to work right away. After such a long time, you should have stayed a little while longer with me. I waited for you so long." I sensed she was suppressing a sob.

"Darling, this job is a big opportunity for me."

The more I tried, the less persuasive I was. I had never given so clumsy a peformance. How could I convince her of my love, of how much I needed and missed her? I could not even give her the real reason for my departure. It would force her to invent her own lies. I preferred to invent them for her. When I saw Erika off to school next morning, the last thing I told her was how much closer Minsk was than Kokchetav and Karaganda. I promised that soon we would really be together.

I slept all the way to Minsk; I was too tired to think and there was no use making plans. Since I had little money, I would phone from the station and try to reach someone if nobody met me. But as the train pulled up to the platform, I could see a small group of people, most of them carrying flowers. The faces grew larger and familiar, and they were waiting for me!

How I had missed that! For so long I had been among strangers.

We stopped at the hotel room my friends had taken for me only long enough to leave my luggage. We were all invited for supper at the home of a composer and musician whom I had known well in Warsaw, and who had played with Adi's band. After supper, I would return to the hotel and rest for a few days. Everything would be just fine.

We ate a lot. We laughed a lot. We drank a lot. It was like old times. After supper our host played the piano while we sang old hits and recalled hilarious moments from our tours. Our laughter grew louder and gayer.

The next morning I awoke ill with grippe. Samuel Abramovich's wife, Shura, phoned to tell me she expected me for dinner. The sound of my voice moved her instead to hasten over with home-cooking and remedies. Next day I felt better but my friends insisted I remain in bed. The following day Samuel Abramovich arrived to talk. I was not to worry about the hotel bill—it had been taken care of. But he needed my documents to report. He looked at them and his face grew long. He would see what could be done. I was not to worry until it was absolutely necessary. It became absolutely necessary next evening.

Running from official to official, Samuel Abramovich realized that no one wanted to take responsibility for granting me permission to remain in Minsk. It was clear that I should not remain at the hotel.

That night Samuel Abramovich took me to a hut on the outskirts of town and told me to remain indoors until he returned. A peasant's hovel, it was a surprising place to find in elegant Minsk. Its occupants came and went but never spoke to me.

Samuel Abramovich was back three days later. He or my other friends could do nothing. They had decided the best thing for me was to go to Gomel; they had heard of plans to open a Jewish theater there.

They gave me the address of the cultural department in Gomel and the name of the official to see. Under cover of night a man sent by Samuel Abramovich saw me to the train.

From the station I phoned Doba. She had spoken to a famous lawyer who, for five thousand rubles, could fix my situation. She had called my mother, and Mama would sell some jewelry to pay him. I was dismayed. The practice of law in Soviet Russia was an absurdity; if the authorities wanted somebody convicted, he was convicted.

I left my luggage at the Gomel station and went to the cultural department. When I told the official whose name I had been given that I had been sent to work with the Jewish theater he looked bewildered.

"Jewish theater in Gomel?" he said softly.

Actually, Yiddish theater was dead. The authorities had decided. But officials who had had good relations with the major Yiddish actors could not bring themselves to say so. Instead they explained away this delay and that postponement as only temporary and assured the actors they would soon be acting again. There was no plan to open a Yiddish theater in Gomel or anywhere else.

But I did not know that at the time, and the official decided to continue the pretense. He gave me a letter to the militia saying that I would be employed by the Gomel Cultural Department, he promised to let me know as soon as my services were needed, and he recommended a place to stay. The place had no vacancy, but the kindly woman owner gave me another name and address. The house was on the outskirts where Gomel, a typical provincial city, became villagelike.

The landlords were an elderly Jewish couple who met me with obvious distrust. Why would a city dweller be interested in sharing their less than modest apartment?

But when I spoke in Yiddish, they were transformed. "Ach, Gott! You should live long and be healthy. Nowadays a young person who is not afraid to use the mother tongue is so rare I can hardly believe it! Come in and talk; you will have a cup of tea with us with homemade kirsch preserves."

The first question was, "Are you sent to work here?"

"Yes, by the Minsk Department of Culture. But I will apply for a transfer to Moscow and I don't know how long it will take."

"And where is your husband, if I may ask? You are not, God forbid, a widow?"

"Oh, no. My husband works in the Far East and my daughter is with her grandparents in Moscow."

Later, I would tell them the truth. But not yet. It was so cozy and warm.

They decided I could stay, and showed me my room. The entrance was through the dining room, in which there was a child's bed.

"A child is with you?" I asked.

"Yes, but he is a very good boy. My daughter is a piano teacher, but her husband is an engineer in a big factory and she stays with him; we are keeping the child with us in the meantime." That was *their* skeleton.

The boy, a charmer, adopted me as a substitute for his absent mother. I adopted him as a substitute for Erika. My landlady proved to be a good and generous cook. Everything worked fine, except that my landlords expected me to go to work every day. So I rose at 6:30 every day and from 7 a.m. until 5:30 p.m. paced the streets of Gomel. Finally I decided to tell them the truth. They were not surprised. Some of their acquaintances had recognized me, but so long as I was not telling, they were not asking.

Erika spent her vacation with me—at eleven, she was old enough to travel alone. We had some wonderful times that summer. At the vacation's end, I called Doba to tell her when to meet Erika, and she said I would probably have to come soon myself because the lawyer—for his five thousand rubles—had written a petition to the Supreme Soviet, and in September I was to submit it personally. He assured Doba the outcome would be favorable.

So at the beginning of September I left for Moscow. I arrived late in the evening and early next morning went to the militia. I explained the purpose of my presence, I showed my petition, and I signed a pledge to leave Moscow unless I received the Supreme Soviet's permission to remain.

Then I went to the Supreme Soviet building. I used to see it from our terrace in the Hotel Moskva. I found the courtyard crowded with people. At the main door a guard asked for my pass. I said I had none but had a personal letter to present to somebody in authority. He told me that without a pass I could forget about seeing anybody. What was my problem? I showed him the petition. He pointed to the crowd. "They have petitions, too." He added that in the crowd I could find people who could tell me how to proceed.

The constitution of the Soviet Union provides that every citizen has the right to appear before the Supreme Soviet. The only difficulty is getting in. When I found a man in charge, he told me the crowd I saw was a remnant of the day's original crowd. Only some of them would be able to enter today. Those who already had got in had been waiting for weeks. I should return next morning as early as possible, register, and receive a number. It would probably be several weeks before my turn came.

I did not mind. As long as it took, I had a legitimate excuse to remain in Moscow.

Erika had thrown herself into my arms when she saw me. A moment later she pushed me away, crying, "Mommy, maybe you should go back! They will arrest you again!"

I explained my visit was legal, that I had come to petition for a permit to remain in Moscow. That calmed her but she could not guess how to handle the situation. She would not even be able to invite anybody home because she would not know how to explain my presence, which I could not hide. Somehow everybody in the building knew about my arrival. They also knew or suspected the purpose, but nobody wanted the truth. We had to invent lies for Erika to tell, lies that everybody expected to hear. If anyone asked, Erika was to say that her mother had come for a short business trip, that during the day I was "very busy," and at night I was too tired to have company.

At dawn the next day, when I approached the Supreme Soviet building, I saw thousands of people. They were mostly parents and relatives of prisoners seeking justice, pardons, or reviews of sentences. The militia did not allow anyone to sit or sleep on the sidewalk and walked about picking up those who had laid down exhausted. Except for people whose numbers admitted them to the courtyard, petitioners were supposed to walk outside the gates or sit on the benches of Alexandrysky Park. The crowd was not supposed to look like a crowd. The American embassy was nearby. Crowds are allowed only when they are organized to cheer or boo.

During my evenings I became involved in Erika's studies. For one thing, I wanted to know why we always had to get new books for her, when Doba's children's books were still on the shelves. The reason, I learned, was that each year the history books incorporated major changes. I compared a history book of Doba's son with Erika's covering the same period. In the older book, Ivan the Terrible symbolized cruelty and tyranny. In Erika's he was virtually a prophet who had been nobly ready to sacrifice anybody for the benefit of the nation. All the other czars, similarly, had been transformed from villains into heroes who had stopped at nothing to achieve their progressive goals.

About the sciences, though, the old and new versions agreed. Newton, Edison, and Marconi had never discovered anything, and Russian scientists like Popov, Yablochkov, and Tsiolkovksy everything. The Russians indeed had distinguished scientists, but I was outraged at the books' silence about science abroad.

If they could alter the past so liberally, I could only imagine what kind of history they were fabricating for the present. I knew some old Bolsheviks had tried to write objective accounts of events since the revolution, and I knew they had been subjected to constant raids in search of their manuscripts.

After three weeks during which I had waited in line from 5 a.m. daily, my turn came. I was allowed into the Supreme Soviet building and told to go to the second floor.

I kept thinking about the moment when I should appear before the Troika, what I should add to my petition, how I would defend myself from all accusations, how I would refute the impossible charges against Adi. When I reached the second floor I saw a young, low-echelon official seated at a table in the corridor.

I presumed he was there to direct petitioners to the right room. But no, he was the one. It was up to him to decide whether or not I would see anybody in the Supreme Soviet. He took my five thousand rubles worth of juridical terminology, put it in his desk without looking at it, asked for my document, and handed me a scrap of paper from a pile on his desk. My plea for pardon was denied. I said I was not pleading for a pardon, I simply wanted rehabilitation. He said only that I no longer could remain in Moscow. He reminded me that I was still an outlaw.

A letter from Adi awaited me at home—how happy he was for me that I was back in Moscow at last.

chapter 27

In the Wilderness
Autumn, 1952

I would have to go at once. The official at the Supreme Soviet probably had already notified the precinct. But whither? I knew I could not find work in Gomel. And I must find work somewhere. How long could I drain Mama? How long could I myself bear idleness?

Doba phoned busily, asking friends to suggest locations just over the hundred-kilometer restriction. One came up with Tula. She had a relative there who could be helpful and who owed her a favor. She would write a letter of recommendation and bring it right over. Waiting two hours for the train, I spent a lot of time in the toilet to keep the militia from asking for my papers and labeling me a vagrant. The toilet was filthy, but I covered the seat with *Pravda,* rested, and drank a beer.

It was the middle of the night when I arrived in Tula. It was unthinkable to go at that hour to the people who had been recommended to me. But it was dangerous to remain at the station. The night was cold and I developed a terrible headache. I suspected I was becoming ill and the suspicion gave me an idea. I boldly asked a militiaman where the city hospital was.

Did I mean the hospital on Stone Street or the one on Stalina Street?

"On Stalina Street. I got a phone call that my sister is there."

"Look, you can't visit her at this hour. Do you have any relatives here?"

"Nobody. My sister just arrived and I don't have her address."

He suggested I go to a hotel and he hailed a taxi for me.

The night clerk, half asleep, did not ask me for documents, just my name. I picked Turkow as the most Russian-sounding. In my room I threw myself into bed. If only I could never wake.

I awoke, face swollen and with an even worse headache. I recognized severe sinusitis, and I spent the day waiting in the hospital corridor until the clinic closed. I was told to come back tomorrow.

At the hotel another clerk was on duty. She informed me I would have to submit my papers. Then she looked at me again. "Go to your room. As soon as you feel better, you will bring the papers down to me."

Two days later, I could delay the papers no longer and took them to her. She said, "Listen, I will allow you to stay one night more, but I would rather not submit these papers." I could not afford to pay for a hotel any longer anyhow.

I was about to go to sleep when a young woman roommate showed up. While we talked, she remembered she had forgotten to ask the desk to wake her in the morning. We had no phone in the room, so she had to go see the desk clerk. When she returned she burst out, "Do you know, the MGB is searching the hotel. Who would hide in a hotel?"

"I can't imagine."

She turned off the light, and we said goodnight. My eyes remained wide open. My heart's pounding accelerated at every sound of footsteps, every opening and closing of a door. Fear had for me a special taste and smell. I had never known how to pray, but I prayed, "Oh, God, save me," and with each passing second I added new words in a silent scream.

This must be the way a hunter's quarry feels. Any living creature should be spared that kind of fear. My roommate was now deep in sleep. How I envied her, and all the people who did not have to fear.

The next morning when I checked out of the hotel, I learned the MGB had searched only rooms occupied by men.

Doba's friend's relative proved to be a young woman with a baby. Her name was Gita. She and her husband fed me well and put me up for the night. Despite their insistence that I take their bed, I slept on the floor of their room, with my bedding partly under the table.

In the morning Gita gave me the address of the local Philharmonia. They remembered me well and promised me a job. I could begin with one hundred fifty rubles per concert, which was a fortune compared with what I earned in Karaganda. They also gave me the addresses of several private rooms. I rented the first one I visited, paid for two weeks in advance, and gave my documents to the landlady to register.

In my room, I found myself singing. I practically had a job. I would ask my Minsk friends to send me some of the music from my repertoire. While I made plans, I washed my hair.

With my head full of suds I was bending to the basin when somebody banged at the window. I heard a man shout, "Rosner lives here?"

"Yes," I yelled back joyously. "But you have to wait a moment until I rinse my hair." It must be somebody from the Philharmonia with good news.

Two militiamen barged in the door, followed by my landlady, who had paled. They ordered me to pack my things.

"Am I arrested? Why? What for?"

"In the precinct they will decide."

My landlady slipped the money I had paid in advance into my pocket. One man took my valise, ordered me to keep my hands behind me as in the old days, and walked beside me. The other followed. I was all wet—I had had no time to change or to dry my hair.

If they put me in prison I will commit suicide, I vowed. This time I will. I have only to think of a way. I tried to recall the name of the song I had been singing, but I could not remember it. Suddenly it became important to me to remember the name of that song.

The precinct room was filthy and filled with drunks and prostitutes, some bleeding heavily from mouths and noses after beatings. One man was stretched out on the floor, and two militiamen were trying to chain his hands and legs. He had an open cut on his face, and his hair was matted with blood. Blood was all over the place. Would they beat me? I almost wished they would. I would resist and maybe they would kill me.

They made room for me on the bench and took my valise into another room. Was there anything in my valise that could incriminate me? What a stupid question. They could say that my bra was a bomb.

I could feel my temperature rising. I heard, "Rosner, Turkow, Kaminska, come in."

What a joke! All the people wondered why only one person rose and went into the other room.

A man sitting behind a table asked, "Why do you have three names?"

M.C.B.W.–Q

"Rosner is my married name. Turkow is my maiden name. Kaminska is my stage name. I am—I mean I was—an actress."

"An artiste, yes? I have an artiste, huh?"

"Yes."

"We have big respect for artistes. You know?"

"Yes, I know."

"So an artiste has to be grateful and not become a criminal."

"I am not a criminal and I am sick."

"If you weren't a criminal, you wouldn't have to serve time. Isn't that so?" he yelled at me, waving my documents before my eyes. "Or maybe you are trying to tell me that we convict innocent people?"

"I am trying to tell you that I am sick." I almost wept. "Am I arrested?"

"No, you can go. And I mean go! As fast and as far as possible out of Tula. We have enough of our own criminals. Take your things and go."

I taxied to the railway station. Should I throw myself under a train? But only my survival could give any meaning to what was happening to me. I boarded a local train to Moscow. It was warm in the compartment, and I fell asleep and dreamed I went from school to a strange apartment where Adi was expecting me. When I walked in he took me in his arms and kissed me ardently. Suddenly he pushed me away and told me, "When you finish school I will make love to you, but not now." In prison, they used to say that when you dreamed about school, it meant prison. So I asked him, "Do you mean school or prison?"

He replied, "But not now. Not now. Not now."

I awoke and it seemed to me that the movement of the train continued to whisper, "Not now. Not now. Not now."

By the time I arrived in Moscow I had a high fever and again the splitting headache. I could barely see. It was too late at night to call Doba. I would phone in the morning after Erika left for school.

Doba's first words were, "What are you doing here?" She was panicky. I explained. After thinking, Doba said, "Wait near the ladies' room. I will come as soon as I make arrangements with the neighbors—then we will think of some place to go." She added, "I will go with you."

Just knowing that somebody was willing to share my burden made me feel better. I wanted to sleep. Sleep was my escape and my healer. But I could not afford it. I could not remain in the ladies' room too long because others needed it. I had to be careful not to attract attention. I was sure the militia had my picture and could have been alerted that I might turn up in Moscow. But perhaps I would be hard to recognize. I had myself bundled up, my face almost covered with a shawl over my head and crossed in a knot on my back; I looked, I was sure, like a peasant. The disguise surely kept my sinuses warm.

A new worry: what if Doba had been followed after my phone call? It seemed to me I had become the Soviet regime's Public Enemy Number One.

The terminal was huge and crowded. The loudspeaker squawked unintelligibly. From time to time I went near the ladies' room, watching for Doba because I was certain she would not recognize me. After almost ten hours on my feet with short intervals in the toilet, I was worn out. All I wanted was rest, sleep, care.

It was two hours more before Doba came, carrying a small valise. As she made her way to the ladies' room, I looked to make certain she was not being followed. She did not recognize me at first. When she did, her chin trembled. I begged her to help me think about what to do. I feared I already had stayed in the terminal too long. It seemed as though everybody were watching me. We looked at the timetable and Doba decided we would go to Ryazan.

"Why Ryazan?"

Because the name rang a bell. Doba had had a relative there before the war. She knew there was good communication by rail, bus, and, as I later learned, even taxi. It met the requirement—over one hundred kilometers from Moscow. So let it be Ryazan.

We bought two tickets, thus legalizing my presence at the terminal. After that we went to the restaurant to await departure time; I had often been there with Adi after performances in the old days. I had not even realized how long it had been since I had eaten, but when the food came I could not swallow it.

It was time to board the train. How good it felt to have Doba beside me. Though I shivered from fever, I soon fell asleep. Everything that happened later was a blur. We went to a hotel by taxi and I found myself in bed, in terrible pain. Hot towels on my head, a doctor painfully draining my sinuses, Doba trying to force me to eat. Everything was tasteless. I could not swallow. But it was a wonderful feeling, being cared for.

After a week, I spoke for the first time with Erika from a phone in our room. Doba had kept in touch, running her home from afar. But as soon as my temperature dropped, I realized how selfish I was, keeping Doba with me. Even though Doba's children and a friendly neighbor were caring for Erika, Doba had to return home and I had to go on my own.

As long as I was in the hotel with Doba, nobody bothered us about my papers. Hers were in order and she said I was her sick daughter.

While Doba shopped during my illness, she had made friends at a food store. The first day I could go out, Doba took me there. After a few words with the woman manager, I realized Doba had told her my story. The manager put us in touch with a widow who would take me in provided I could get a residence permit.

Doba did not want me to see her off, and I started at once for the precinct. The moment I entered the room I attacked the official with arguments. I told him about Tula. I told him that if he refused to register me, I would commit suicide in his office. I acted absolutely out of character—almost hysterical, but whatever I did must have been the right thing because I succeeded.

chapter **28**

"I Would Rather Carry Stones"
Autumn, 1952

My new landlady, Rosa Yefimovna, was small and a bit stooped, but her black eyes sparkled, her smile dazzled, and her long, thick black hair tied in a big knot showed only the first signs of gray. She had been a beauty. Her husband had been a top engineer in the municipal building department and had been awarded a three-room apartment in a project he constructed. After he was killed in action, Rosa Yefimovna was informed that she was entitled to only one room and would have to share the flat. As the widow of a war hero, she was assigned management of a haberdashery stand in the market and she had a widow's pension; but even so, she found it difficult to feed herself and her son, who was about to be graduated from high school. That was how she came to accept me as a boarder in her one room.

To provide me with a bit of privacy, my part of the room, near the window, was partitioned by a wardrobe. Behind the wardrobe was the boy's bed, and close to the wall, Rosa Yefimovna's. At the head of my bed stood a small table where Rosa Yefimovna kept her kitchen utensils and provisions which she cooked at night, her time to use the kitchen. The other two rooms were occupied by two families that never had anything to do with one another.

Rosa's life consisted of standing all day in the open market, whatever the weather, and of cooking, cleaning, and washing clothes at night. To work she wore a warm brown coat, a heavy shawl bundled around her head and neck, and boots. But the first Sunday I was there she dressed up, transformed herself into a society lady, and announced she was taking me to visit old friends who had asked to meet me. They were influential.

Rosa's friends assured me that "in spite of the present situation" they could find me a position as a salesperson. I knew what they meant by the "present situation." Each day every newspaper carried items such as "Comrade Kuznetzov, whose actual name is Rosenblatt, was caught redhanded with his fat hand in the socialistic property of the people." Every edition of every paper warned against "Jewish nationalists" and "Jewish economic spies."

A job as a salesperson was lucrative. I remembered how things used to be brought out from under the counter for me, in return for tickets to a performance or a tip, and everyone knew that the take was shared with managers, bookkeepers, inspectors. We decided that a sales job was not for me; it could get me into trouble. Before the evening ended I said, "I would rather carry stones."

I got my preference. After several weeks of searching for work as a photographic laboratory assistant or a hair washer in a beauty salon, I wound up carrying stones—loading brick and cement at a construction site. The pay was determined by the number of wheelbarrows filled, pushed over a narrow plank, and unloaded. By the end of the week I knew I would have to quit.

As I lay in bed I realized that in my preoccupation with my everyday struggle to survive, I had concentrated on tactics rather than strategy. I reviewed mentally all the people I had known. Some former friends were influential and would want to ease my plight, I was sure, if they knew of it. But did I have the right to involve them? Because of their positions, they still believed that if one sought justice in the system, justice could be achieved. No, I could not appeal to them.

Then I reminded myself of the MVD official, the theatrical buff, who had admired our group and sought our company. Adi had been a little jealous of him, because he felt his interest in me was too specific. Irene had mentioned in Karaganda that he had moved high up in the MVD. I decided to seek him out.

As soon as I was back on my feet, I took an early train to Moscow. As I approached the MVD building I recalled I had often seen people cross the street rather than pass close to it, as though they feared an invisible hand would reach out to snatch them. At the time it had seemed funny. Now butterflies fluttered in my stomach.

A security officer behind a table asked if I had a pass or an appointment. I had neither. I told him only that I had come from out of town to see Colonel G—insky. The colonel would not see anybody without an appointment, the officer said, but I persuaded him to send in my name. The officer answered several phone calls, then got one that caused him to look up at me sharply. "Yes, she is right here." He gave me a pass and directions.

The colonel looked even more impressive than he had years ago. He had grown in might as well as weight. He did not rise to greet me; he did not respond to my greeting. He murmured to me to be seated and continued to look down at his papers as he asked why I had come.

I said I was sure he knew what had happened to us, but now I had served my time and was back. My child was in Moscow and the woman who was caring for her would not mind if I stayed in her apartment, if I had the legal right to be in Moscow. So I had come for a residence permit.

When he looked up at me, his eyes were glassy and expressed nothing. "You wouldn't be able to obtain such a permit," he said brusquely.

Knowing I had only a moment more in his presence, I appealed. "You see, there is actually no place where I can live and support myself. I've been through a lot. I was not allowed to go to Poland where my mother is. And now you are not allowing me to stay in Moscow with my child."

"That's right."

"Maybe I can get a temporary permit, so I can do something about it, appeal to the proper authorities. I really need a roof over my head. I want to be with my child, at least for a while."

"Not allowed."

"Maybe a couple of days? I am so tired. I don't feel well."

"Not allowed."

"So perhaps you can at least suggest what I can do?"

Again looking through me, he said, "The only thing that I can suggest is that you hang yourself."

He was in deadly earnest. I rose and said something like, "Sorry to have bothered you."

I went through all the motions like a puppet, buying a ticket, boarding a train, and traveling back to Ryazan. For more than a week I could not speak to anybody or even call Doba. When I did snap out of it and called Doba, I sensed she was worried about something but she insisted she simply had a headache. I doubted that. Something was being hidden from me.

At the flat, Rosa's son, home from school, greeted me breathlessly. "You have to get in touch with my mother; she has an important message."

I ran to the market. My landlady was surrounded by customers but managed to tell me to go to the office of the City Electrical Network and see the head bookkeeper. They were hiring people. It was nearly closing time when I arrived, but the head bookkeeper was willing to see me. He had the most unusual name I had ever heard. I had met Revolutsia, Lenina, Stalina, and even Piatiletka (Five Year Plan). But he was Autonom Stepanovitch, christened in celebration of the establishment of an "autonomous republic."

He must have been desperate for people because he hired me on the spot as a bookkeeping clerk. I told him I had no bookkeeping experience and had never been good with figures, but would do my best. He assured me that I would be given all the help I needed and that with an abacus I would manage. I was to begin work early next morning. I did not know how to use an abacus, but Rosa Yefimovna gave me a lesson that night.

I arrived at the office before anyone. My duties were to convert kilowatts consumed into currency, and record them in the books. Almost all of the books that passed through my hands were unintelligible, kept by illiterates. From the first day, I took them one by one and rewrote the names and pertinent data.

The sudden need for clerks, it developed, resulted from a bureaucratic bumble. The Ryazan region had long been known for excellent onions, and since collectivization of farms all *kolkhozes* had prospered cultivating onions. Then the agricultural authorities at the highest level ruled that potatoes should replace onions. The collectives failed and most of the families in them nearly starved. Young people left to find jobs in cities and towns, such as Ryazan. The authorities tracked them down and returned them to the farms. The loss of the refugee workers disrupted Ryazan's employment pattern. The head bookkeeper had hired me on sight because I was not a refugee from a farm and would not be snatched away.

I was paid meagerly—one hundred rubles per month of which fifty went to Rosa for rent. I decided to save as much as I could of the remaining fifty—which turned out to be somewhat less than fifty because on my second day on the job I found myself drafted into the Union of Communal Workers and had dues to pay.

But I had a permanent residence in Ryazan and I had a job. Therefore there was nothing illegal about visiting Moscow, though I could not live there.

Moscow had thousands of visitors every day who came to buy such things as flour, rice, and bread that were unavailable where they lived. I decided to surprise Erika and Doba with a visit, legally and by daylight. Ever since my last conversation with Doba I had wanted to find out what was bothering her. So one Sunday morning I rang their doorbell.

Their first reaction was a mixture of delight and fear. I assured them my presence was legal and said I planned to visit them every week. After breakfast Doba insisted on going to the housing management to register me and to show them my permanent residence document for Ryazan. She returned elated that nobody had objected. But Doba seemed to avoid every chance to be alone with me. Only after Erika had gone to bed did I corner her and ask what was bothering her.

She admitted that at about the time of my call, she had learned that some famous physicians—she did not want to mention names but I knew some of them personally—had been arrested. All were Jewish. There were other unpleasant occurrences. In cases of mixed marriages, the non-Jewish partner had been called in by the authorities and asked to invalidate the marriage. Nobody knew what to think. Doba herself had been pushed out of lines at stores and mocked, for she spoke Russian with a Yiddish accent.

I murmured that this was reminiscent of the Nazis. "How can you compare?" she asked indignantly.

I spent New Year's Eve with Erika, Doba's family, and some friends and neighbors of theirs. I found the moods of Moscow and Ryazan vastly different. In Ryazan, people went about their business normally, joking, taking pleasure from a good buy on a blouse or telling a friend about where to obtain a rare food item. In Moscow, people had stopped joking. At the New Year's celebration we drank a lot, but the toasts had changed. Now they were "to the hope that everything will be well," "to peace and better times," or just "to the good life!" Nobody trusted himself to say, "To the end of anti-Semitic excesses!" That would have been an admission that they existed.

chapter *29*

Appeal to Ehrenburg
Winter, 1953

On January 13 *Pravda* publicized the names of nine well-known doctors, six of them Jews, who had turned out to be traitors, spies, foreign agents, white-coated murderers. One—Professor Feldman— had treated me, and Professors Vovsi and Kogan I knew. In the next few days the whole country was signing petitions, urging the government to "settle the matter in the appropriate way."

The USSR seemed athirst for blood. The authorities had initiated the whole thing with the death of Mikhoels. But what were they out to achieve? I could not understand either the reaction of some Jews: "How could they (the doctors) do such things? They certainly deserve to rot!" Were they really so obtuse? Or did they simply not want to acknowledge the new terror they faced?

On March 4 a communique announced that on the night of March 1-2 Stalin had suffered a massive brain hemhorrage. Bulletins from his bedside, signed by a constellation of doctors—none Jewish— dominated newspaper extras. Stalin's speeches, especially those stressing the unity and strength of the Communist party and the Soviet system, were reprinted at length. On March 6 the newspapers had black borders. Stalin had died the evening of March 5.

All over Ryazan and everywhere in the Soviet Union radio stations broadcast dirges and church bells rang continually. At work we gathered in a meeting to mourn. A deep baritone voice from a loudspeaker told us of our loss and our grief. People in the streets and in my office stood sobbing, tears streaming down their faces.

I wept too. I, who had lost so much, suffered so much during his era, wept. Since I had been in Russia I had heard endlessly about Father

Stalin's might. I had witnessed the war in which masses of people had fought and died believing in him. Now the ship had lost its captain. In inexperienced hands, it might be wrecked. It was not the wreck that troubled me, but how many innocents would drown as a result.

Next day the new government was introduced. Georgy Maksimilianovich Malenkov had been appointed chairman of the Council of Ministers and Lavrenty Pavlovich Beria first vice-chairman. Newspapers pictured the new government around Stalin's open coffin.

My coworkers snatched the pictures from each other's hands and tried to identify the subjects. "Now, let me see, this one is Zhukov, and this is Molotov. And this one to the right, that's Beria. But this stuffed goose?" It was Malenkov. Nobody knew him, and people rushed to libraries and bookshops for his *curriculum vitae*. Nothing was available, but within a few days the bookshelves were full of such stuff.

At the Ryazan movies, crowds waited in line to see the funeral films. I went myself. At that, it was better than in Moscow where the vast throng at the actual ceremonies suffered hundreds of casualties. In the aftermath, the Soviet Union seemed a kingdom without a king. The party reasoned and pleaded, urging the people to rededicate themselves to the Communist cause, as Comrade Stalin would have wished. "We are sure that we can count on the solidarity of the people," they repeated.

They forgot about abusing Jews. For a while they even stopped sniping at American and British imperialists and became engrossed instead with a famine in Brazil, emphasizing the contrast with Russia, where everything was going so well.

Indeed, the new leadership, such as it was, was trying hard to keep store shelves well stocked and to signal that better times were at hand. The reassurances climaxed on March 28 with a proclamation of amnesty that credited the population's obedience to law, reflected in declining crime.

I had been avoiding Moscow since the height of the anti-Semitic crusade, but now seemed the time to try again to obtain a residence permit for Moscow. Millions of other people had the same idea. Wherever I went I turned back, discouraged by the long lines.

Instead I wrote petitions for rehabilitation to the MVD, to the Troika of the Supreme Soviet, to members of the Politburo, to Beria, and to Tzanava—a Georgian who had held high rank in Byelorussia, whom I personally knew and who was, socially, a likable fellow.

From Beria, who seemed to be the most powerful of them all, I received only an acknowledgement that my petition had been received. From the others, I got no answers.

But in April the accusations against the Jewish doctors were denounced as a fraud; the "mistake" was blamed on a woman physician who had borne false witness. Beria signed an order rehabilitating the victims. Once again, I dared to hope.

Talk began to be heard about the "errors" of Stalin's era. I was sure we—Adi and I—were one of them, and that soon our turn would come. But the errors, apparently, had been easier to make than to undo, and there had been so many of them.

Was there to be no end to this? However, one thing changed—it was no longer a matter of shame to admit that one was a former convict. Even Autonom Stepanovich said, "I suppose you will soon be rehabilitated and then, of course, you will leave us. We certainly will miss you."

When I visited Moscow I received phone calls and invitations from former acquaintances. Some claimed to have just learned that I was in the area and had managed to obtain Doba's phone number and address. A few said, "Shame on you! How could you! You come back to Moscow and don't even get in touch with us?"

A few others said, "Believe me, we often thought of you." I believed them. When they added, "Whenever we planned to call you something happened, either I got sick or I had to go away," I did not believe them. But I never blamed any of them and I could not even tell them there was no need for excuses.

One beautiful July day I was visiting with Erika at the *dacha* of a famous actor. It was so like a daydream I used to have in the darkest days. My daughter was with me. I was surrounded by colleagues who were totally relaxed. We discussed the new developments in art. We gossiped and I caught up with whatever had happened in their personal lives during my absence. We talked about the last festive performance at the Bolshoi at which my host and some of the guests had been present. Members of the Politburo had been there, too, adding importance to the occasion. The most impressive of them had been Beria, sitting in his box. He was rumored to be involved with a young dancer, but who ever knew for sure what went on in the personal lives of such officials?

Then one guest, a prominent comedian, carried away by the spirit of free speech, recounted something that puzzled us all. He also had

had an invitation to the Bolshoi, but he had just received a part in a movie, had wanted to read the script, and had stayed home. He lived in the Arbat, in the center of Moscow, and his windows overlooked Beria's well-guarded mansion. Every window in the Beria mansion had been lit up, and men had been rushing in and out. Beria was at the Bolshoi, so he could not have been giving a party—and it had not looked like a party.

When the comedian finished, quiet fell. No one commented on his story. Those who had no cars looked at their watches and reminded themselves of train schedules. Everyone rose to go. The spirit of free speech had had a short life.

On July 10 I read in *Izvestia* that Beria was a traitor and an imperialist and capitalist agent. He had been dismissed from all his posts and was under investigation by the Supreme Soviet. Now the comedian's story made sense.

The gossips said that Beria had been preparing a coup d'etat and had organized MVD forces to take over the Kremlin. But the party's vigilance had foiled him.

I found myself thinking about the petitions I had addressed to Beria, to Tzanava (who was allegedly involved in the plot), and others.

The newspapers began to report the dismissal of people in government who were linked with Beria, and I felt no regret when I learned that the colonel who had suggested I hang myself was among them.

Changes came with breathtaking speed. Malenkov even started to flirt with President Eisenhower, and about July 20, almost on my birthday, I received a document informing me that I had been rehabilitated and all my rights restored. It did not impress the militia of the precinct in which Doba lived. I still could not get a residence permit for Moscow. But now I could ask for help from friends who had never lost their influence.

I went down a list of them. Then somebody suggested, "Why not Ilya Ehrenburg? He survived all the purges. He is a member of the Supreme Soviet, he knew you and your family, and your mother was of such help to him."

Of course! How could I have overlooked him? I phoned. His elderly secretary, whom I knew well, had died and his present secretary was on vacation. Comrade Ehrenburg was out of town. But a high-pitched male voice asked me to leave my name and phone number, and I would be notified when Ehrenburg returned.

I left Moscow Sunday evening and on Tuesday I called Doba. Full of excitement, she told me Ehrenburg was expecting me on Saturday at 2 p.m. I took Erika with me, to give her the opportunity to meet a giant of contemporary literature and to spare me the explanation of a grieving mother who could not be with her child. Seeing Erika, he would understand.

A tall, thin, very shortsighted young man opened the door for us, ushered us into Ehrenburg's study, and told us Comrade Ehrenburg would be with us in a moment. The young man kept his head to one side as he spoke, his Adam's apple bobbed, and he constantly brushed his disheveled hair out of his eyes with his fingers. He introduced himself as a student of literature who now had the great honor of filling in for Ehrenburg's vacationing secretary. He told us to make ourselves comfortable and returned to his typing.

Soon the door opened and the young man jumped up from behind his typewriter. Ilya Ehrenburg had not changed much since I had last seen him, except for the gray in his hair. He told me I looked well, but he must have been guessing, for he did not look at me.

I told him that I had not asked to see him until I had received my rehabilitation papers, because I had not wanted to compromise him. But now the charges against me had been voided and my rights restored. The only thing I lacked was a residence permit for Moscow. "I am so sure you can help me," I told him.

Ehrenburg stood facing a bookshelf filled with editions of his works. He had not changed his position. I began to speak quickly. "I hope that you understand what I have gone through. I am tired of running. I am tired of years of vagrancy, with no permanent place, being hunted from place to place. Here, in Moscow, I have a place to stay, together with my child. I know that I am not involving anybody in anything, I only hope—"

He interrupted. "There is no need to explain your problem. I receive hundreds of letters every day, telling me the same story. Phone calls with similar requests. I have never agreed to see anybody. I made an exception for you. But the only thing I can do—" He turned to face me, holding his hands behind him as he used to do when he lectured. "The only thing I can do for you is to write that you asked me for the permit to be granted. But don't expect any recommendations from me."

I stood there with Erika holding my hand.

He looked at his watch, peered out the window, and told me he had to leave because his driver was waiting to take him to his *dacha*.

To the young man who had been sitting behind the typewriter all this time, he said brusquely, "Let me have a piece of my stationery." He signed his name at the bottom of the sheet and said, "You have heard our conversation. Write the letter and give it to Ruth Zigmundovna." Then he asked me how my mother was, shook my hand, and breezed out of the room.

Only then did I look at the young man's face. His strong glasses magnified the tears welling in his eyes. He tried to say something but his voice cracked. Finally he told me Comrade Ehrenburg had not expressed himself precisely, but he understood how to write the letter.

He discreetly wiped the corners of his eyes and sat down. While he was typing, I walked over to the bookshelf which Ehrenburg had been staring at while he was speaking to me. I saw none of his early books, written when he lived in France and which had made him world famous. Those books had never been published in Russia. The young man put the note into an envelope and handed it to me. The envelope was addressed to the head of the Moscow militia. Emotionally, he pumped my hand up and down and patted Erika's head.

He then murmured there was no need to mention the incident to anybody, wished us all the luck, and ushered us to the door. Outside, I looked at the letter. It recommended in the strongest terms that I be permitted to live in Moscow.

Early Monday morning Doba accompanied me to the precinct. A new man was in charge. He was most polite and accommodating, in keeping with the moment's political fashion. He suggested I leave my letter with him. "Don't worry, I'll make sure it goes through the proper channels," he said. If I wished to wait in Moscow for the answer, he would see that nobody bothered me.

Four days later the head of the precinct called me. "I wish to have the personal pleasure of notifying you that your application for residency has been granted. Your new passport is waiting here for you. Of course, I could have a militia man deliver it to you, but I prefer to avoid an unpleasant association . . . ." Here he laughed at his own joke. "And also there's no need to risk any misinterpretation by the neighbors. I am sure you'll prefer to come down here in person to sign it and pick it up."

I went to the precinct with the speed of light. When I arrived back in the apartment I was greeted by shouts, hurrahs, and glasses of vodka in all hands. We clinked our glasses and drank to the end of the nightmare. Everyone looked over my passport as though they had never seen anything like it. We celebrated all day, and each time I raised my glass, I had in mind Ehrenburg's young secretary whom I did not dare to thank.

I telephoned Mama who told me she would try to get permission to visit me. There was no point in mentioning my ultimate goal, leaving Russia, but even that miracle now seemed possible.

But first I had to find a job in Moscow. I remembered the words I had heard long before in Leningrad—the higher you rise, the lower you fall. I wanted a job that would provide just subsistence. The lower the profile I kept, the easier it would be one day to reunite with my family in Poland. This was not the time to return to show business. But the actors' union, VTO (Soviet Unionwide Theatrical Society), had a workshop for disabled and retired actors who did all sorts of jobs, from making envelopes to painting boxes, silk, or plates, all on a piecework basis.

Since my rights had been restored, I was still a member of VTO. But I was not disabled or retired. So I wrote to Yablochkina, the famous actress who headed VTO, and explained that I did not feel ready to return to the stage, but that a job painting would allow me time with my child. So I became a painter of plates, working at home for a ruble per large plate, and seventy-five kopeks per smaller plate. All winter, drying plates filled the apartment.

For Erika my new status meant a dream come true. I had gone with her immediately to meet her teacher, and to be introduced to everyone else, too. I was asked to join the school's parents' committee, and when I attended its meetings, Erika would run toward me with open arms, calling from afar, "Mama!" to make sure everyone knew I was hers. She would run ahead of me as we walked just to be able to turn around and call "Mama" aloud. I sensed she wanted to prove to herself that I really existed.

Erika was turning out to be a tall, handsome girl. She was intelligent and well read, but whatever knowledge she could absorb from books, school, and environment was limited by the Soviet Reality. She was a typical Soviet product: she cared nothing about her personal appearance and wore heavy, ribbed cotton stockings and her hair in unbecoming thick braids. She never giggled and gossiped with her peers, as young girls do in most of the world. Her social life was confined to the Pioneers, who were instructed to inform on their parents as a patriotic duty. So Soviet parents and their children never talked together about anything but the routine of daily life.

One evening about that time, Erika was invited to a girlfriend's birthday party. I was to pick her up at ten o'clock, and when I arrived at the party Erika was so happy to have me there she went around introducing me to everybody. The birthday girl insisted that I meet her brother and knocked on an adjoining door explaining, "My brother had to go back to his studies." Proudly she added, "He is in the military academy, you see."

A nice-looking boy opened the door, a book in his hand. The title was something about strategy, but it was the author's name that interested me—Pavlovsky.

I remembered the mysterious, quiet accountant of that name whom I had met in Kokchetav, and recalled rumors that she was the wife of a very important Polish military man. Now, seeing that book, I made up my mind to find out as much as I could.

I discovered the truth in a way I cannot disclose even now. She was indeed the wife of a Polish military officer who, with a subordinate named Rokossovsky, had defected to Russia years before. Both had risen to high military rank in Byelorussia. Then they had been arrested on charges of treason. Pavlovsky had been sent to one concentration camp and Rokossovsky to Vorkuta, where he was made a supervisor at the *sanobrabodka*. In the war, when the Russians organized Poles into fighting forces, they yanked Rokossovsky from his bathhouse post and elevated him to the rank of Marshal. Pavlosky, Rokossovsky's old superior, remained a prisoner throughout the war and afterward. But the Russians did not entirely waste his talents: his textbooks on strategy were required reading for military academy cadets. Mrs. Pavlovska, when I met her, had been sentenced to exile in Kokchetav.

chapter 30

Reunion with Adi
1954

A jubilant telegram from Adi. He was free! Rehabilitated! Ready to come! But he needed money for two plane tickets. *Two* plane tickets?

All my life I had had exaggerated ideas about human duties and responsibilites. They had got me into pretty messes at times. But this was the final thing I had to do.

Our marriage had been on the rocks long before our arrest. Shortly before our planned return to Poland, I had explained to Adi that since we had come together, we would leave together, but that in Poland, we would part. I loved him but his infidelities had hurt me so much that I could not continue. He had not believed me; I was so dependent on him, he said, that I would be lost without him. He assured me constantly of his love for me and brushed off his escapades as meaningless. They never were to me.

When he was arrested I could perhaps have found an easy way out for myself by telling the authorities I planned to divorce him anyhow. It might not have surprised them for they probably knew more about our marriage than I did. In the first days after Adi's arrest, some people strongly urged me to stop going to inquire for him, to abandon him to his fate, and to leave with the baby for Moscow. But Adi had needed my support, and that was no time to turn away.

When we had been able to correspond during his imprisonment and exile, he had sent me encouraging and endearing letters, and I had sent such letters to him. Now, at the beginning of 1954, he was about to return to Moscow. He was able to do so only on the grounds of my residency there. I owed it to our daughter to help him come. I called friends and asked for a loan. They wondered why I needed so much money and I explained it was for two plane tickets.

"Did *you* come from Karaganda by plane?" they asked pointedly.
"No, but *they* have a baby with them."

Early one morning Adi arrived, loving and tender, his suitcase
filled with mementos of his new family. He had sent "them" away to
"her" home town. "She" had always known that if it became possible,
he would return to me and "she" had accepted the condition.

Erika, of course, was ecstatic at having her father back, and
naturally we concealed the situation from her. For her sake, Adi
remained with us a while, then moved to the Hotel Moskva. We told
Erika that he needed more comfort and space as he was organizing a
band, but that because of her school it would be better if we remained
where we were. Whether or not she believed the story, I never knew.

Adi really had been entrusted with organizing a new orchestra.
He made a triumphant comeback on the stage and again earned big
money. Almost immediately he became involved in a new love affair,
but that did not stop him from seeing us almost every day and pleading
with me to return to him. At least I stopped painting my plates!

I longed, of course, to see Mama. But she could not come. The
Polish authorities always included her name and Mel's on lists of
delegates to Russian artistic events, and each time the Soviet
authorities struck their names from the list. Mama was refused as a
visitor to her daughter and granddaughter; she was refused as a
tourist.

It was not because the Russians wanted to prevent Mama from
seeing us. It was because she and her own mother had earned their
fame primarily as promoters of Jewish culture in the Yiddish language.
If Mama, a popular and world-renowned personality were to come—
especially officially—it would be difficult to conceal her presence.
Since virtually all Yiddish cultural enterprises had been suppressed,
the Russians would be embarrassed. The very existence of a Jewish
state theater in Poland and my mother's position in it would be too
difficult to explain.

The Soviet leadership was entangled in its own contradictions. At
home it had encouraged nationalistic pride among some of the small
nations making up the Soviet Union, had even created written
languages where none had existed and had founded newspapers in
those languages. But the Jews, who had a rich language and a culture,
were persecuted and even killed.

Abroad, Soviet policy was equally contradictory. The Soviet
Union had been among the earliest nations to recognize the State of
Israel. But Israel had become the most dangerous theme in Soviet

Russia, because the desire of Jews to go there would have made "bad propaganda," as the major had said to me when he sent me off to prison.

But eventually the Soviet authorities compromised. My brother Viktor, who was fourteen, was granted a visa to visit us.

I had always considered Viktor more of a son than a brother. In my telephone conversations with Mama, we had often discussed what a blessing his very existence was to all of us. During all the years of hardship, Viktor had been their consolation. He had grown up aware of the existence of great wrongs. When he was very small, a friend of the family asked him why he was always so serious. "How can I smile," he answered, "when Mother always cries because Rutja is in jail? And Erika is alone and unhappy."

Once Mama told him, "Soon I will buy you a new pair of shoes." He replied, "I can walk in old shoes. Better to send the money to Rutja."

I had last seen Viktor when he was four and one-half, as Erika was, at the time of my arrest. They had had the same teddy bear fur coats—the niece and the uncle, my daughter and my kid brother. I could still picture him in that teddy bear coat. Now, finally, the two would meet again. Excitement reigned. Doba started cooking, calling me into the kitchen constantly to taste this and sample that. And did I think he would like it? The last thing I could remember, he was partial to noodles with milk.

Then came the sunny summer day when Doba, her children, Adi, Erika, and I went to meet the train from Warsaw.

I had not been to the terminal since my last trip from Ryazan. The terminal had been grim, terrifying, aswarm with people who were after me. Now it was a joyous place where I would be reunited with my little brother. We saw him waving from the distance. He was taller than I.

The moment he stepped down from the train, people stared at him. He was dressed in shorts, European style. He wore a watch! He had a Western haircut. Rather shy, Viktor was tormented by the attention he attracted and he soon announced he would not leave the apartment until he acquired long pants. By phone, we arranged for Mama to send him a pair.

I was determined to make the most of Viktor's stay with us. Adi reserved a lavish suite at Leningrad's Astoria Hotel and I took the children sightseeing to the Winter Palace, the Hermitage, the Peterhof (the Versailles-like summer residence of the czars), and the *Petropavlovskaya Krepost*—the Fortress of Peter and Paul. In the czars times the fortress was a political prison. On the inevitable tour, which included many foreigners, the guide told the story of the Decembrist rebels—intelligent young princes, army officers, and economists among them—who had attempted Russia's first popular revolution in December 1825. In a voice filled with emotion, he pointed out the cells in which they had been held.

Each cell had a bed covered with a mattress, pillow, and blankets. Each cell had a table with a lamp, pen, and ink. At each table stood a chair. Books lay on the shelves. As the guide described the suffering and humiliation of the cells' inmates, I suppressed hysterical laughter until I had to go out into the yard.

When we returned to Moscow, I phoned Mama. She and Mel had finally received visitors' visas. Why and how the Soviet Union had changed its mind remained a mystery. At last, to see them! After almost ten years.

The day of their expected arrival was sunny and hot, but my hands were icy cold and I could only whisper.

As we approached the platform, Adi had a firm grip on my arm. I could feel the tension in the air, and nobody said a word. Someone spotted the train. As it puffed toward the platform, I broke away from Adi and took off in the opposite direction, toward the terminal. I was terrified, as when I had first attempted to speak to Erika from Kokchetav. Adi, Viktor, and Erika dragged me back.

Finally there they were. I could see Mel leading Mama down the steps. I ran to them. We clung to one another. We assured one another that we would not cry. We won't! We won't! I was vaguely aware, through tears, of Mel hugging me, embracing Erika.

The first day we kept repeating, "Let's not talk yet. Not yet!" The time finally came when we were able to give vent to the long-withheld torrent. We spoke chaotically, one voice over the other, interrupting, in half sentences. Mama related how back in 1946 she had reserved rooms for Adi and me in the hotel in which she and Mel were staying; how she had met every train, waited for a letter and phone calls, until she heard from Doba.

She told of her countless attempts to have us freed, and of the promises that had kept her going. And only now did I learn the full extent of her activities as an actress and an anti-fascist. Censorship had prevented her writing about them or discussing them on the phone.

I preferred to skip my more dramatic moments, and we finally caught up with the present. I explained how I felt toward Adi. It was painful for all of us. I knew that in his way he loved me, but I also knew that I could not cope with his split personality. We persuaded him finally to let me go my own way; without his assent, I could not get an exit visa even to visit Mama in Poland. That was all Erika and I dared to apply for, though I was determined that once out of Russia, I would never return.

I had one more difficult task—to explain my decision about Adi to Erika. I told her I was sure she must have guessed the truth. I told her I was sorry to have to hurt her and begged her to have confidence that my decision would prove to be the right one. I offered to remain in Russia if that was what she really wanted, but it still would not mean that we would live with her father. Her father would always remain her father, though, and she would be able to visit him.

Next morning, in tears, she told me, "Mommy, I know you wouldn't do this if you didn't have to. I also know that maybe someday I will be able to understand more. But however it is, wherever you go, I go."

chapter **31**

The Road Back
1955-1956

Laden with documents, I went to the OVIR, the office in charge of issuing passports and visas. They asked for more documents. I obtained more documents. Just going to the OVIR kept me busy. They postponed and postponed and postponed the decision. Then they decided: the answer was no. I would have to wait a year before reapplying. That was the rule.

The year passed. I reapplied, starting afresh with the documents. They asked for different documents. Finally, with Mama pulling strings in Poland and me pushing in Moscow, I was informed that I would receive an exit passport with a visa good for a visit abroad.

A few days before our scheduled departure, the OVIR had an afterthought. Where was my birth certificate? Without it they could not grant the visa. Since I had been born in Kiev, I could get the certificate there.

Could I write for it? No, I would have to go in person to the Kiev office of archives.

Time was short. Besides, I lacked the money for the trip to Kiev, and friends warned me that long lines of people waited at the Kiev archives for days.

I decided on a desperate tactic. I asked the telephone operator to connect me with the director of the office of archives in Kiev. I got through. An actress again, I said officiously: "You are director of the office of archives, comrade?"

"Yes, comrade." He did not ask who was speaking.

"We have an urgent matter for you." I did not say who "we" were. "We are sending Ruth Zigmundovna Turkow abroad and she must leave in two days. We require her birth certificate so that we can complete her documents. See that we get it immediately. And to speed things, deliver it directly to her." I gave my address. "That is all, comrade."

I got the certificate.

We said our good-byes to Erika's friends and to my friends. I had said good-bye so often, to so many friends. And why, my friends asked, did I want to go to Warsaw, a city in ruins? But I knew from Mama and Mel that, though Warsaw had been reduced to rubble, private initiative had given it a higher standard of living than Moscow's. And if one wanted to leave Warsaw, that too was possible.

When we were all packed and dressed to travel, we sat down in Doba's apartment, silent. It is an old Russian custom, for good luck before a journey. (The godless Russians cherish more superstitions than any other people I know.)

I looked around at the sad faces. Adi. Doba. Her children. People who had done so much for us and would always mean so much to us. I was afraid to look at Erika. I knew she was trying to suppress her tears. To her it was not going back, it was leaving. She had been born in Russia. And Russian was the only language she spoke.

I could not overcome my fear that something might happen at the last moment. Would they really let us go?

We boarded the train and Erika and I stood by the open window. On the platform were friends who had come to see us off. Words stuck in my throat when I tried to talk to them. As the train began to move, the people on the platform moved with it. The train picked up speed and they ran after us. Only then did we shout our assurances that we would visit them, that they would visit us, that we would never forget them. The last to stop running was Adi.

And finally, he too stood only waving and wiping the tears. Soon everyone vanished from view.

We were alone in our compartment. By now the train was racing along, but even then I could not believe that we would reach Warsaw. Every time I saw a KGB uniform in the corridor outside our compartment, my heart stopped. The conductor frightened me when he opened the door to ask if we wanted anything. I could only shake my head. But I was determined that Erika would not know my terror. Erika asked me to promise that I would allow her to finish in a Russian school because she did not want to lose years studying in a new language. I nodded. Clearly she had many questions but I asked her to please read a book. I had a terrible headache and there would be time to talk later.

I could not take my eyes from the door. At any moment I expected a uniformed man to open it and announce that I had to go back—if not worse. Would they let Erika continue on if they arrested me? What would I do if that happened? What *could* I do?

Every outcry, every stop, every new passenger heightened my foreboding. Finally we arrived at Brest-Litovsk, once Polish and now the last Soviet city before the border. This was where they changed the train tracks to fit the narrower gauge rails of Western Europe; it was also the last checkpoint for documents and luggage. The border guards climbed on the train from both ends, closed doors, and checked thoroughly until they all met in our middle compartment. They went through our valises systematically and found nothing remarkable. Then they told me to follow them. I had to be present in the terminal while they examined the belongings we had in the baggage car. Those consisted chiefly of a combination television-radio-record player— that had been and still was way ahead of its time—and books belonging to Erika, who had subscribed for years to a Masters of Russian Literature series. I had to leave Erika alone. I told her not to worry. Even if the train moved to another platform, I would find her. Then I followed the guards.

Most passengers were led by border guards, but some were taken over by KGB men. The terminal swarmed with them.

All of the passengers had fear in their eyes. They all tried to mask it. I knew how they felt. The guards checked every page of Erika's books. I begged them to hurry because I was afraid the train would leave without me. "So what? You'll take the next train tomorrow."

"But my child is on that train, alone." I could not think how Mama would feel if I were not on the expected train.

"I can leave the books here," I offered. They ignored me.

Finally, having found nothing interesting, they just shook each book, holding it by one corner of the cover. That speeded the procedure but wrecked most of the bindings.

After an interminable time, they took my luggage back to the baggage car and I ran to Erika, who was hanging out the window. She tried to hide from me how frightened she was, but I understood without words and held her in my arms.

The train's doors were locked, with the border guards standing in place. Slowly the train began to move. My daughter wanted to make sure. "Mom, can we talk now? Or do you still have the headache?"

"It'll go away soon," I said, smiling.

The first signs in Polish appeared.

Polish border guards took over. An officer checked our papers against a list he held in his hand. When had we left Poland? he asked. Nineteen thirty-nine. Had we ever considered repatriation as Poles? Yes, indeed! He returned our passports with repatriation papers between the leaves.

When the officer and the guards left and the train was moving again, I said, "Erika, my headache is gone. Now we can talk!" I kissed her and hugged her, as though I had regained her only then.

She asked, "Are there many people in Poland who speak Russian? How will I be able to make new friends without knowing the language? Will we live together with Mama Ida?"

I tried to answer every question, but exhaustion was overtaking us both. Her last question before she fell asleep was, "Mommy, how will our life be there?"

I covered her and let her sleep. I did not know the answer. I had never thought that far ahead. First, mere survival had been my only objective. Then going back had become the goal. This was the happy ending of something. Of what it was the beginning, I could not tell. I was tired. So very tired. I knew only that I did not want to be brave anymore.

Postscript

Mama—Ida Kaminska—and Mel now divide their time between Israel and New York and remain active on stage. Mama was an Academy Award nominee as the best actress in 1967, for her role in the film *Shop on Main Street*.

Adi Rosner managed to leave Russia in 1973 and died in his native Berlin in 1976.

Erika and her nine-year-old daughter, my grandchild Amaris, now live in Florida.

Victor and his family live in New York.

My father, Zygmund Turkow, spent his last years in Israel, acting in Hebrew and Yiddish until his death in 1970.

Doba died in Moscow in 1970.

Hymie is living in Israel. Retired from show business, he makes himself available whenever my family needs his help.

Mr. Blaustein died in Israel where he lived out his last years, reunited with a surviving son.

Lopek disappeared finally, as mysteriously as he used to appear.

Zosia and a daughter were brought to America by Zosia's religious brethren, Jehovah's Witnesses.

Of my Russian friends, the two actors who risked a great deal to visit me in Kharkov and offered to care for Erika are now living happily in Israel and so are the Levines.

Some of Adi's former bandsmen live in New York, some in Israel. Other of my Russian friends remain in the Soviet Union, and though I have given fictitious names to those who figure importantly in this story and have obscured some incidents by which they might be identified, I must not endanger them by disclosing their current status.

Index